G000144290

The MCSE™ Windows® 2000 Server Cram Sheet

This Cram Sheet contains the distilled, key facts about the Windows 2000 Server exam. Review this information last thing before entering the test room, paying special attention to those areas where you feel you need the most review. You can transfer any of the facts onto a blank piece of paper before beginning the exam.

INSTALLING WINDOWS 2000 SERVER

1. Winnt.exe is used for upgrading 16-bit operating systems. Remember these switches:
   - **/e**—executes a command
   - **/s**—specifies the source of the installation files
   - **/u**—specifies the unattended answer file
   - **/udf**—specifies the Uniqueness Database File (UDF)

2. Winnt32.exe is used for upgrading 32-bit operating systems. Remember these switches:
   - **/s**—specifies the source of the installation files
   - **/unattend**—specifies the unattended answer file
   - **/udf**—specifies the Uniqueness Database File (UDF)

3. Setup Manager is used to automatically install Windows 2000 Professional and Windows 2000 Server.

4. System Preparation Tool, sysprep, removes the security identifiers (SIDs) so that the disk can be duplicated.

5. DCPROMO is the command used to promote a member server to a domain controller.

6. When upgrading to Windows 2000 Server:
   - Upgrade the PDC first, BDCs after the PDC, and member servers at any time.
   - Upgrade NT 3.51-4.0 Servers straight to Windows 2000 Servers.
   - Upgrade NT 3.1-3.5 Servers to NT 4.0 or 3.51 Servers, and then upgrade to Windows 2000 Server.

HARDWARE DEVICES

7. Device Manager is used to configure hardware, update drivers, and install system devices. Use the Update Driver button to update drivers.

8. IRQ settings:

IRQ	Device	IRQ	Device
0	System Timer	8	Realtime Clock
1	Keyboard	9	Unassigned
2	Secondary IRQ	10	Primary SCSI controller
3	COM 2 and 4	11	Secondary SCSI controller
4	COM 1 and 3	12	PS/2 Mouse
5	LPT2 or sound	13	Unassigned
6	Floppy	14	Primary hard drive controller
7	LPT1	15	Unassigned

9. Driver signing verifies that a digital signature was added to the driver by Microsoft.
   - Windows File Protection—prevents system files from being replaced by files that are not signed
   - System File Checker (sfc.exe)—verifies correct system file versions
   - File Signature Verification (sigverify)—scans and logs file signature information

NETWORKING SERVICES

10. DHCP—dynamically assigns TCP/IP addresses to client computers
    - If a router does not support DHCP traffic, a DHCP/BOOTP Relay Agent must be configured.

- ARC path in the BOOT.INI can be edited to boot to another location. multi(0)disk(0)rdisk(0)partition(1) or scsi(0)disk(0)rdisk(0)partition(1)
  - multi(0) signifies the first controller, multi(1) signifies the second controller, and so on.
  - scsi(0) signifies the first controller without the SCSI BIOS enabled, scsi(1) signifies the second controller without the SCSI BIOS enabled, and so on.
  - rdisk(0) signifies the first disk on the controller, rdisk(1) signifies the second disk on the controller, and so on.
  - disk(0) signifies the first disk on the controller without the SCSI BIOS enabled, disk(1) signifies the second disk on the controller, and so on.
  - partition(1) signifies the first partition on the disk or rdisk, partition(2) signifies the second partition on the disk or rdisk, and so on.

48. The Performance tool consists of System Monitor and Performance Logs And Alerts. It is used to monitor objects and counters.

49. Task Manager is used to monitor programs, track system performance, and maintain processes. Process priority can be set using Task Manager or the command line: /realtime, /high, /abovenormal, /normal, /below normal, /low.

50. Disk Defragmenter scans the hard drive for data that is fragmented and tries to relocate the data to contiguous space for better read/write performance.

51. Disk Cleanup is used to scan a selected hard drive, reports how much disk space it can free up, and then prompts for input on files to delete.

52. Network Monitor is used to view network statistics and packet information.

53. Event Viewer is used to access log files that are being compiled by the server.

54. Regedit and Regedt32 are used to edit the Windows 2000 registry.

28. Copying and moving NTFS permissions or compressed files and folders.

Same NTFS Volume	Different NTFS Volume
Copy	Inherits NTFS permissions. Inherits NTFS permissions.
Move	Retains its NTFS permissions. Inherits NTFS permissions.

29. Disk quotas are used to set space restrictions on users. Quotas can only be implemented on an NTFS volume, are tracked independently for each volume assigned, are calculated by the uncompressed, and are based on file ownership.

PRINTERS AND IIS 5.0

30. Internet Printing Protocol (IPP) is used to access, manage, and print to print devices through a Web page.

31. To manage a network printer, type "http://*servername*/ printers".

32. To find a network printer, type "http://*servername*/ printers/*share_name*.print".

NETWORK RESOURCES

33. Windows Installer is used to manage the installation of software on remote computers. Uses a file with an .msi extension, which replaces the setup.exe.

34. Software Installation And Maintenance is used to deploy and manage the software throughout an organization. Can use GPOs to widely distribute.

35. Remote Installation Services (RIS) is used to remotely install Windows 2000 Professional.

36. Distributed file system (Dfs) is used to create a logical hierarchical file system, made up of shared folders from different locations, but they are seen by the users as one common logical file system.

37. Terminal Services is used to run applications on the server's desktop from a client, without using client resources. The two modes are: Application Server mode and Remote Administration mode.

38. Routing and Remote Access is a program that is a software router and a program used to authenticate and access resources using different types of connections.
   • Remote Access Server—provides dial-in access to the network
   • Virtual Private Network (VPN)—provides a secure connection to the network through an Internet connection
   • Network Router—facilitates communication between different networks

SECURITY

39. Security Configuration And Analysis Tool is used to configure a server against security holes and attacks, and uses different security templates to analyze and secure the computer.

40. Security permissions, only available on NTFS volumes, should be used to secure local resources.

41. Group Policy Objects (GPOs) are implemented to control user's local desktops, computer settings, and user rights.

42. Encrypting File System (EFS) uses public key encryption to secure files and folders on an NTFS volume. Only the user who encrypts a file or folder can access it. A recovery agent is used to decrypted files that have lost their keys or the original owner is unavailable to decrypted.

TROUBLESHOOTING

43. Backup Program is used to back up and recover data.
   • Supports hard drives, floppies, tape drives, CDROM, and removable disks.
   • System State data: the Registry, system startup files, Component Services Class Registration database, Certificate Services database, Active Directory database, and sysvol.
   • ntdsutil.exe is used to perform an authoritative restore of Active Directory database information.

44. Advanced Startup options accessed using the F8 key on bootup: Safe Mode, Safe Mode With Networking, Safe Mode With Command Prompt, Enable Boot Logging, Enable VGA Mode, Last Known Good Configuration, Directory Services Restore Mode, Debugging Mode, and Boot Normal.

45. Recovery Console, used after the Advanced Startup options fail, starts and stops services, accesses the server's drives, copies files, deletes files, logs on to the server, and formats a server's hard drives. To preinstall, run winnt32.exe /cmdcons.

46. The emergency repair disk (ERD), used after Advanced Startup and Recovery Console have failed, contains information about Windows 2000 Server system settings that helps repair damaged boot sector and system files using the Windows 2000 Server CD-ROM.

47. Boot disk, used to boot a computer with a corrupt master boot record (MBR), a corrupt boot sector, a missing NTLDR file, a missing ntdetect.com, or a failed mirror.
   • Contains the NTLDR, BOOT.INI, and NTDETECT.COM files.

- Automatic Private IP Addressing (APIPA)—Windows 2000 computers automatically assign themselves an IP address (169.254.0.1 to 169.254.255.254) if they cannot obtain one from a DHCP server

11. DNS resolves computer and domain names to IP addresses.
    - Active Directory Integrated Zones—replicate DNS information throughout the domain increasing the fault tolerance of DNS information
    - Full zone transfer—sends all of the zone data to receiving servers
    - Incremental zone transfer—sends only zone data that has changed, reducing zone transfer traffic

12. NWLink is the protocol used to communicate with systems using IPX/SPX. The correct frame type must be configured for communication between systems.

13. CSNW enables clients to use file and print resources of NetWare servers.

14. GSNW (includes CSNW and NWLink) enables servers to act as a gateway, for Microsoft servers and clients, to NetWare servers, acts as a gateway for file and printer resources.

USERS AND GROUPS

15. Domain Local Group Scope can have users from any domain in the forest, but they can only access recourses in the local domain.

16. Global Group Scope can only have users from the local domain, but they can access resources in any domain in the forest.

17. Universal Group Scope can have users, global groups, and other universal groups from any domain in the forest, and they can access resource in any domain in the forest. Only available in native mode.

18. Group Policy Objects (GPOs) implementation order: Windows NT system policies, local group policy, site policy, domain policy, OU policy, child OU policy.

STORAGE

19. Basic and dynamic storage can be formatted in FAT, FAT32, and NTFS 5.0. When creating sets or volumes the storage types must be the same.
    - Volumes, sets, striped sets, and striped volume are not fault tolerant. If one disk fails all the data is lost.
    - Mirrored sets and mirrored volumes are fault tolerant. If one disk fails, all of the data is available on the other half of the mirror. If both disks fail, all the data is lost.
    - Striped set with parity (RAID 5 set) and striped volume with parity (RAID 5 volume) are fault

tolerant. If one disk fails, the data is still available. If two or more disks fail, all the data is lost.

20. Basic storage can use either four primary partitions or three primary partitions with extended partitions as space allows. Use the Upgrade To Dynamic option to convert to dynamic storage without data loss.
    - To repair a mirrored set, use the options: Repair Volume and Resynchronize Mirror.
    - To repair a RAID 5 set, use the options: Repair Volume and Regenerate Parity.
    - A partition or striped set cannot be repaired. The data must be recovered from a backup.

21. Dynamic storage enables you to create volumes, spanned volumes, mirrored volumes, striped volumes, and RAID 5. It was developed to expand storage, increase fault tolerance in the storage, and improve your ability to recover damaged storage.
    - To repair a mirrored volume, use the option: Reactivate Mirror.
    - To repair a RAID 5 volume, use the options: Reactivate Disk and Repair Volume.
    - A volume, spanned volume, or striped volume cannot be repaired. The data must be recovered from a backup.

22. The following errors and fixes may occur when adding storage from other computers.
    - Failed: Incomplete Volume—part of a volume has been imported. The rest of the volume must be imported for data on the disks to be accessible.
    - Failed Redundancy—part of a mirrored volume or RAID-5 has been imported. Data is accessible, but there is no fault tolerance in the imported volume.

23. A mounted volume represents a folder in an existing directory. File system must be NTFS. Used to save drive letters and add space to existing volumes.

PERMISSIONS

24. When combining share and security permissions: Calculate the total share permissions and the total security permissions, then take the most restrictive permission for the total access permission to the resource.

25. Share permissions are assigned to a folder that will be a network resource for users. Share permissions do not affect locally accessing resources. Combine and take the highest access level to calculate share permissions.

26. Security permissions, only accessible on an NTFS volume, protects files and folders at the local computer and over the network. Combine and take the highest access level to calculate security permissions.

27. Deny Access means that the user cannot access the resources regardless of other permissions.

MCSE™
Windows® 2000
Server

Natasha Knight

MCSE™ Windows® 2000 Server Exam Cram

Limits of Liability and Disclaimer of Warranty

The author and publisher of this book have used their best efforts in preparing the book and the programs contained in it. These efforts include the development, research, and testing of the theories and programs to determine their effectiveness. The author and publisher make no warranty of any kind, expressed or implied, with regard to these programs or the documentation contained in this book.

The author and publisher shall not be liable in the event of incidental or consequential damages in connection with, or arising out of, the furnishing, performance, or use of the programs, associated instructions, and/or claims of productivity gains.

Trademarks

Trademarked names appear throughout this book. Rather than list the names and entities that own the trademarks or insert a trademark symbol with each mention of the trademarked name, the publisher states that it is using the names for editorial purposes only and to the benefit of the trademark owner, with no intention of infringing upon that trademark.

The Coriolis Group, LLC
14455 N. Hayden Road
Suite 220
Scottsdale, Arizona 85260

(480)483-0192
FAX (480)483-0193
www.coriolis.com

Library of Congress Cataloging-in-Publication Data
Knight, Natasha
    MCSE Windows 2000 Server exam cram /by Natasha Knight
        p.   cm.
    Includes index.
    ISBN 1-57610-713-2
    1. Electronic data processing personnel--Certification.   2. Microsoft software--Examinations--Study guides.   3. Microsoft Windows Server   I. Title.
QA76.3.K595   2000
005.7'13769--dc21

00-058990
CIP

President and CEO
Keith Weiskamp

Publisher
Steve Sayre

Acquisitions Editor
Shari Jo Hehr

Development Editor
Deborah Doorley

Marketing Specialist
Cynthia Caldwell

Project Editor
Sharon Sanchez McCarson

Technical Reviewers
Jim Bloomingdale
Rick Horowitz

Production Coordinator
Wendy Littley

Cover Designer
Jesse Dunn

Layout Designer
April Nielsen

Printed in the United States of America
10 9 8 7 6 5 4 3 2

The Coriolis Group, LLC • 14455 North Hayden Road, Suite 220 • Scottsdale, Arizona 85260

ExamCram.com Connects You to the Ultimate Study Center!

Our goal has always been to provide you with the best study tools on the planet to help you achieve your certification in record time. Time is so valuable these days that none of us can afford to waste a second of it, especially when it comes to exam preparation.

Over the past few years, we've created an extensive line of *Exam Cram* and *Exam Prep* study guides, practice exams, and interactive training. To help you study even better, we have now created an e-learning and certification destination called **ExamCram.com**. (You can access the site at **www.examcram.com**.) Now, with every study product you purchase from us, you'll be connected to a large community of people like yourself who are actively studying for their certifications, developing their careers, seeking advice, and sharing their insights and stories.

I believe that the future is all about collaborative learning. Our **ExamCram.com** destination is our approach to creating a highly interactive, easily accessible collaborative environment, where you can take practice exams and discuss your experiences with others, sign up for features like "Questions of the Day," plan your certifications using our interactive planners, create your own personal study pages, and keep up with all of the latest study tips and techniques.

I hope that whatever study products you purchase from us—*Exam Cram* or *Exam Prep* study guides, *Personal Trainers*, *Personal Test Centers*, or one of our interactive Web courses—will make your studying fun and productive. Our commitment is to build the kind of learning tools that will allow you to study the way you want to, whenever you want to.

Visit ExamCram.com now to enhance your study program.

Help us continue to provide the very best certification study materials possible. Write us or email us at **learn@examcram.com** and let us know how our study products have helped you study. Tell us about new features that you'd like us to add. Send us a story about how we've helped you. We're listening!

Good luck with your certification exam and your career. Thank you for allowing us to help you achieve your goals.

Keith Weiskamp

Keith Weiskamp
President and CEO

Look for these other products from The Coriolis Group:

MCSE Windows 2000 Accelerated Exam Prep By Lance Cockcroft, Erik Eckel, and Ron Kauffman	**MCSE Windows 2000 Professional Exam Cram** By Dan Balter, Dan Holme, Todd Logan, and Laurie Salmon
MCSE Windows 2000 Server Exam Prep By David Johnson and Dawn Rader	**MCSE Windows 2000 Network Exam Cram** By Hank Carbeck, Derek Melber, and Richard Taylor
MCSE Windows 2000 Professional Exam Prep By Michael D. Stewart, James Bloomingdale, and Neall Alcott	**MCSE Windows 2000 Directory Services Exam Cram** By Will Willis, David V. Watts, and J. Peter Bruzzese
MCSE Windows 2000 Network Exam Prep By Tammy Smith and Sandra Smeeton	**MCSE Windows 2000 Security Design Exam Cram** By Phillip G. Schein
MCSE Windows 2000 Directory Services Exam Prep By David V. Watts, Will Willis, and Tillman Strahan	**MCSE Windows 2000 Network Design Exam Cram** By Kim Simmons, Jarret W. Buse, and Todd Halping
MCSE Windows 2000 Security Design Exam Prep By Richard Alan McMahon and Glen Bicking	**MCSE Windows 2000 Directory Services Design Exam Cram** By Dennis Scheil and Diana Bartley
MCSE Windows 2000 Network Design Exam Prep By Geoffrey Alexander, Anoop Jalan, and Joseph Alexander	**MCSE Windows 2000 Core Four Exam Cram Pack**

MCSE Migrating from NT 4 to Windows 2000 Exam Prep
By Glen Bergen, Graham Leach, and David Baldwin

and...
MCSE Windows 2000 Foundations
By James Michael Stewart and Lee Scales

MCSE Windows 2000 Directory Services Design Exam Prep
By J. Peter Bruzzese and Wayne Dipchan

MCSE Windows 2000 Core Four Exam Prep Pack

For my husband, Scott Knight, the most wonderful, loving, supportive husband in the world. I love you.

☙

About the Author

Natasha Knight grew up in the small Oregon coast town of Cannon Beach. She graduated from Linfield College in McMinnville, Oregon, with a Bachelor of Science degree in physics and minors in mathematics and philosophy. After working in the semiconductor/surface physics industry for two years, she became a network systems administrator at the University of Montana Mansfield Library. Most recently, Tasha and her husband moved to Salt Lake City, Utah, where she is a fulltime MCT of Windows NT 4.0 MCSE track and the new Windows 2000 track.

Tasha is MCT-, MCSE-, and A+-certified, and is a network systems administrator. She has worked with Microsoft server products since NT 3.51, Unix products for over 4 years, and desktop operating systems for over 10 years. In her spare time, she enjoys time with her husband, Scott Knight. They love to camp, hike, and fly-fish. They are currently getting ready to welcome their first child into the world.

Acknowledgments

Thank you to my wonderful, loving husband, Scott Knight, without whose help and support this book would have never been possible. Scott, I love you with all of my heart—thank you for supporting me, helping me grow as a writer and a person, and taking the time to review my work so that this book would be a success.

Thank you to my family and friends who have always loved and supported me regardless of which road I decided to take in life. A special thanks to my mom, Nancy Littell; I hope that I can be as wonderful a mom as you are. And special thanks to my dad, Ira Kent; I hope that if we have a son, he will grow up to be as great a man as his grandpa. Also a special thanks to my stepdad, Mike Littell; my mother-in-law, Nancy Knight; my father-in-law, Bob Knight; Grandma Lilly; Grandma Betty; Grandma Jackie; Noah; Leslie; Rob; Lisa; Katie; and Dakota.

I would also like to thank all of the wonderful people at Coriolis. A special thanks to the acquisitions editor, Shari Jo Hehr, who made this book possible, and to my wonderful project editor, Sharon McCarson, who held my hand throughout the process, answered all of my questions, and was a friend along the way. A big thank you to my copyeditor, Cheri Robinson, for all of your thoughtful insight, and to my technical reviewers, Jim Bloomingdale and Rick Horowitz. Thank you to all the other people at Coriolis who helped make this book possible, including Wendy Littley, April Nielsen, Jesse Dunn, and Paula Kmetz.

Contents at a Glance

Table of Contents

. . . .

Introduction

Welcome to *MCSE Windows 2000 Server Exam Cram*! Whether this is your first or your fifteenth *Exam Cram* book, you'll find information here and in Chapter 1 that will help ensure your success as you pursue knowledge, experience, and certification. This book aims to help you get ready to take—and pass—the Microsoft certification Exam 70-215, titled "Installing, Configuring, and Administering Microsoft Windows 2000 Server." This Introduction explains Microsoft's certification programs in general and talks about how the *Exam Cram* series can help you prepare for Microsoft's Windows 2000 certification exams.

Exam Cram books help you understand and appreciate the subjects and materials you need to pass Microsoft certification exams. *Exam Cram* books are aimed strictly at test preparation and review. They do not teach you everything you need to know about a topic. Instead, I (the author) present and dissect the questions and problems I've found that you're likely to encounter on a test. I've worked to bring together as much information as possible about Microsoft certification exams.

Nevertheless, to completely prepare yourself for any Microsoft test, I recommend that you begin by taking the Self-Assessment included in this book immediately following this Introduction. This tool will help you evaluate your knowledge base against the requirements for an MCSE under both ideal and real circumstances.

Based on what you learn from that exercise, you might decide to begin your studies with some classroom training or some background reading. On the other hand, you might decide to pick up and read one of the many study guides available from Microsoft or third-party vendors on certain topics, including The Coriolis Group's *Exam Prep* series. I also recommend that you supplement your study program with visits to **ExamCram.com** to receive additional practice questions, get advice, and track the Windows 2000 MCSE program.

I also strongly recommend that you install, configure, and fool around with the software that you'll be tested on, because nothing beats hands-on experience and familiarity when it comes to understanding the questions you're likely to encounter on a certification test. Book learning is essential, but hands-on experience is the best teacher of all!

The Microsoft Certified Professional (MCP) Program

The MCP Program currently includes the following separate tracks, each of which boasts its own special acronym (as a certification candidate, you need to have a high tolerance for alphabet soup of all kinds):

➤ *MCP (Microsoft Certified Professional)*—This is the least prestigious of all the certification tracks from Microsoft. Passing one of the major Microsoft exams qualifies an individual for the MCP credential. Individuals can demonstrate proficiency with additional Microsoft products by passing additional certification exams.

➤ *MCP+SB (Microsoft Certified Professional + Site Building)*—This certification program is designed for individuals who are planning, building, managing, and maintaining Web sites. Individuals with the MCP+SB credential will have demonstrated the ability to develop Web sites that include multimedia and searchable content and Web sites that connect to and communicate with a back-end database. It requires one MCP exam, plus two of these three exams: "70-055: Designing and Implementing Web Sites with Microsoft FrontPage 98," "70-057: Designing and Implementing Commerce Solutions with Microsoft Site Server, 3.0, Commerce Edition," or "70-152: Designing and Implementing Web Solutions with Microsoft Visual InterDev 6.0."

➤ *MCSE (Microsoft Certified Systems Engineer)*—Anyone who has a current MCSE is warranted to possess a high level of networking expertise with Microsoft operating systems and products. This credential is designed to prepare individuals to plan, implement, maintain, and support information systems, networks, and internetworks built around Microsoft Windows 2000 and its BackOffice Server 2000 family of products.

To obtain an MCSE, an individual must pass four core operating system exams, one optional core exam, and two elective exams. The operating system exams require individuals to prove their competence with desktop and server operating systems and networking/internetworking components.

For Windows NT 4 MCSEs, the Accelerated exam, "70-240: Microsoft Windows 2000 Accelerated Exam for MCPs Certified on Microsoft Windows NT 4.0," is an option. This free exam covers all of the material tested in the Core Four exams. The hitch in this plan is that you can take the test only once. If you fail, you must take all four core exams to recertify. The Core Four exams are: "70-210: Installing, Configuring and Administering Microsoft Windows 2000 Professional," "70-215: Installing, Configuring and Administering Microsoft Windows 2000 Server," "70-216: Implementing and

Administering a Microsoft Windows 2000 Network Infrastructure," and "70-217: Implementing and Administering a Microsoft Windows 2000 Directory Services Infrastructure."

To fulfill the fifth core exam requirement, you can choose from three design exams: "70-219: Designing a Microsoft Windows 2000 Directory Services Infrastructure," "70-220: Designing Security for a Microsoft Windows 2000 Network," or "70-221: Designing a Microsoft Windows 2000 Network Infrastructure." You are also required to take two elective exams. An elective exam can fall in any number of subject or product areas, primarily BackOffice Server 2000 components. The two design exams that you don't select as your fifth core exam also qualify as electives. If you are on your way to becoming an MCSE and have already taken some exams, visit **www.microsoft.com/ trainingandservices/** for information about how to complete your MCSE certification.

In September 1999, Microsoft announced its Windows 2000 track for MCSE and also announced retirement of Windows NT 4.0 MCSE core exams on 12/31/2000. Individuals who wish to remain certified MCSEs after 12/31/ 2001 must "upgrade" their certifications on or before 12/31/2001. For more detailed information than is included here, visit **www.microsoft.com/ trainingandservices/**.

New MCSE candidates must pass seven tests to meet the MCSE requirements. It's not uncommon for the entire process to take a year or so, and many individuals find that they must take a test more than once to pass. The primary goal of the *Exam Prep* series and the *Exam Cram* series is to make it possible, given proper study and preparation, to pass all Microsoft certification tests on the first try. Table 1 shows the required and elective exams for the Windows 2000 MCSE certification.

➤ *MCSD (Microsoft Certified Solution Developer)*—The MCSD credential reflects the skills required to create multi-tier, distributed, and COM-based solutions, in addition to desktop and Internet applications, using new technologies. To obtain an MCSD, an individual must demonstrate the ability to analyze and interpret user requirements; select and integrate products, platforms, tools, and technologies; design and implement code, and customize applications; and perform necessary software tests and quality assurance operations.

To become an MCSD, you must pass a total of four exams: three core exams and one elective exam. Each candidate must choose one of these three desktop application exams—"70-016: Designing and Implementing Desktop Applications with Microsoft Visual C++ 6.0," "70-156: Designing and Implementing Desktop Applications with Microsoft Visual FoxPro 6.0," or

Table 1   MCSE Windows 2000 Requirements

Core

If you have not passed these 3 Windows NT 4 exams	
Exam 70-067	Implementing and Supporting Microsoft Windows NT Server 4.0
Exam 70-068	Implementing and Supporting Microsoft Windows NT Server 4.0 in the Enterprise
Exam 70-073	Microsoft Windows NT Workstation 4.0
then you must take these 4 exams	
Exam 70-210	Installing, Configuring and Administering Microsoft Windows 2000 Professional
Exam 70-215	Installing, Configuring and Administering Microsoft Windows 2000 Server
Exam 70-216	Implementing and Administering a Microsoft Windows 2000 Network Infrastructure
Exam 70-217	Implementing and Administering a Microsoft Windows 2000 Directory Services Infrastructure
If you have already passed exams 70-067, 70-068, and 70-073, you may take this exam	
Exam 70-240	Microsoft Windows 2000 Accelerated Exam for MCPs Certified on Microsoft Windows NT 4.0

5th Core Option

Choose 1 from this group	
Exam 70-219*	Designing a Microsoft Windows 2000 Directory Services Infrastructure
Exam 70-220*	Designing Security for a Microsoft Windows 2000 Network
Exam 70-221*	Designing a Microsoft Windows 2000 Network Infrastructure

Elective

Choose 2 from this group	
Exam 70-019	Designing and Implementing Data Warehouse with Microsoft SQL Server 7.0
Exam 70-219*	Designing a Microsoft Windows 2000 Directory Services Infrastructure
Exam 70-220*	Designing Security for a Microsoft Windows 2000 Network
Exam 70-221*	Designing a Microsoft Windows 2000 Network Infrastructure
Exam 70-222	Migrating from Microsoft Windows NT 4.0 to Microsoft Windows 2000
Exam 70-028	Administering Microsoft SQL Server 7.0
Exam 70-029	Designing and Implementing Databases on Microsoft SQL Server 7.0
Exam 70-080	Implementing and Supporting Microsoft Internet Explorer 5.0 by Using the Internet Explorer Administration Kit
Exam 70-081	Implementing and Supporting Microsoft Exchange Server 5.5
Exam 70-085	Implementing and Supporting Microsoft SNA Server 4.0
Exam 70-086	Implementing and Supporting Microsoft Systems Management Server 2.0
Exam 70-088	Implementing and Supporting Microsoft Proxy Server 2.0

This is not a complete listing—you can still be tested on some earlier versions of these products. However, we have included mainly the most recent versions so that you may test on these versions and thus be certified longer. We have not included any tests that are scheduled to be retired.

* The 5th Core Option exam does not double as an elective.

"70-176: Designing and Implementing Desktop Applications with Microsoft Visual Basic 6.0"—*plus* one of these three distributed application exams— "70-015: Designing and Implementing Distributed Applications with Microsoft Visual C++ 6.0," "70-155: Designing and Implementing Distributed Applications with Microsoft Visual FoxPro 6.0," or "70-175: Designing and Implementing Distributed Applications with Microsoft Visual Basic 6.0." The third core exam is "70-100: Analyzing Requirements and Defining Solution Architectures." Elective exams cover specific Microsoft applications and languages, including Visual Basic, C++, the Microsoft Foundation Classes, Access, SQL Server, Excel, and more.

➤ *MCDBA (Microsoft Certified Database Administrator)*—The MCDBA credential reflects the skills required to implement and administer Microsoft SQL Server databases. To obtain an MCDBA, an individual must demonstrate the ability to derive physical database designs, develop logical data models, create physical databases, create data services by using Transact-SQL, manage and maintain databases, configure and manage security, monitor and optimize databases, and install and configure Microsoft SQL Server.

To become an MCDBA, you must pass a total of three core exams and one elective exam. The required core exams are "70-028: Administering Microsoft SQL Server 7.0," "70-029: Designing and Implementing Databases with Microsoft SQL Server 7.0," and "70-215: Installing, Configuring and Administering Microsoft Windows 2000 Server."

The elective exams that you can choose from cover specific uses of SQL Server and include "70-015: Designing and Implementing Distributed Applications with Microsoft Visual C++ 6.0," "70-019: Designing and Implementing Data Warehouses with Microsoft SQL Server 7.0," "70-155: Designing and Implementing Distributed Applications with Microsoft Visual FoxPro 6.0," "70-175: Designing and Implementing Distributed Applications with Microsoft Visual Basic 6.0," and two exams that relate to Windows 2000: "70-216: Implementing and Administering a Microsoft Windows 2000 Network Infrastructure," and "70-087: Implementing and Supporting Microsoft Internet Information Server 4.0."

If you have taken the three core Windows NT 4 exams on your path to becoming an MCSE, you qualify for the Accelerated exam (it replaces the Network Infrastructure exam requirement). The Accelerated exam covers the objectives of all four of the Windows 2000 core exams. In addition to taking the Accelerated exam, you must take only the two SQL exams—Administering and Database Design.

Note that the exam covered by this book is a core requirement for the MCDBA certification. Table 2 shows the requirements for the MCDBA certification.

Table 2 MCDBA Requirements
Core

If you have not passed these 3 Windows NT 4 exams	
Exam 70-067	Implementing and Supporting Microsoft Windows NT Server 4.0
Exam 70-068	Implementing and Supporting Microsoft Windows NT Server 4.0 in the Enterprise
Exam 70-073	Microsoft Windows NT Workstation 4.0
you must take this exam	
Exam 70-215	Installing, Configuring and Administering Microsoft Windows 2000 Server
plus these 2 exams	
Exam 70-028	Administering Microsoft SQL Server 7.0
Exam 70-029	Designing and Implementing Databases with Microsoft SQL Server 7.0

Elective

Choose 1 of the following exams	
Exam 70-015	Designing and Implementing Distributed Applications with Microsoft Visual C++ 6.0
Exam 70-019	Designing and Implementing Data Warehouses with Microsoft SQL Server 7.0
Exam 70-087	Implementing and Supporting Microsoft Internet Information Server 4.0
Exam 70-155	Designing and Implementing Distributed Applications with Microsoft Visual FoxPro 6.0
Exam 70-175	Designing and Implementing Distributed Applications with Microsoft Visual Basic 6.0
Exam 70-216	Implementing and Administering a Microsoft Windows 2000 Network Infrastructure

OR

If you have already passed exams 70-067, 70-068, and 70-073, you may take this exam	
Exam 70-240	Microsoft Windows 2000 Accelerated Exam for MCPs Certified on Microsoft Windows NT 4.0
plus these 2 exams	
Exam 70-028	Administering Microsoft SQL Server 7.0
Exam 70-029	Designing and Implementing Databases with Microsoft SQL Server 7.0

➤ *MCT (Microsoft Certified Trainer)*—Microsoft Certified Trainers are deemed able to deliver elements of the official Microsoft curriculum, based on technical knowledge and instructional ability. Thus, it is necessary for an individual seeking MCT credentials (which are granted on a course-by-course basis) to pass the related certification exam for a course and complete the official Microsoft training in the subject area, and to demonstrate an ability to teach.

This teaching skill criterion may be satisfied by proving that one has already attained training certification from Novell, Banyan, Lotus, the Santa Cruz Operation, or Cisco, or by taking a Microsoft-sanctioned workshop on instruction. Microsoft makes it clear that MCTs are important cogs in the Microsoft training channels. Instructors must be MCTs before Microsoft will allow them to teach in any of its official training channels, including Microsoft's affiliated Certified Technical Education Centers (CTECs) and its online training partner network. As of January 1, 2001, MCT candidates must also possess a current MCSE.

Microsoft has announced that the MCP+I and MCSE+I credentials will not be continued when the MCSE exams for Windows 2000 are in full swing because the skill set for the Internet portion of the program has been included in the new MCSE program. Therefore, details on these tracks are not provided here; go to **www.microsoft.com/trainingandservices/** if you need more information.

Once a Microsoft product becomes obsolete, MCPs typically have to recertify on current versions. (If individuals do not recertify, their certifications become invalid.) Because technology keeps changing and new products continually supplant old ones, this should come as no surprise. This explains why Microsoft has announced that MCSEs have 12 months past the scheduled retirement date for the Windows NT 4 exams to recertify on Windows 2000 topics. (Note that this means taking at least two exams, if not more.)

The best place to keep tabs on the MCP Program and its related certifications is on the Web. The URL for the MCP program is **www.microsoft.com/ trainingandservices/**. But Microsoft's Web site changes often, so if this URL doesn't work, try using the Search tool on Microsoft's site with either "MCP" or the quoted phrase "Microsoft Certified Professional" as a search string. This will help you find the latest and most accurate information about Microsoft's certification programs.

Taking a Certification Exam

Once you've prepared for your exam, you need to register with a testing center. Each computer-based MCP exam costs $100, and if you don't pass, you may retest for an additional $100 for each additional try. In the United States and Canada, tests are administered by Prometric and by Virtual University Enterprises (VUE). Here's how you can contact them:

➤ *Prometric*—You can sign up for a test through the company's Web site at **www.prometric.com**. Or, you can register by phone at 800-755-3926 (within the United States or Canada) or at 410-843-8000 (outside the United States and Canada).

➤ *Virtual University Enterprises*—You can sign up for a test or get the phone numbers for local testing centers through the Web page at **www.vue.com/ms/**.

To sign up for a test, you must possess a valid credit card, or contact either company for mailing instructions to send them a check (in the U.S.). Only when payment is verified, or a check has cleared, can you actually register for a test.

To schedule an exam, call the number or visit either of the Web pages at least one day in advance. To cancel or reschedule an exam, you must call before 7 P.M. pacific standard time the day before the scheduled test time (or you may be charged, even if you don't appear to take the test). When you want to schedule a test, have the following information ready:

➤ Your name, organization, and mailing address.

➤ Your Microsoft Test ID. (Inside the United States, this means your Social Security number; citizens of other nations should call ahead to find out what type of identification number is required to register for a test.)

➤ The name and number of the exam you wish to take.

➤ A method of payment. (As we've already mentioned, a credit card is the most convenient method, but alternate means can be arranged in advance, if necessary.)

Once you sign up for a test, you'll be informed as to when and where the test is scheduled. Try to arrive at least 15 minutes early. You must supply two forms of identification—one of which must be a photo ID—to be admitted into the testing room.

All exams are completely closed-book. In fact, you will not be permitted to take anything with you into the testing area, but you will be furnished with a blank sheet of paper and a pen or, in some cases, an erasable plastic sheet and an erasable pen. I suggest that you immediately write down on that sheet of paper all the information you've memorized for the test. In *Exam Cram* books, this information appears on a tear-out sheet inside the front cover of each book. You will have some time to compose yourself, record this information, and take a sample orientation exam before you begin the real thing. I suggest you take the orientation test before taking your first exam, but because they're all more or less identical in layout, behavior, and controls, you probably won't need to do this more than once.

When you complete a Microsoft certification exam, the software will tell you whether you've passed or failed. If you need to retake an exam, you'll have to schedule a new test with Prometric or VUE and pay another $100.

 The first time you fail a test, you can retake the test the next day. However, if you fail a second time, you must wait 14 days before retaking that test. The 14-day waiting period remains in effect for all retakes after the second failure.

Tracking MCP Status

As soon as you pass any Microsoft exam (except Networking Essentials), you'll attain Microsoft Certified Professional (MCP) status. Microsoft also generates transcripts that indicate which exams you have passed. You can view a copy of your transcript at any time by going to the MCP secured site and selecting Transcript Tool. This tool will allow you to print a copy of your current transcript and confirm your certification status.

Once you pass the necessary set of exams, you'll be certified. Official certification normally takes anywhere from six to eight weeks, so don't expect to get your credentials overnight. When the package for a qualified certification arrives, it includes a Welcome Kit that contains a number of elements (see Microsoft's Web site for other benefits of specific certifications):

➤ A certificate suitable for framing, along with a wallet card and lapel pin.

➤ A license to use the MCP logo, thereby allowing you to use the logo in advertisements, promotions, and documents, and on letterhead, business cards, and so on. Along with the license comes an MCP logo sheet, which includes camera-ready artwork. (Note: Before using any of the artwork, individuals must sign and return a licensing agreement that indicates they'll abide by its terms and conditions.)

➤ A subscription to *Microsoft Certified Professional Magazine*, which provides ongoing data about testing and certification activities, requirements, and changes to the program.

Many people believe that the benefits of MCP certification go well beyond the perks that Microsoft provides to newly anointed members of this elite group. We're starting to see more job listings that request or require applicants to have an MCP, MCSE, and so on, and many individuals who complete the program can qualify for increases in pay and/or responsibility. As an official recognition of hard work and broad knowledge, one of the MCP credentials is a badge of honor in many IT organizations.

How to Prepare for an Exam

Preparing for any Windows 2000 Server-related test (including "Installing, Configuring, and Administering Microsoft Windows 2000 Server") requires that you obtain and study materials designed to provide comprehensive information about the product and its capabilities that will appear on the specific exam for which you are preparing. The following list of materials will help you study and prepare:

➤ The Windows 2000 Server product CD includes comprehensive online documentation and related materials; it should be a primary resource when you are preparing for the test.

➤ The exam preparation materials, practice tests, and self-assessment exams on the Microsoft Training & Services page at **www.microsoft.com/ trainingandservices/default.asp?PageID=mcp**. The Testing Innovations link offers samples of the new question types found on the Windows 2000 MCSE exams. Find the materials, download them, and use them!

➤ The exam preparation advice, practice tests, questions of the day, and discussion groups on the **ExamCram.com** e-learning and certification destination Web site (**www.examcram.com**).

In addition, you'll probably find any or all of the following materials useful in your quest for Windows 2000 Server expertise:

➤ *Microsoft training kits*—Microsoft Press offers a training kit that specifically targets Exam 70-215. For more information, visit: **http://mspress.microsoft.com/ findabook/list/series_ak.htm**. This training kit contains information that you will find useful in preparing for the test.

➤ *Microsoft TechNet CD*—This monthly CD-based publication delivers numerous electronic titles that include coverage of Directory Services Design and related topics on the Technical Information (TechNet) CD. Its offerings include product facts, technical notes, tools and utilities. A subscription to TechNet costs $299 per year, but it is well worth the price. Visit **www.microsoft.com/ technet/** and check out the information under the "TechNet Subscription" menu entry for more details.

➤ *Study guides*—Several publishers—including The Coriolis Group—offer Windows 2000 titles. The Coriolis Group series includes the following:

  ➤ *The Exam Cram series*—These books give you information about the material you need to know to pass the tests.

  ➤ *The Exam Prep series*—These books provide a greater level of detail than the *Exam Cram* books and are designed to teach you everything you need to know from an exam perspective. Each book comes with a CD that contains interactive practice exams in a variety of testing formats.

  Together, the two series make a perfect pair.

➤ *Multimedia*—These Coriolis Group materials are designed to support learners of all types—whether you learn best by reading or doing:

  ➤ *The Exam Cram Personal Trainer*—Offers a unique, personalized self-paced training course based on the exam.

  ➤ *The Exam Cram Personal Test Center*—Features multiple test options that simulate the actual exam, including Fixed-Length, Random, Review, and Test All. Explanations of correct and incorrect answers reinforce concepts learned.

➤ *Classroom training*—CTECs, online partners, and third-party training companies (like Wave Technologies, Learning Tree, Data-Tech, and others) all offer classroom training on Windows 2000. These companies aim to help you prepare to pass Exam 70-215. Although such training runs upwards of $350 per day in class, most of the individuals lucky enough to partake find it to be quite worthwhile.

➤ *Other publications*—There's no shortage of materials available about Windows 2000 Server. The resource sections at the end of each chapter should give you an idea of where we think you should look for further discussion.

By far, this set of required and recommended materials represents a nonpareil collection of sources and resources for Windows 2000 Server and related topics. I anticipate that you'll find that this book belongs in this company

About this Book

Each topical *Exam Cram* chapter follows a regular structure, along with graphical cues about important or useful information. Here's the structure of a typical chapter:

➤ *Opening hotlists*—Each chapter begins with a list of the terms, tools, and techniques that you must learn and understand before you can be fully conversant with that chapter's subject matter. I follow the hotlists with one or two introductory paragraphs to set the stage for the rest of the chapter.

➤ *Topical coverage*—After the opening hotlists, each chapter covers a series of topics related to the chapter's subject title. Throughout this section, I highlight topics or concepts likely to appear on a test using a special Exam Alert layout, like this:

This is what an Exam Alert looks like. Normally, an Exam Alert stresses concepts, terms, software, or activities that are likely to relate to one or more certification test questions. For that reason, I think any information found offset in Exam Alert format is worthy of unusual attentiveness on your part. Indeed, most of the information that appears on The Cram Sheet appears as Exam Alerts within the text.

Pay close attention to material flagged as an Exam Alert; although all the information in this book pertains to what you need to know to pass the exam, I flag certain items that are really important. You'll find what appears in the meat of each chapter to be worth knowing, too, when preparing for the test. Because this book's material is very condensed, I recommend that you use this book along with other resources to achieve the maximum benefit.

In addition to the Exam Alerts, I have provided tips that will help you build a better foundation for Windows 2000 Server knowledge. Although the information may not be on the exam, it is certainly related and will help you become a better test-taker.

This is how tips are formatted. Keep your eyes open for these, and you'll become a Windows 2000 Server guru in no time!

➤ *Practice questions*—Although I talk about test questions and topics throughout the book, a section at the end of each chapter presents a series of mock test questions and explanations of both correct and incorrect answers.

➤ *Details and resources*—Every chapter ends with a section titled "Need to Know More?". This section provides direct pointers to Microsoft and third-party resources offering more details on the chapter's subject. In addition, this section tries to rank or at least rate the quality and thoroughness of the topic's coverage by each resource. If you find a resource you like in this collection, use it, but don't feel compelled to use all the resources. On the other hand, I recommend only resources I use on a regular basis, so none of my recommendations will be a waste of your time or money (but purchasing them all at once probably represents an expense that many network administrators and would-be MCPs and MCSEs might find hard to justify).

The bulk of the book follows this chapter structure slavishly, but there are a few other elements that I'd like to point out. Chapter 14 includes a sample test that provides a good review of the material presented throughout the book to ensure you're ready for the exam. Chapter 15 is an answer key to the sample test that appears in Chapter 14. In addition, you'll find a handy glossary and an index.

Finally, the tear-out Cram Sheet attached next to the inside front cover of this *Exam Cram* book represents a condensed and compiled collection of facts and tips that I think you should memorize before taking the test. Because you can dump this information out of your head onto a piece of paper before taking the exam, you can master this information by brute force—you need to remember it only long enough to write it down when you walk into the test room. You might even want to look at it in the car or in the lobby of the testing center just before you walk in to take the test.

How to Use this Book

I've structured the topics in this book to build on one another. Therefore, some topics in later chapters make more sense after you've read earlier chapters. That's why I suggest you read this book from front to back for your initial test preparation. If you need to brush up on a topic or you have to bone up for a second try, use the index or table of contents to go straight to the topics and questions that you need to study. Beyond helping you prepare for the test, I think you'll find this book useful as a tightly focused reference to some of the most important aspects of Windows 2000 Server.

Given all the book's elements and its specialized focus, I've tried to create a tool that will help you prepare for—and pass—Microsoft Exam 70-215. Please share your feedback on the book, especially if you have ideas about how we can improve it for future test-takers.

Send your questions or comments to The Coriolis Group at **learn@examcram.com**. Please remember to include the title of the book in your message. Also, be sure to check out the Web pages at **www.examcram.com**, where you'll find information updates, commentary, and certification information.

Thanks, and enjoy the book!

Self-Assessment

The reason I included a Self-Assessment in this *Exam Cram* book is to help you evaluate your readiness to tackle MCSE certification. It should also help you understand what you need to know to master the topic of this book—namely, Exam 70-215, "Installing, Configuring, and Administering Microsoft Windows 2000 Server." But before you tackle this Self-Assessment, let's talk about concerns you may face when pursuing an MCSE for Windows 2000, and what an ideal MCSE candidate might look like.

MCSEs in the Real World

In the next section, I describe an ideal MCSE candidate, knowing full well that only a few real candidates will meet this ideal. In fact, my description of that ideal candidate might seem downright scary, especially with the changes that have been made to the program to support Windows 2000. But take heart: Although the requirements to obtain an MCSE may seem formidable, they are by no means impossible to meet. However, be keenly aware that it does take time, involves some expense, and requires real effort to get through the process.

Increasing numbers of people are attaining Microsoft certifications, so the goal is within reach. You can get all the real-world motivation you need from knowing that many others have gone before, so you will be able to follow in their footsteps. If you're willing to tackle the process seriously and do what it takes to obtain the necessary experience and knowledge, you can take—and pass—all the certification tests involved in obtaining an MCSE. In fact, The Coriolis Group has designed *Exam Preps*, the companion *Exam Crams*, *Exam Cram Personal Trainers*, and *Exam Cram Personal Test Centers* to make it as easy on you as possible to prepare for these exams. The Coriolis Group has also greatly expanded its Web site, **www.examcram.com,** to provide a host of resources to help you prepare for the complexities of Windows 2000.

Besides MCSE, other Microsoft certifications include:

➤ MCSD, which is aimed at software developers and requires one specific exam, two more exams on client and distributed topics, plus a fourth elective exam drawn from a different, but limited, pool of options.

➤ Other Microsoft certifications, whose requirements range from one test (MCP) to several tests (MCP+SB, MCDBA).

The Ideal Windows 2000 MCSE Candidate

Just to give you some idea of what an ideal MCSE candidate is like, here are some relevant statistics about the background and experience such an individual might have. Don't worry if you don't meet these qualifications, or don't come that close—this is a far from ideal world, and where you fall short is simply where you'll have more work to do.

➤ Academic or professional training in network theory, concepts, and operations. This includes everything from networking media and transmission techniques through network operating systems, services, and applications.

➤ Three-plus years of professional networking experience, including experience with Ethernet, token ring, modems, and other networking media. This must include installation, configuration, upgrade, and troubleshooting experience.

Note: The Windows 2000 MCSE program is much more rigorous than the previous NT MCSE program; therefore, you'll really need some hands-on experience. Some of the exams require you to solve real-world case studies and network design issues, so the more hands-on experience you have, the better.

➤ Two-plus years in a networked environment that includes hands-on experience with Windows 2000 Server, Windows 2000 Professional, Windows NT Server, Windows NT Workstation, and Windows 95 or Windows 98. A solid understanding of each system's architecture, installation, configuration, maintenance, and troubleshooting is also essential.

➤ Knowledge of the various methods for installing Windows 2000, including manual and unattended installations.

➤ A thorough understanding of key networking protocols, addressing, and name resolution, including TCP/IP, IPX/SPX, and NetBEUI.

➤ A thorough understanding of NetBIOS naming, browsing, and file and print services.

➤ Familiarity with key Windows 2000-based TCP/IP-based services, including HTTP (Web servers), DHCP, WINS, DNS, plus familiarity with one or more of the following: Internet Information Server (IIS), Index Server, and Proxy Server.

➤ An understanding of how to implement security for key network data in a Windows 2000 environment.

➤ Working knowledge of NetWare 3.x and 4.x, including IPX/SPX frame formats, NetWare file, print, and directory services, and both Novell and Microsoft client software. Working knowledge of Microsoft's Client Service For NetWare (CSNW), Gateway Service For NetWare (GSNW), the NetWare Migration Tool (NWCONV), and the NetWare Client For Windows (NT, 95, and 98) is essential.

➤ A good working understanding of Active Directory. The more you work with Windows 2000, the more you'll realize that this new operating system is quite different than Windows NT. New technologies like Active Directory have really changed the way that Windows is configured and used. I recommend that you find out as much as you can about Active Directory and acquire as much experience using this technology as possible. The time you take learning about Active Directory will be time very well spent!

Fundamentally, this boils down to a bachelor's degree in computer science, plus three years' experience working in a position involving network design, installation, configuration, and maintenance. I believe that well under half of all certification candidates meet these requirements, and that, in fact, most meet less than half of these requirements—at least, when they begin the certification process. But because all the people who already have been certified have survived this ordeal, you can survive it too—especially if you heed what the Self-Assessment can tell you about what you already know and what you need to learn.

Put Yourself to the Test

The following series of questions and observations is designed to help you figure out how much work you must do to pursue Microsoft certification and what kinds of resources you may consult on your quest. Be absolutely honest in your answers, or you'll end up wasting money on exams you're not yet ready to take. There are no right or wrong answers, only steps along the path to certification. Only you can decide where you really belong in the broad spectrum of aspiring candidates.

Two things should be clear from the outset, however:

➤ Even a modest background in computer science will be helpful.

➤ Hands-on experience with Microsoft products and technologies is an essential ingredient to certification success.

Educational Background

1. Have you ever taken any computer-related classes? [Yes or No]

   If Yes, proceed to question 2; if No, proceed to question 4.

2. Have you taken any classes on computer operating systems? [Yes or No]

   If Yes, you will probably be able to handle Microsoft's architecture and system component discussions. If you're rusty, brush up on basic operating system concepts, especially virtual memory, multitasking regimes, user mode versus kernel mode operation, and general computer security topics.

   If No, consider some basic reading in this area. I strongly recommend a good general operating systems book, such as *Operating System Concepts, 5th Edition*, by Abraham Silberschatz and Peter Baer Galvin (John Wiley & Sons, 1998, ISBN 0-471-36414-2). If this title doesn't appeal to you, check out reviews for other, similar titles at your favorite online bookstore.

3. Have you taken any networking concepts or technologies classes? [Yes or No]

   If Yes, you will probably be able to handle Microsoft's networking terminology, concepts, and technologies (brace yourself for frequent departures from normal usage). If you're rusty, brush up on basic networking concepts and terminology, especially networking media, transmission types, the OSI Reference Model, and networking technologies such as Ethernet, token ring, FDDI, and WAN links.

   If No, you might want to read one or two books in this topic area. The two best books that I know of are *Computer Networks, 3rd Edition*, by Andrew S. Tanenbaum (Prentice-Hall, 1996, ISBN 0-13-349945-6) and *Computer Networks and Internets, 2nd Edition*, by Douglas E. Comer (Prentice-Hall, 1998, ISBN 0-130-83617-6).

   Skip to the next section, "Hands-on Experience."

4. Have you done any reading on operating systems or networks? [Yes or No]

   If Yes, review the requirements stated in the first paragraphs after questions 2 and 3. If you meet those requirements, move on to the next section. If No, consult the recommended reading for both topics. A strong background will help you prepare for the Microsoft exams better than just about anything else.

Hands-on Experience

The most important key to success on all of the Microsoft tests is hands-on experience, especially with Windows 2000 Server and Professional, plus the many add-on services and BackOffice components around which so many of the Microsoft certification exams revolve. If you are left with only one realization after taking this Self-Assessment, it should be that there's no substitute for time spent installing, configuring, and using the various Microsoft products upon which you'll be tested repeatedly and in depth.

5. Have you installed, configured, and worked with:

➤ Windows 2000 Server? [Yes or No]

If Yes, make sure you understand basic concepts as covered in Exam 70-215. You should also study the TCP/IP interfaces, utilities, and services for Exam 70-216, plus implementing security features for Exam 70-220.

 You can download objectives, practice exams, and other data about Microsoft exams from the Training and Certification page at **www. Microsoft.com/trainingandservices/default.asp?PageID=mcp/**. Use the "Exams" link to obtain specific exam information.

If you haven't worked with Windows 2000 Server, you must obtain one or two machines and a copy of Windows 2000 Server. Then, learn the operating system and whatever other software components on which you'll also be tested.

In fact, I recommend that you obtain two computers, each with a network interface, and set up a two-node network on which to practice. With decent Windows 2000-capable computers selling for about $500 to $600 apiece these days, this shouldn't be too much of a financial hardship. You may have to scrounge to come up with the necessary software, but if you scour the Microsoft Web site you can usually find low-cost options to obtain evaluation copies of most of the software that you'll need.

➤ Windows 2000 Professional? [Yes or No]

If Yes, make sure you understand the concepts covered in Exam 70-210.

If No, you will want to obtain a copy of Windows 2000 Professional and learn how to install, configure, and maintain it. You can use *MCSE Windows 2000 Professional Exam Cram* to guide your activities and studies, or work straight from Microsoft's test objectives if you prefer.

For any and all of these Microsoft exams, the Resource Kits for the topics involved are a good study resource. You can purchase softcover Resource Kits from Microsoft Press (search for them at **http://mspress. microsoft.com/**), but they also appear on the TechNet CDs (**www.microsoft.com/technet**). Along with *Exam Crams* and *Exam Preps*, we believe that Resource Kits are among the best tools you can use to prepare for Microsoft exams.

6. For any specific Microsoft product that is not itself an operating system (for example, SQL Server), have you installed, configured, used, and upgraded this software? [Yes or No]

If the answer is Yes, skip to the next section. If it's No, you must get some experience. Read on for suggestions on how to do this.

Experience is a must with any Microsoft product exam, be it something as simple as FrontPage 2000 or as challenging as SQL Server 7.0. For trial copies of other software, search Microsoft's Web site using the name of the product as your search term. Also, search for bundles like "BackOffice" or "Small Business Server."

If you have the funds, or your employer will pay your way, consider taking a class at a Certified Training and Education Center (CTEC) or at an Authorized Academic Training Partner (AATP). In addition to classroom exposure to the topic of your choice, you get a copy of the software that is the focus of your course, along with a trial version of whatever operating system it needs, with the training materials for that class.

Before you even think about taking any Microsoft exam, make sure you've spent enough time with the related software to understand how it may be installed and configured, how to maintain such an installation, and how to troubleshoot that software when things go wrong. This will help you in the exam, and in real life!

Testing Your Exam-Readiness

Whether you attend a formal class on a specific topic to get ready for an exam or use written materials to study on your own, some preparation for the Microsoft certification exams is essential. At $100 a try, pass or fail, you want to do everything you can to pass on your first try. That's where studying comes in.

I have included a practice exam in this book, so if you don't score that well on the test, you can study more and then tackle the test again. The Coriolis Group also has exams that you can take online through the **ExamCram.com** Web site at **www.examcram.com**. If you still don't hit a score of at least 80 percent after these tests, you'll want to investigate the other practice test resources we mention in this section.

For any given subject, consider taking a class if you've tackled self-study materials, taken the test, and failed anyway. The opportunity to interact with an instructor and fellow students can make all the difference in the world, if you can afford that privilege. For information about Microsoft classes, visit the Training and Certification page at **www.microsoft.com/education/partners/ctec.asp** for Microsoft Certified Education Centers or **www.microsoft.com/aatp/default.htm** for Microsoft Authorized Training Providers.

If you can't afford to take a class, visit the Training and Certification page anyway, because it also includes pointers to free practice exams and to Microsoft Certified Professional Approved Study Guides and other self-study tools. And even if you can't afford to spend much at all, you should still invest in some low-cost practice exams from commercial vendors.

7. Have you taken a practice exam on your chosen test subject? [Yes or No]

   If Yes, and you scored 70 percent or better, you're probably ready to tackle the real thing. If your score isn't above that threshold, keep at it until you break that barrier.

   If No, obtain all the free and low-budget practice tests you can find and get to work. Keep at it until you can break the passing threshold comfortably.

When it comes to assessing your test readiness, there is no better way than to take a good-quality practice exam and pass with a score of 80 percent or better. When we're preparing ourselves, we shoot for 90-plus percent, just to leave room for the "weirdness factor" that sometimes shows up on Microsoft exams.

Assessing Readiness for Exam 70-215

In addition to the general exam-readiness information in the previous section, there are several things you can do to prepare for the Installing, Configuring, and Administering Microsoft Windows 2000 Server exam. As you're getting ready for Exam 70-215, visit the Exam Cram Windows 2000 Resource Center at **www.examcram. com/studyresource/w2kresource/**. Another valuable resource is the Exam Cram Insider newsletter. Sign up at **www.examcram.com** or send a blank email message to **subscribe-ec@mars.coriolis.com**. I also suggest that you join an active MCSE mailing list. One of the better ones is managed by Sunbelt Software. Sign up at **www.sunbelt-software.com** (look for the Subscribe To button).

You can also cruise the Web looking for "braindumps" (recollections of test topics and experiences recorded by others) to help you anticipate topics you're likely to encounter on the test. The MCSE mailing list is a good place to ask where the useful braindumps are, or you can check Shawn Gamble's list at **www. commandcentral.com.**

 You can't be sure that a braindump's author can provide correct answers. Thus, use the questions to guide your studies, but don't rely on the answers in a braindump to lead you to the truth. Double-check everything you find in any braindump.

Microsoft exam mavens also recommend checking the Microsoft Knowledge Base (available on its own CD as part of the TechNet collection, or on the Microsoft Web site at **http://support.microsoft.com/support/**) for "meaningful technical support issues" that relate to your exam's topics. Although I'm not sure exactly what the quoted phrase means, I have also noticed some overlap between technical support questions on particular products and troubleshooting questions on the exams for those products.

Onward, through the Fog!

Once you've assessed your readiness, undertaken the right background studies, obtained the hands-on experience that will help you understand the products and technologies at work, and reviewed the many sources of information to help you prepare for a test, you'll be ready to take a round of practice tests. When your scores come back positive enough to get you through the exam, you're ready to go after the real thing. If you follow my assessment regime, you'll not only know what you need to study, but when you're ready to make a test date at Prometric or VUE. Good luck!

Microsoft Certification Exams

Terms you'll need to understand:

✓ Case study
✓ Multiple-choice question formats
✓ Build-list-and-reorder question format
✓ Create-a-tree question format
✓ Drag-and-connect question format
✓ Select-and-place question format
✓ Fixed-length tests
✓ Simulations
✓ Adaptive tests
✓ Short-form tests

Techniques you'll need to master:

✓ Assessing your exam-readiness
✓ Answering Microsoft's varying question types
✓ Altering your test strategy depending on the exam format
✓ Practicing (to make perfect)
✓ Making the best use of the testing software
✓ Budgeting your time
✓ Guessing (as a last resort)

Exam taking is not something that most people anticipate eagerly, no matter how well prepared they may be. In most cases, familiarity helps offset test anxiety. In plain English, this means you probably won't be as nervous when you take your fourth or fifth Microsoft certification exam as you'll be when you take your first one.

Whether it's your first exam or your tenth, understanding the details of taking the new exams (how much time to spend on questions, the environment you'll be in, and so on) and the new exam software will help you concentrate on the material rather than on the setting. Likewise, mastering a few basic exam-taking skills should help you recognize—and perhaps even outfox—some of the tricks and snares you're bound to find in some exam questions.

This chapter, besides explaining the exam environment and software, describes some proven exam-taking strategies that you should be able to use to your advantage.

Assessing Exam-Readiness

I strongly recommend that you read through and take the Self-Assessment included with this book (it appears just before this chapter, in fact). This will help you compare your knowledge base to the requirements for obtaining an MCSE, and it will also help you identify parts of your background or experience that may be in need of improvement, enhancement, or further learning. If you get the right set of basics under your belt, obtaining Microsoft certification will be that much easier.

Once you've gone through the Self-Assessment, you can remedy those topical areas where your background or experience may not measure up to an ideal certification candidate. But you can also tackle subject matter for individual tests at the same time, so you can continue making progress while you're catching up in some areas.

Once you've worked through an *Exam Cram*, have read the supplementary materials, and have taken the practice test, you'll have a pretty clear idea of when you should be ready to take the real exam. Although we strongly recommend that you keep practicing until your scores top the 75 percent mark, 80 percent would be a good goal to give yourself some margin for error in a real exam situation (where stress will play more of a role than when you practice). Once you hit that point, you should be ready to go. But if you get through the practice exam in this book without attaining that score, you should keep taking practice tests and studying the materials until you get there. You'll find more pointers on how to study and prepare in the Self-Assessment. But now, on to the exam itself!

The Exam Situation

When you arrive at the testing center where you scheduled your exam, you'll need to sign in with an exam coordinator. He or she will ask you to show two forms of identification, one of which must be a photo ID. After you've signed in and your time slot arrives, you'll be asked to deposit any books, bags, or other items you brought with you. Then, you'll be escorted into a closed room.

All exams are completely closed book. In fact, you will not be permitted to take anything with you into the testing area, but you will be furnished with a blank sheet of paper and a pen or, in some cases, an erasable plastic sheet and an erasable pen. Before the exam, you should memorize as much of the important material as you can, so you can write that information on the blank sheet as soon as you are seated in front of the computer. You can refer to this piece of paper anytime you like during the test, but you'll have to surrender the sheet when you leave the room.

You will have some time to compose yourself, to record this information, and to take a sample orientation exam before you begin the real thing. I suggest you take the orientation test before taking your first exam, but because they're all more or less identical in layout, behavior, and controls, you probably won't need to do this more than once.

Typically, the room will be furnished with anywhere from one to half a dozen computers, and each workstation will be separated from the others by dividers designed to keep you from seeing what's happening on someone else's computer. Most test rooms feature a wall with a large picture window. This permits the exam coordinator to monitor the room, to prevent exam-takers from talking to one another, and to observe anything out of the ordinary that might go on. The exam coordinator will have preloaded the appropriate Microsoft certification exam—for this book, that's Exam 70-215—and you'll be permitted to start as soon as you're seated in front of the computer.

All Microsoft certification exams allow a certain maximum amount of time in which to complete your work (this time is indicated on the exam by an on-screen counter/clock, so you can check the time remaining whenever you like). All Microsoft certification exams are computer generated. In addition to multiple choice, you'll encounter select and place (drag and drop), create a tree (categorization and prioritization), drag and connect, and build list and reorder (list prioritization) on most exams. Although this may sound quite simple, the questions are constructed not only to check your mastery of basic facts and figures about Windows 2000 Server, but they also require you to evaluate one or more sets of circumstances or requirements. Often, you'll be asked to give more than one answer to a question. Likewise, you might be asked to select the best or most effective solution to a problem from a range of choices, all of which technically are correct. Taking the exam is quite an adventure, and it involves real thinking. This book shows you what to expect and how to deal with the potential problems, puzzles, and predicaments.

In the next section, you'll learn more about how Microsoft test questions look and how they must be answered.

Exam Layout and Design

The format of Microsoft's Windows 2000 exams is different from that of its previous exams. For the design exams (70-219, 70-220, 70-221), each exam consists entirely of a series of case studies, and the questions can be of six types. For the Core Four exams (70-210, 70-215, 70-216, 70-217), the same six types of questions can appear, but you are not likely to encounter complex multiquestion case studies.

For design exams, each case study or "testlet" presents a detailed problem that you must read and analyze. Figure 1.1 shows an example of what a case study looks like. You must select the different tabs in the case study to view the entire case.

Following each case study is a set of questions related to the case study; these questions can be one of six types (which are discussed next). Careful attention to details provided in the case study is the key to success. Be prepared to toggle frequently between the case study and the questions as you work. Some of the case studies also include diagrams, which are called *exhibits*, that you'll need to examine closely to understand how to answer the questions.

Once you complete a case study, you can review all the questions and your answers. However, once you move on to the next case study, you may not be able to return to the previous case study and make any changes.

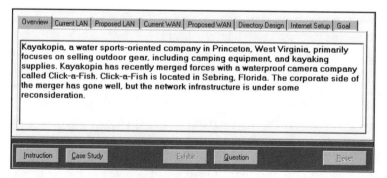

Figure 1.1   This is how case studies appear.

The six types of question formats are:

➤ Multiple choice, single answer

➤ Multiple choice, multiple answers

➤ Build list and reorder (list prioritization)

➤ Create a tree

➤ Drag and connect

➤ Select and place (drag and drop)

Note: Exam formats may vary by test center location. You may want to call the test center or visit ExamCram.com to see if you can find out which type of test you'll encounter.

Multiple-Choice Question Format

Some exam questions require you to select a single answer, whereas others ask you to select multiple correct answers. The following multiple-choice question requires you to select a single correct answer. Following the question is a brief summary of each potential answer and why it is either right or wrong.

Question 1

Of the following types of programs, which one is used for an unattended installation of Windows 2000 Server?

○ a. DCPROMO

○ b. Setup Manager

○ c. Setup Wizard

○ d. winnt.exe

The correct answer is b. Answer a is incorrect because DCPROMO is used to promote a member server to a domain controller. Answer c is incorrect because the Setup Wizard is used for an attended installation. Answer d is incorrect because winnt.exe is the program used to install Windows 2000 Server.

This sample question format corresponds closely to the Microsoft certification exam format—the only difference on the exam is that questions are not followed by answer keys. To select an answer, you would position the cursor over the radio button next to the answer. Then, click the mouse button to select the answer.

Let's examine a question where one or more answers are possible. This type of question provides checkboxes rather than radio buttons for marking all appropriate selections.

Question 2

Which of the following files systems can be implemented using Windows 2000 Server? [Check all correct answers]

❑ a. FAT

❑ b. FAT32

❑ c. NTPS

❑ d. NTFS

❑ e. HPFS

The correct answers are a, b and d. Answer c is incorrect because it is a made up file system. Answer e is incorrect because Windows 2000 does not support HPFS.

For this particular question, three answers are required. For Question 2, you have to check the boxes next to items a b and d to obtain credit for a correct answer. Notice that picking the right answers also means knowing why the other answers are wrong!

Build-List-and-Reorder Question Format

Questions in the build-list-and-reorder format present two lists of items—one on the left and one on the right. To answer the question, you must move items from the list on the right to the list on the left. The final list must then be reordered into a specific order.

These questions can best be characterized as "From the following list of choices, pick the choices that answer the question. Arrange the list in a certain order." To give you practice with this type of question, some questions of this type are included in this study guide. Here's an example of how they appear in this book; for a sample of how they appear on the test, see Figure 1.2.

Question 3

From the following list of famous people, pick those that have been elected President of the United States. Arrange the list in the order that they served.

Thomas Jefferson

Ben Franklin

Abe Lincoln

George Washington

Andrew Jackson

Paul Revere

The correct answer is:

George Washington

Thomas Jefferson

Andrew Jackson

Abe Lincoln

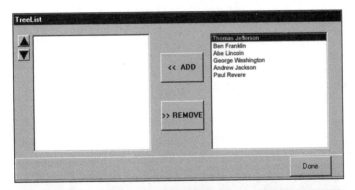

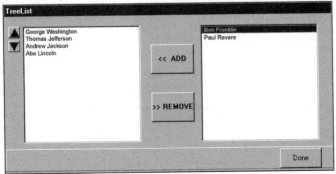

Figure 1.2 This is how build-list-and-reorder questions appear.

On an actual exam, the entire list of famous people would initially appear in the list on the right. You would move the four correct answers to the list on the left, and then reorder the list on the left. Notice that the answer to the question did not include all items from the initial list. However, this may not always be the case.

To move an item from the right list to the left list, first select the item by clicking on it, and then click on the Add button (left arrow). Once you move an item from one list to the other, you can move the item back by first selecting the item and then clicking on the appropriate button (either the Add button or the Remove button). Once items have been moved to the left list, you can reorder an item by selecting the item and clicking on the up or down button.

Create-a-Tree Question Format

Questions in the create-a-tree format also present two lists—one on the left side of the screen and one on the right side of the screen. The list on the right consists of individual items, and the list on the left consists of nodes in a tree. To answer the question, you must move items from the list on the right to the appropriate node in the tree.

These questions can best be characterized as simply a matching exercise. Items from the list on the right are placed under the appropriate category in the list on the left. Here's an example of how they appear in this book; for a sample of how they appear on the test, see Figure 1.3.

Question 4

The calendar year is divided into four seasons:

    Winter

    Spring

    Summer

    Fall

Identify the season when each of the following holidays occurs:

    Christmas

    Fourth of July

    Labor Day

    Flag Day

    Memorial Day

    Washington's Birthday

    Thanksgiving

    Easter

The correct answer is:

Winter

    Christmas

    Washington's Birthday

Spring

    Flag Day

    Memorial Day

    Easter

Summer

    Fourth of July

    Labor Day

Fall

    Thanksgiving

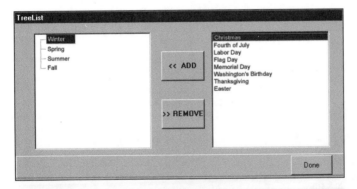

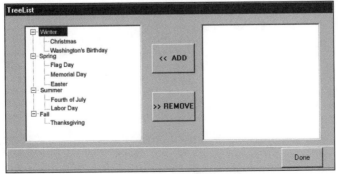

Figure 1.3 This is how create-a-tree questions appear.

In this case, all the items in the list were used. However, this may not always be the case.

To move an item from the right list to its appropriate location in the tree, you must first select the appropriate tree node by clicking on it. Then, you select the item to be moved and click on the Add button. If one or more items have been added to a tree node, the node will be displayed with a "+" icon to the left of the node name. You can click on this icon to expand the node and view the item(s) that have been added. If any item has been added to the wrong tree node, you can remove it by selecting it and clicking on the Remove button.

Drag-and-Connect Question Format

Questions in the drag-and-connect format present a group of objects and a list of "connections." To answer the question, you must move the appropriate connections between the objects.

This type of question is best described using graphics. Here's an example.

Question 5

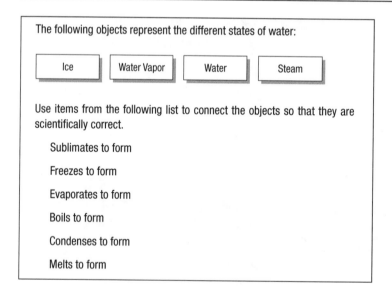

The correct answer is:

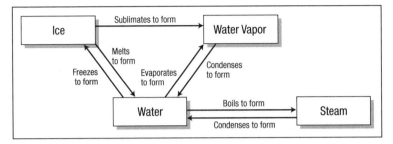

For this type of question, it's not necessary to use every object, and each connection can be used multiple times.

Select-and-Place Question Format

Questions in the select-and-place (drag-and-drop) format present a diagram with blank boxes, and a list of labels that need to be dragged to correctly fill in the blank boxes. To answer the question, you must move the labels to their appropriate positions on the diagram.

This type of question is best described using graphics. Here's an example.

Question 6

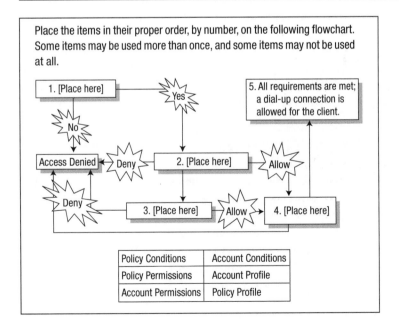

The correct answer is:

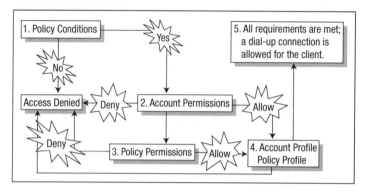

Microsoft's Testing Formats

Currently, Microsoft uses four different testing formats:

➤ Case study

➤ Fixed length

➤ Adaptive

➤ Short form

As we mentioned earlier, the case study approach is used with Microsoft's design exams. These exams consist of a set of case studies that you must analyze to enable you to answer questions related to the case studies. Such exams include one or more case studies (tabbed topic areas), each of which is followed by 4 to 10 questions. The question types for design exams and for Core Four Windows 2000 exams are multiple choice, build list and reorder, create a tree, drag and connect, and select and place. Depending on the test topic, some exams are totally case-based, whereas others are not.

Other Microsoft exams employ advanced testing capabilities that might not be immediately apparent. Although the questions that appear are primarily multiple choice, the logic that drives them is more complex than older Microsoft tests, which use a fixed sequence of questions, called a *fixed-length test*. Some questions employ a sophisticated user interface, which Microsoft calls a *simulation*, to test your knowledge of the software and systems under consideration in a more or less "live" environment that behaves just like the original. The Testing Innovations link at **www.microsoft.com/trainingandservices/default.asp?PageID=mcp** includes a downloadable practice simulation.

For some exams, Microsoft has turned to a well-known technique, called *adaptive testing*, to establish a test-taker's level of knowledge and product competence. Adaptive exams look the same as fixed-length exams, but they discover the level of difficulty at which an individual test-taker can correctly answer questions. Test-takers with differing levels of knowledge or ability therefore see different sets of questions; individuals with high levels of knowledge or ability are presented with a smaller set of more difficult questions, whereas individuals with lower levels of knowledge are presented with a larger set of easier questions. Two individuals may answer the same percentage of questions correctly, but the test-taker with a higher knowledge or ability level will score higher because his or her questions are worth more.

Also, the lower-level test-taker will probably answer more questions than his or her more-knowledgeable colleague. This explains why adaptive tests use ranges of values to define the number of questions and the amount of time it takes to complete the test.

Adaptive tests work by evaluating the test-taker's most recent answer. A correct answer leads to a more difficult question (and the test software's estimate of the test-taker's knowledge and ability level is raised). An incorrect answer leads to a less difficult question (and the test software's estimate of the test-taker's knowledge and ability level is lowered). This process continues until the test targets the test-taker's true ability level. The exam ends when the test-taker's level of accuracy meets a statistically acceptable value (in other words, when his or her performance demonstrates an acceptable level of knowledge and ability), or when the maximum number of items has been presented (in which case, the test-taker is almost certain to fail).

Microsoft also introduced a short-form test for its most popular tests. This test delivers 25 to 30 questions to its takers, giving them exactly 60 minutes to complete the exam. This type of exam is similar to a fixed-length test, in that it allows readers to jump ahead or return to earlier questions, and to cycle through the questions until the test is done. Microsoft does not use adaptive logic in this test, but claims that statistical analysis of the question pool is such that the 25 to 30 questions delivered during a short-form exam conclusively measure a test-taker's knowledge of the subject matter in much the same way as an adaptive test. You can think of the short-form test as a kind of "greatest hits exam" (that is, the most important questions are covered) version of an adaptive exam on the same topic.

Note: Some of the Microsoft exams can appear as a combination of adaptive and fixed-length questions.

Microsoft tests can come in any one of these forms. Whatever you encounter, you must take the test in whichever form it appears; you can't choose one form over another. If anything, it pays more to prepare thoroughly for an adaptive exam than for a fixed-length or a short-form exam: The penalties for answering incorrectly are built into the test itself on an adaptive exam, whereas the layout remains the same for a fixed-length or short-form test, no matter how many questions you answer incorrectly.

 The biggest difference between an adaptive test and a fixed-length or short-form test is that on a fixed-length or short-form test, you can revisit questions after you've read them over one or more times. On an adaptive test, you must answer the question when it's presented and will have no opportunities to revisit that question thereafter.

Strategies for Different Testing Formats

Before you choose a test-taking strategy, you must know if your test is case study based, fixed length, short form, or adaptive. When you begin your exam, you'll know right away if the test is based on case studies. The interface will consist of a tabbed Window that allows you to easily navigate through the sections of the case.

If you are taking a test that is not based on case studies, the software will tell you that the test is adaptive, if in fact the version you're taking is an adaptive test. If your introductory materials fail to mention this, you're probably taking a fixed-length test (50 to 70 questions). If the total number of questions involved is 25 to 30, you're taking a short-form test. Some tests announce themselves by indicating that they will start with a set of adaptive questions, followed by fixed-length questions.

 You'll be able to tell for sure if you are taking an adaptive, fixed-length, or short-form test by the first question. If it includes a checkbox that lets you mark the question for later review, you're taking a fixed-length or short-form test. If the total number of questions is 25 to 30, it's a short-form test; if more than 30, it's a fixed-length test. Adaptive test questions can be visited (and answered) only once, and they include no such checkbox.

The Case Study Exam Strategy

Most test-takers find that the case study type of test used for the design exams (70-219, 70-220, and 70-221) is the most difficult to master. When it comes to studying for a case study test, your best bet is to approach each case study as a standalone test. The biggest challenge you'll encounter is that you'll feel that you won't have enough time to get through all of the cases that are presented.

Each case provides a lot of material that you'll need to read and study before you can effectively answer the questions that follow. The trick to taking a case study exam is to first scan the case study to get the highlights. Make sure you read the overview section of the case so that you understand the context of the problem at hand. Then, quickly move on and scan the questions.

As you are scanning the questions, make mental notes to yourself so that you'll remember which sections of the case study you should focus on. Some case studies may provide a fair amount of extra information that you don't really need to answer the questions. The goal with this scanning approach is to avoid having to study and analyze material that is not completely relevant.

When studying a case, carefully read the tabbed information. It is important to answer each and every question. You will be able to toggle back and forth from case to questions, and from question to question within a case testlet. However, once you leave the case and move on, you may not be able to return to it. You may want to take notes while reading useful information so you can refer to them when you tackle the test questions. It's hard to go wrong with this strategy when taking any kind of Microsoft certification test.

The Fixed-Length and Short-Form Exam Strategy

A well-known principle when taking fixed-length or short-form exams is to first read over the entire exam from start to finish while answering only those questions you feel absolutely sure of. On subsequent passes, you can dive into more complex questions more deeply, knowing how many such questions you have left.

Fortunately, the Microsoft exam software for fixed-length and short-form tests makes the multiple-visit approach easy to implement. At the top-left corner of each question is a checkbox that permits you to mark that question for a later visit.

Note: Marking questions makes review easier, but you can return to any question by clicking the Forward or Back button repeatedly.

As you read each question, if you answer only those you're sure of and mark for review those that you're not sure of, you can keep working through a decreasing list of questions as you answer the trickier ones in order.

There's at least one potential benefit to reading the exam over completely before answering the trickier questions: Sometimes, information supplied in later questions sheds more light on earlier questions. At other times, information you read in later questions might jog your memory about Windows 2000 Server facts, figures, or behavior that helps you answer earlier questions. Either way, you'll come out ahead if you defer those questions about which you're not absolutely sure.

Here are some question-handling strategies that apply to fixed-length and short-form tests. Use them if you have the chance:

➤ When returning to a question after your initial read-through, read every word again—otherwise, your mind can fall quickly into a rut. Sometimes, revisiting a question after turning your attention elsewhere lets you see something you missed, but the strong tendency is to see what you've seen before. Try to avoid that tendency at all costs.

➤ If you return to a question more than twice, try to articulate to yourself what you don't understand about the question, why answers don't appear to make sense, or what appears to be missing. If you chew on the subject awhile, your subconscious might provide the details you lack, or you might notice a "trick" that points to the right answer.

As you work your way through the exam, another counter that Microsoft provides will come in handy—the number of questions completed and questions outstanding. For fixed-length and short-form tests, it's wise to budget your time by making sure that you've completed one-quarter of the questions one-quarter of the way through the exam period, and three-quarters of the questions three-quarters of the way through.

If you're not finished when only five minutes remain, use that time to guess your way through any remaining questions. Remember, guessing is potentially more valuable than not answering, because blank answers are always wrong, but a guess may turn out to be right. If you don't have a clue about any of the remaining questions, pick answers at random, or choose all a's, b's, and so on. The important thing is to submit an exam for scoring that has an answer for every question.

At the very end of your exam period, you're better off guessing than leaving questions unanswered.

The Adaptive Exam Strategy

If there's one principle that applies to taking an adaptive test, it could be summed up as "Get it right the first time." You cannot elect to skip a question and move on to the next one when taking an adaptive test, because the testing software uses your answer to the current question to select whatever question it plans to present next. Nor can you return to a question once you've moved on, because the software gives you only one chance to answer the question. You can, however, take notes, because sometimes information supplied in earlier questions will shed more light on later questions.

Also, when you answer a question correctly, you are presented with a more difficult question next, to help the software gauge your level of skill and ability. When you answer a question incorrectly, you are presented with a less difficult question, and the software lowers its current estimate of your skill and ability. This continues until the program settles into a reasonably accurate estimate of what you know and can do, and takes you on average through somewhere between 15 and 30 questions as you complete the test.

The good news is that if you know your stuff, you'll probably finish most adaptive tests in 30 minutes or so. The bad news is that you must really, really know your stuff to do your best on an adaptive test. That's because some questions are so convoluted, complex, or hard to follow that you're bound to miss one or two, at a minimum, even if you do know your stuff. So the more you know, the better you'll do on an adaptive test, even accounting for the occasionally weird or unfathomable questions that appear on these exams.

 Because you can't always tell in advance if a test is fixed-length, short form, or adaptive, you will be best served by preparing for the exam as if it were adaptive. That way, you should be prepared to pass no matter what kind of test you take. But if you do take a fixed-length or short-form test, remember the tips from the preceding section. They should help you improve on what you could do on an adaptive test.

If you encounter a question on an adaptive test that you can't answer, you must guess an answer immediately. Because of how the software works, you may suffer for your guess on the next question if you guess right, because you'll get a more difficult question next!

Question-Handling Strategies

For those questions that take only a single answer, usually two or three of the answers will be obviously incorrect, and two of the answers will be plausible—of course, only one can be correct. Unless the answer leaps out at you (if it does, reread the question to look for a trick; sometimes those are the ones you're most likely to get wrong), begin the process of answering by eliminating those answers that are most obviously wrong.

Almost always, at least one answer out of the possible choices for a question can be eliminated immediately because it matches one of these conditions:

➤ The answer does not apply to the situation.

➤ The answer describes a nonexistent issue, an invalid option, or an imaginary state.

After you eliminate all answers that are obviously wrong, you can apply your retained knowledge to eliminate further answers. Look for items that sound correct but refer to actions, commands, or features that are not present or not available in the situation that the question describes.

If you're still faced with a blind guess among two or more potentially correct answers, reread the question. Try to picture how each of the possible remaining answers would alter the situation. Be especially sensitive to terminology; sometimes the choice of words ("remove" instead of "disable") can make the difference between a right answer and a wrong one.

Only when you've exhausted your ability to eliminate answers, but remain unclear about which of the remaining possibilities is correct, should you guess at an answer. An unanswered question offers you no points, but guessing gives you at least some chance of getting a question right; just don't be too hasty when making a blind guess.

Note: If you're taking a fixed-length or a short-form test, you can wait until the last round of reviewing marked questions (just as you're about to run out of time, or out of unanswered questions) before you start making guesses. You will have the same option within each case study testlet (but once you leave a testlet, you may not be allowed to return to it). If you're taking an adaptive test, you'll have to guess to move on to the next question if you can't figure out an answer some other way. Either way, guessing should be your technique of last resort!

Numerous questions assume that the default behavior of a particular utility is in effect. If you know the defaults and understand what they mean, this knowledge will help you cut through many Gordian knots.

Mastering the Inner Game

In the final analysis, knowledge breeds confidence, and confidence breeds success. If you study the materials in this book carefully and review all the practice questions at the end of each chapter, you should become aware of those areas where additional learning and study are required.

After you've worked your way through the book, take the practice exam in the back of the book. Taking this test will provide a reality check and help you identify areas to study further. Make sure you follow up and review materials related to the questions you miss on the practice exam before scheduling a real exam. Only when you've covered that ground and feel comfortable with the whole scope of the practice exam should you set an exam appointment. Only if you score 80 percent or better should you proceed to the real thing (otherwise, obtain some additional practice tests so you can keep trying until you hit this magic number).

If you take a practice exam and don't score at least 80 to 85 percent correct, you'll want to practice further. Microsoft provides links to practice exam providers and also offers self-assessment exams at **www.microsoft.com/trainingandservices/**. You should also check out **ExamCram.com** for downloadable practice questions.

Armed with the information in this book and with the determination to augment your knowledge, you should be able to pass the certification exam. However, you need to work at it, or you'll spend the exam fee more than once before you finally pass. If you prepare seriously, you should do well. We are confident that you can do it!

The next section covers other sources you can use to prepare for the Microsoft certification exams.

Additional Resources

A good source of information about Microsoft certification exams comes from Microsoft itself. Because its products and technologies—and the exams that go with them—change frequently, the best place to go for exam-related information is online.

If you haven't already visited the Microsoft Certified Professional site, do so right now. The MCP home page resides at **www.microsoft.com/trainingandservices** (see Figure 1.4).

Note: This page might not be there by the time you read this, or may be replaced by something new and different, because things change regularly on the Microsoft site. Should this happen, please read the sidebar titled "Coping with Change on the Web."

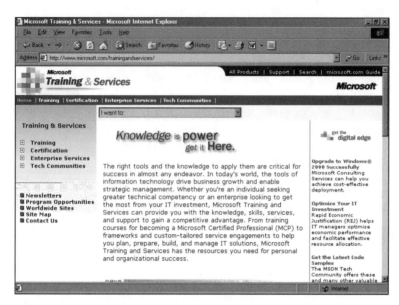

Figure 1.4 The Microsoft Certified Professional home page.

Coping with Change on the Web

Sooner or later, all the information we've shared with you about the Microsoft Certified Professional pages and the other Web-based resources mentioned throughout the rest of this book will go stale or be replaced by newer information. In some cases, the URLs you find here might lead you to their replacements; in other cases, the URLs will go nowhere, leaving you with the dreaded "404 File not found" error message. When that happens, don't give up.

There's always a way to find what you want on the Web if you're willing to invest some time and energy. Most large or complex Web sites—and Microsoft's qualifies on both counts—offer a search engine. On all of Microsoft's Web pages, a Search button appears along the top edge of the page. As long as you can get to Microsoft's site (it should stay at **www.microsoft.com** for a long time), use this tool to help you find what you need.

The more focused you can make a search request, the more likely the results will include information you can use. For example, you can search for the string

```
"training and certification"
```

to produce a lot of data about the subject in general, but if you're looking for the preparation guide for Exam 70-215, "Installing, Configuring, and Administering

Microsoft Windows 2000 Server," you'll be more likely to get there quickly if you use a search string similar to the following:

```
"Exam 70-215" AND "preparation guide"
```

Likewise, if you want to find the Training and Certification downloads, try a search string such as this:

```
"training and certification" AND "download page"
```

Finally, feel free to use general search tools—such as **www.search.com**, **www.altavista.com**, and **www.excite.com**—to look for related information. Although Microsoft offers great information about its certification exams online, there are plenty of third-party sources of information and assistance that need not follow Microsoft's party line. Therefore, if you can't find something where the book says it lives, intensify your search.

Introduction to Windows 2000 Active Directory

Terms you'll need to understand:

✓ Active Directory

✓ Domain controller

✓ Object

✓ Attributes

✓ Organizational Unit (OU)

✓ Domain

✓ Tree

✓ Forest

✓ Distinguished name

✓ Relative distinguished name

✓ User principle name

✓ Schema

✓ Global Catalog Server

✓ Operation Masters

✓ Two-way transitive trust

✓ One-way nontransitive trust

Techniques you'll need to master:

✓ Working with the Microsoft Management Console (MMC)

✓ Adding snap-ins to the MMC

✓ Understanding the naming conventions of the Active Directory

✓ Understanding domains and their roles in an organization

This chapter briefly reviews some of the new concepts and organizational features of Windows 2000 Server, helping to establish a foundation for the new operating system, as well as introducing the new domain structure of Windows 2000. This chapter also gives you the knowledge and vocabulary needed for many of the topics covered in this book and on the exam.

Active Directory

One of the enhanced concepts deeply integrated into Windows 2000 Server is Microsoft's version of a directory service: *Active Directory*. Directory services are not new to operating systems. They have actually been around for years, and they are not new to Microsoft. The Active Directory in Windows 2000, however, is a more advanced feature than seen in previous Microsoft products. The Active Directory is an organization's directory with a service that makes the information available to authenticated users on the network. It is the *directory service* database that allows users easy access to information and resources.

Directory Database

The directory database in the Active Directory is made up of objects. *Objects* are items such as servers, users, computers, printers, network devices, files, and folders. These objects are stored in the Active Directory in a hierarchical order. The storage of objects makes them easy to administer and easy to access. It is also easy to add objects to this hierarchy. The objects make up all of the information in the Active Directory database.

Domain Controllers

A *domain controller* holds security and directory database information for a domain in the Active Directory. Whereas Windows NT 4.0 used the *backup domain controller (BDC)* and *primary domain controller (PDC)* model, Windows 2000 no longer maintains these different levels of controllers. The domain controllers in Windows 2000 share their information with all the domain controllers in an organization and the information can be edited from any domain controller. No domain controller in the organization has more authority than any other; all the domain controllers participate at the same level. The Active Directory database is formed by a combination of all domain controllers. The information on each domain controller, including servers, users, and other objects, is replicated to other domain controllers to form the Active Directory database for that organization.

Fault Tolerance

Once a computer becomes a domain controller, that computer participates in what is called *multiple master replication*. Multiple master replication dictates that the domain controllers share their directory information with the rest of the domain controllers in the organization.

When a domain controller is added to a domain, that controller is recognized as being part of the Active Directory. Its information is replicated throughout the organization, and the organization's information is replicated back to the newly added domain controller. The domain controllers in an organization recognize each other, replicate their information to each other, and provide fault tolerance for each other. In this manner, all the domain controllers in the organization have a copy of the directory service database. Fault tolerant storage of information throughout the organization helps minimize data loss. If a domain controller goes down, information can be retrieved from another domain controller because they share the same information.

The Scalability of Active Directory

Windows 2000 scales to suit an organization's growing needs. The Active Directory gives administrators the ability to add domain controllers to handle the server loads and gives the expansion needed to add millions of objects. With multiple master replication, it is easy to add a new domain controller to an organization. It also does not disrupt the flow of the organization, and it integrates seamlessly. The ease of adding domain controllers makes Windows 2000 scalable.

Windows 2000 also allows an organization to be scaled so that millions of objects can be added to the Active Directory. As an organization grows, it can add not only more domain controllers but also more domains, users, groups, printers, files, and folders. Windows 2000 far exceeds the 40MB file size restrictions that applied to the NT 4.0 Security Accounts Manager (SAM).

The Active Directory is a central point of entry into a Windows 2000 organization. After users log on to a domain controller, they have access to anything in the organization to which the administrator has granted them privileges. This centralized access makes all objects in the organization available to users, no matter how large the organization becomes.

Central Administration

Central administration is another advantage for all administrators implementing Windows 2000. Because the Active Directory replicates all of the domain information throughout an organization, all the information is central for an administrator with the correct permissions. The administrator centrally controls servers, users, groups, printers, policies, and many other objects that we will discuss later in this book.

Security Model

Windows 2000 provides a security model that far exceeds other Windows operating systems. The security is controlled through the Active Directory. It can be controlled down to a particular user or object, or it can be set at a high level in the Active Directory and flow through an organization. The administrator dictates security procedures, but can delegate responsibility. The administrator easily can delegate control to other individuals at a general or a very specific level. The security model also includes policies and permissions. *Policies* restrict users from certain actions, and *permissions* restrict access to resources. Chapters 6 and 8 discuss these topics in depth.

Technologies Supported in Windows 2000

One of the advantages to Windows 2000 is the use of standards and protocols. Standards and protocols enable administrators to integrate Windows 2000 with many different types of networks regardless of operating system. It also gives the Windows 2000 operating system flexibility to be administered, changed, and configured from anywhere in the organization. In addition, it is compatible with systems outside of the Windows operating system. This compatibility is the result of components such as X.500, Lightweight Directory Access Protocol (LDAP), and Domain Name System (DNS).

X.500

X.500 is a naming recommendation put forth by the *International Telecommunications Union (ITU)*. This recommendation allows different directory services to communicate using common naming conventions. X.500 dictates that when the naming convention is followed, it can be integrated with other standards such as LDAP and DNS to form a fully functional directory service. This directory service integration allows objects to be queried by other operating systems.

Lightweight Directory Access Protocol (LDAP)

Windows 2000 uses LDAP to connect and communicate with other directory services. *LDAP* is the Internet protocol standard used for querying a directory service. After a common naming convention is established, such as X.500, LDAP can use the convention to query all objects in the directory service and publish the results. It enables you to search for resources, users, objects, and attribute fields. An example of a Windows 2000 LDAP query is a user who wants to find all the printers in an organization. The LDAP query returns all printers that are located in the Active Directory.

Domain Name System (DNS)

Domain Name System is used to manage computers in Windows 2000. DNS resolves host names to Internet Protocol (IP) addresses. Computers in a Windows 2000 domain are referred to by their DNS name. DNS stores information on computers, computer names, IPs, Internet addresses, and frequently qualified domain names (FQDN).

Transmission Control Protocol/Internet Protocol (TCP/IP)

TCP/IP is the Internet transmission protocol that allows communication between computer systems. Using TCP/IP enables global communication with any other computer running TCP/IP. Chapter 5 discusses TCP/IP configuration in more depth.

Microsoft Management Console (MMC)

Microsoft Management Console (MMC) is the main administrative tool for Windows 2000. MMC is the interface used in Windows 2000, and Microsoft provides snap-ins for different administrative tasks. A *snap-in* is a tool used to administer computers from MMC. Table 2.1 lists some common snap-in tools. Snap-ins include tools to configure services, configure objects, and administer computers. A list of snap-ins can be found in MMC by clicking Console|Add/ Remove Snap-Ins, and then clicking Add.

Microsoft also provides administrative consoles that are preconfigured with snap-ins. You can find these consoles under Start|Programs|Administrative Tools. Sometimes you may find that it's to your advantage to create your own MMC. Creating your own MMC allows you to have all the tools needed to administer your organization in one handy console. Figure 2.1 displays a newly created MMC console with snap-ins added to administer an organization. To create your own MMC, perform the following steps:

1. Click on Start|Run.

2. In the Run dialog box at the Location prompt, type "MMC".

3. In MMC, select Console|Add/Remove Snap-in, and click Add.

4. Choose the snap-in from the Add Standalone Snap-In box, and click Add.

5. Add the snap-ins needed to administer Windows 2000.

6. Click OK.

7. Select Console|Save As to save your snap-ins as your personal MMC for future use.

Table 2.1 Provided snap-ins.

Name of Snap-In	Function
Active Directory Domains and Trusts	Manages domains and trust relationships
Active Directory Sites and Services	Manages sites and computer services
Active Directory Users and Computers	Manages users, computers, and groups
Computer Management	Manages storage devices, drives, folders, system information, and computer events
Device Manager	Manages hardware devices: CD-ROMs, floppies, monitors, displays, ports, sound cards, controllers, and hard drives
Disk Management	Manages hard drives, file systems, volumes, and mounted volumes
DNS	Domain Name System configuration
Event Viewer	Logged events: application, directory service, DNS, file replication, security, and system events
Group Policies	Computer and user policy control
Services	All services and the status of these services
Shared Folders	All shares, sessions, and open files
System Information	System summary, hardware resources, computer components, software, and IE information

Logical Structure of a Domain

The *logical structure* is the way a domain is configured for administrative purposes. This structure is centered around objects, organizational units, domains, trees, and forests. The logical structure of a domain can be large or small. Windows 2000 allows small organizations to have a few servers in a single domain forest; whereas a large organization that has expanded can have a multiple tree forest for its logical structure. The logical structure does not take into account the physical location or network connectivity in the domain; thus the logical structure does not depend on the size or complexity of your physical network. The logical structure includes the following items that must be familiar to you: objects, attributes, organizational units, domains, trees, forests, and the schema.

Objects and Attributes

Objects are the most basic unit of organization in a network. Objects are items like a user, a printer, a group, or a computer. An object is defined by the *attributes* that are associated with it. All objects have attributes, and these attributes define the object. A user object may have attributes of first name, last name, phone, extension, address, and many more. Chapter 6 takes a closer look at objects and attributes.

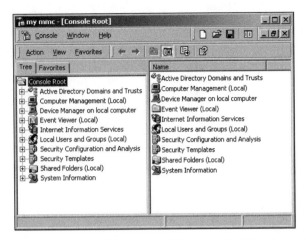

Figure 2.1   Microsoft Management Console with additional snap-ins.

Note: Objects cannot contain other objects. Attributes are the only items that are associated with an object.

Organizational Units (OU)

An *Organizational Unit* (OU) is a container that organizes objects. An OU can contain items such as users, printers, groups, computers, objects, and other OUs. OUs are used for administrative purposes to organize objects within a domain. OUs can also be used to aid administrators in delegating control of OUs for administrative purposes.

Domains

A *domain* in Windows 2000 is a group of computers that share a common security and user database. A domain must have one domain controller: A Windows 2000 Server. Using domains enables administrators to divide the network into security boundaries. In addition, they make it easy for administrators from other domains to have their own security models. Security from one domain can then be isolated so that other domains security models are not affected.

Trees

A *tree* is a logical structure that has more than one domain. The first domain in a logical structure is the *root* domain, regardless of how small or how large your logical structure becomes. The next domain that you add becomes a domain in a tree. The expandability of Windows 2000 makes it possible to have many domains in a tree. In a tree hierarchy all the domains share a common namespace or domain name. Figure 2.2 displays the onedomain.com tree hierarchy.

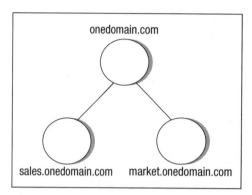

Figure 2.2 Onedomain.com tree diagram.

Forests

In Windows 2000 a *forest* is two or more trees that do not share the same domain namespace. An example of a forest is one company that has two domain names: onedomain.com and twodomain.com. Onedomain.com and twodomain.com keep their own namespace, and they share the same Active Directory database, schema, and Global Catalog. Figure 2.3 diagrams the onedomain.com forest with the two namespaces.

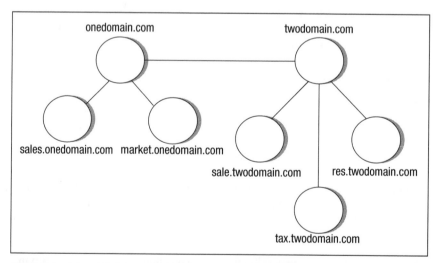

Figure 2.3 A forest that does not share the same domain namespace.

Naming Conventions

Naming conventions exist in Windows 2000 so that all objects in an organization can be located in a quick, easy manner. LDAP is the industry standard for naming schemes. LDAP defines a common way to refer to objects in the Active Directory. Using this standard, an object is defined by the object's name, the container the object is in, and all of the domain components that make up the logical structure. You can refer to an object in the Active Directory by distinguished name, relative distinguished name, and user principle name.

Distinguished Name (DN)

A *distinguished name (DN)* identifies the location of an object in the domain. The distinguished name is the most complex of the naming schemes because it identifies all of the components to quickly locate the object anywhere in the Active Directory. A distinguished name consists of fields that correspond with acronyms. The following fields and their corresponding acronyms have been defined by the X.500 standard:

➤ *CN*—The common name of the object or container.

➤ *DC*—The domain component of the object or container.

An example of a distinguished name is CN=JohnDoe,CN=Users, DC= onedomain,DC=com. This distinguished name can be interpreted by X.500 and LDAP and shows that John Doe can be found in the Users container in the domain onedomain.com.

Note: Distinguished names must be unique in a forest.

Relative Distinguished Name (RDN)

The *relative distinguished name (RDN)* refers to the object in a distinguished name. The relative distinguished name is a shorthand version of the distinguished name, which makes it easier to interpret. The relative distinguished name of the distinguished name CN=JohnDoe,CN=Users,DC=onedomain,DC=com is John Doe.

You use the relative distinguished name when you do more focused searches using LDAP. You use this name when the LDAP search has already narrowed the criteria to a certain domain. When the domain is already defined in the search, the only criterion needed is the name of the object in that domain being queried.

User Principle Name (UPN)

You can think of the *user principle name (UPN)* as the user's logon name. The name is accessed in the Active Directory as a login account. The user principle name for the distinguished name CN=JohnDoe,CN=Users,DC=onedomain, DC=com is JohnDoe@onedomain.com.

Downlevel Login Name

The *downlevel login name* refers to the domain and the object being referred to in the domain. This name is used for backwards compatibility with Windows. The NetBIOS name for the distinguished name CN=JohnDoe,CN=Users, DC=onedomain,DC=com is onedomain\JohnDoe.

 Becoming familiar with these naming strategies is important with the Active Directory. Administrators should be able to interpret the relative distinguished name, user principle name, and downlevel login name from the distinguished name that is given, and vice versa.

The Schema

The *schema* is a set of rules for objects and attributes stored in the Active Directory. The schema contains information on the different kinds of objects and the attributes for those objects. Remember that each object has a set of attributes associated with it. A user object has attributes such as first name, last name, phone, address, and ZIP code. These attributes are defined in the schema. The schema is the standard for all objects and attributes.

The schema is used any time that an administrator adds a new object to the Active Directory. When a new object is added to the Active Directory, the schema defines the fields that are available for the object. The new user object screen, by definition of the schema, allows attributes such as first name, last name, and other attribute fields. The schema defines the attributes associated with each object. Therefore, the user object does not have an attribute field of printer type because printer type is not an attribute associated with a user object in the schema.

Physical Structure of a Domain

The logical structure of a domain takes into account the Active Directory and the hierarchical structure of domains. The *physical structure* of a domain is defined by the location of computers and network connections to those computers. It also defines network traffic and how it is configured and managed. The logical and physical structures of a network should be thought of as two separate structures that do not relate to one another.

The physical structure is critical to network function in a domain, tree, and forest environment. It dictates how network traffic flows and how replication occurs throughout an organization. Sites and domain controllers define the physical structure of an organization. The site dictates network traffic, replication, and logon validation; whereas the domain controllers are the computers that form and define the sites.

The Physical Structure and Sites

A *site* is the main component of the physical structure in an organization. A physical structure can consist of one site or many sites. A site consists of a combination of one or more IP subnets connected by a high-speed link. Sites are used to segment a network into manageable parts depending on the *local area network (LAN)* or *wide area network (WAN)* speeds. A network is segmented by sites to help logon and replication traffic over slow network connections. When users log on to a network, they first attempt to log on to a local domain controller in their site. This enables the users to log on to a local domain controller rather than crossing slow LAN links to a domain controller in a remote site. The local site is always the first choice of computers within that site.

Sites also enable administrators to optimize networks. Traffic can be managed to the full network potential by organizing high-speed networks into sites. Setting up scheduled replication times between sites with slow or congested LANs or WANs can reduce logon and replication traffic. This ability to manage allows the administrators to have control over connections and how traffic is replicated through the organization. The segmenting of networks into sites is at the discretion of the administrator.

Domain Controllers

When Windows 2000 Server is first installed, the server has the potential to be one of two kinds of servers. It can be a *member server*, which does not participate in the Active Directory and domain security. It also can be a *domain controller*, which does hold the Active Directory and security information for an organization. All domain controllers in a forest hold a copy of the Active Directory database. This copy adds redundancy to the network. Every domain must have at least one domain controller. It is recommended that you have more than one domain controller per domain for redundancy and fault tolerance.

Some domain controllers in the organization have special roles. They are assigned to domain controllers by default, but an administrator can alter the role if justification is warranted. The most critical roles are the Global Catalog Server and the Operation Masters. The Global Catalog Server is responsible for searches and logins that take place in a domain. The Operations Masters have special roles that are either forest wide or domain wide.

Global Catalog Servers

A *Global Catalog Server* is the domain controller that maintains a global catalog. The main role of the Global Catalog Server is to allow users universal logon authentication. The global catalog is also the mechanism in Windows 2000 that coordinates and responds to queries of the Active Directory database.

The first domain controller in the root domain is automatically the Global Catalog Server. As domains are added to the organization, each site should contain a Global Catalog Server. It is recommended that each site have a least two Global Catalog Servers. If a Global Catalog Server is unavailable, it cannot refer users to a domain controller for logon authentication, and the users cannot logon to the domain. If more than one Global Catalog Server exists on a network, traffic is routed to the other available Global Catalog Servers.

The Global Catalog Server automatically caches default information for the organization. The cache contains information that has been previously queried or information that is predefined for every Global Catalog such as first and last names. An administrator can control the attributes given as results in a query and which objects cannot be queried. If searching becomes too slow because of the size of the organization, an administrator can configure another domain controller to be a Global Catalog Server to help balance the searching load. Global catalogs can also be moved to other domain controllers or added to multiple domain controllers throughout the organization.

 Operation Masters may be covered on the exam. Be prepared to explain how many of them there are, and how to optimize them.

Operation Masters

Operation Masters are domain controllers that are assigned to complete certain tasks for the domain or forest. The Operation Masters' duties are always specific to the domain or forest, and no other computer is allowed to complete these tasks. The tasks are separated into manageable areas, and because one server is responsible for one task, no other computer can take on that role. An administrator can transfer the roles of the Operation Masters to other computers to balance the computer loads. Operation Masters can perform two different roles: Forest-wide roles and domain-wide roles. The forest-wide roles are Operation Masters for the whole forest, whereas domain-wide roles are Operation Masters for the domain in which they reside.

Forest-Wide Operation Masters

Two types of forest-wide Operation Masters exist. The first is the Schema Master, discussed in the previous section, and the second is the Domain Naming Master:

➤ The *Schema Master* is the domain controller in the forest that is responsible for maintaining and distributing the schema to the rest of the forest. The first domain controller in the forest is the Schema Master. It maintains all of the object types and the attributes to those types. If the schema needs to be updated or changed (which is not recommended), it must be updated on the Schema Master by a schema administrator. It is also not recommended that the Schema Master role be moved to another computer, although it can be done.

➤ The *Domain Naming Master* is the domain controller for the forest that records the additions and deletions of domains to the forest. This Operation Master is important in keeping the integrity of the domain. The Domain Naming Master is queried when new domains are added to the forest.

Domain-Wide Operation Masters

The *domain-wide Operation Masters'* role is to control activity inside of the domain. These roles range in scope from keeping track of domain controllers in a domain to assisting non Windows 2000 users.

➤ The *Relative Identifier (RID) Master* is responsible for assigning blocks of RIDs to all domain controllers in a domain. A Security Identifier (SID) is a unique identifier for each object in a domain. A RID uniquely defines the domain in which the SID was created. A RID and unique SID represent each object in a domain. They uniquely define the object and specify where it was created.

➤ The *Primary Domain Controller (PDC) Emulator* is responsible for emulating NT 4.0 for clients that have not migrated to Windows 2000. One of the PDC emulator's primary responsibility is to logon non Windows 2000 clients. The PDC emulator will also be consulted if a client fails to logon. This gives the PDC emulator a chance to check for any last minute password changes for non-2000 clients in the domain before it rejects the logon request.

➤ The *Infrastructure Master* records changes made concerning objects in a domain. All changes are reported to the Infrastructure Master first, and then they are replicated out to the other domain controllers. It is also the Infrastructure Master's role to update other domains with changes that have been made to objects.

Trust Relationships

Trust relationships are the last topic we will discuss regarding the overview of Windows 2000 Active Directory. A trust is an agreement established between domains that allows them to have access and permissions to each others resources. A *trust* allows for rights to be assigned to administrators, users, and groups. Trusts have vastly changed since NT 4.0. One of the main differences is that now trusts by default are transitive. A transitive trust means that a trust relation can pass from one trust to another. In Windows 2000, the default is no longer the one-to-one trust relationship, it is a many-to-many trust relationship. There are two kinds of trusts in Windows 2000: two-way transitive trusts and one-way nontransitive trusts.

Two-Way Transitive Trusts

A *two-way transitive* is the default trust relationship for all domains in a Windows 2000 tree or forest. A two-way transitive trust is the automatic default for a multiple domain configuration. This allows other trusting domains access to all trusted domain resources. All trusts by default are not only transitive; they are also two-way. This implies that when a trust is set up between two domains they are both the trusted domain and the trusting domain, as shown in Figure 2.4.

An example of a two-way transitive trust is:

> DomainA trusts DomainB; therefore, DomainB trusts DomainA.
>
> DomainB trusts DomainC; therefore, DomainC trusts DomainB.
>
> Therefore:
>
> DomainA trusts DomainC, and DomainC trusts DomainA.

One-Way Nontransitive Trust

A *one-way nontransitive trust* can still be set up in Windows 2000 for compatibility with NT 4.0 domains. The one-way nontransitive trusts are the same trusts used in NT 4.0. In Windows 2000 these trust relationships must be manually created by the administrators from both domains. A one-way trust means that only one domain trusts another domain. It does not mean they both trust each other. A nontransitive trust relationship does not flow through an organization; it is a one-to-one commitment, as shown in Figure 2.5.

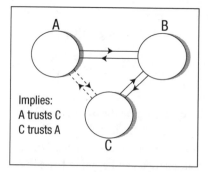

Figure 2.4   A two-way transitive trust relationship.

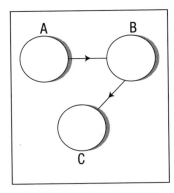

Figure 2.5   One-way nontransitive trust relationship.

An example of a one-way nontransitive trust is:

DomainA trusts DomainB.

DomainB trusts DomainC.

But,

DomainA does not trust DomainC.

DomainC does not trust DomainA.

DomainB does not trust DomainA.

DomainC does not trust DomainB.

Practice Questions

Question 1

> Which of the following are used as standards or recommendations in Windows
> 2000 Server to implement the Active Directory? [Check all correct answers]
>
> ❑ a. X.400
>
> ❑ b. X.500
>
> ❑ c. DIP
>
> ❑ d. LDAP
>
> ❑ e. IPX
>
> ❑ f. TCP/IP
>
> ❑ g. DNS
>
> ❑ h. DHCP

Answers b, d, f, and g are correct. Answer a is incorrect because it is an email standard. C is incorrect because DIP is a made up protocol. E is incorrect because the protocol IPX is not needed to make the Active Directory. H is incorrect because dynamically assigning an IP address is not a standard or recommendation used for the Active Directory, although Windows 2000 does support DHCP.

Question 2

> If DomainA has a default trust with DomainB, DomainB has a default trust
> with DomainC, DomainZ has a default trust with DomainQ, and DomainQ
> has a one-way nontransitive trust that trusts DomainA, what is the trust
> relationship between DomainB and DomainZ?
>
> ○ a. DomainB trusts DomainZ and DomainZ trusts DomainB.
>
> ○ b. DomainZ trusts DomainB and DomainB trusts DomainZ.
>
> ○ c. DomainB trusts DomainZ.
>
> ○ d. DomainZ trusts DomainB.
>
> ○ e. No trust exists.

Answer e is correct. The one-way trust of DomainQ trusting DomainA is exclusive to those two domains. Therefore, no other trusts between the domains exist.

Question 3

What is the relative distinguished name of the user: CN=SueJ, CN=Users, DC=onedomain, DC=com?

- ○ a. Sue
- ○ b. SueJ
- ○ c. Sue@onedomain.com
- ○ d. SueJ@onedomain.com
- ○ e. onedomain\sue
- ○ f. onedomain\SueJ

Answer b is correct. Answer a is missing the letter J in the name. Answers c and d are user principle names, and answers e and f are NetBIOS names.

Question 4

What is the user principle name of the user: CN=SueJ, CN= backupusers, DC=twodomain, DC=com?

- ○ a. Sue@backupusers.twodomain.com
- ○ b. SueJ@backupusers.twodomain.com
- ○ c. Sue@domain.com
- ○ d. SueJ@domain.com
- ○ e. Sue@twodomain.com
- ○ f. SueJ@twodomain.com

Answer f is correct. Answers a and b are incorrect because the backupusers common name is not used in the domain name component. Answers c and d do not have the twodomain.com. Answer e is incorrect because the letter J has been dropped from the username.

Question 5

> How many Schema Masters are in a forest?
>
> ○ a. 0
>
> ○ b. 1
>
> ○ c. 2
>
> ○ d. 5
>
> ○ e. 1 plus a backup Schema Master
>
> ○ f. 1 plus 2 backup Schema Master

Answer b is correct. Answer a is incorrect because you must have a Schema Master. Answers c and d are incorrect because you can have only one Schema Master per forest. Answers e and f are incorrect because there is no such thing as a backup Schema Master.

Question 6

> How many RID Masters are in a forest?
>
> ○ a. There are none in the forest.
>
> ○ b. There is one for the forest.
>
> ○ c. There are as many as the domain needs.
>
> ○ d. There are as many as there are domains.
>
> ○ e. There are as many as there are domain controllers.
>
> ○ f. There are as many as there are trees.
>
> ○ g. There are as many as there are sites.

Answer d is correct. Answers a and b are incorrect because a forest that has multiple trees must contain more than one RID Master. Answers c and e are incorrect because there can only be one RID Master per domain. Answers f and g are incorrect because there can only be one RID Master per domain.

Question 7

Who can edit the schema? [Check all correct answers]

- ❑ a. Users
- ❑ b. Administrators
- ❑ c. Backup Operators
- ❑ d. Schema Administrators
- ❑ e. Domain Administrators

Answer d is correct. Schema Administrators are the only users allowed to edit the schema.

Question 8

Which of the following are forest wide Operations Masters? [Check all correct answers]

- ❑ a. Domain Naming Master
- ❑ b. Infrastructure Master
- ❑ c. Primary Domain Controller Emulator
- ❑ d. Relative Identifier Master
- ❑ e. Schema Master

Answers a and e are correct. Schema Master and Domain Naming Master are the only forest-wide Operation Masters. Answers b, c, and d are incorrect because Infrastructure Master, Primary Domain Controller Emulator, and Relative Identifier Master are domain-wide Operation Masters.

Question 9

What trust is the default for Windows 2000?

- ○ a. One-way transitive
- ○ b. One-way nontransitive
- ○ c. Two-way transitive
- ○ d. Two-way nontransitive

Answer c is correct. A two-way transitive trust is the default for Windows 2000.

Need to Know More?

 Russel, Charlie, and Sharon Crawford: *Microsoft Windows 2000 Server Administrator's Companion*. Microsoft Press, Redmond, Washington, 2000. ISBN 1-57231-819-8. This is a valuable resource for information about implementing a forest, trusts, Active Directory, and Operation Masters.

 Search **www.ietf.org/rfc.html** for RFC 2052 for information on DNS SRV records.

 Search **www.ietf.org/rfc.html** for RFC 2163 for information on Internet DNS and X.500.

 Search **www.ietf.org/rfc.html** for RFC 2251 for information on LDAP V3 and X.500.

 Information on the TCP/IP protocol can be found by searching **www.ietf.org/rfc.html** for RFC 791 and 793.

 Search TechNet on the Internet at **www.microsoft.com/technet/default.asp** or the TechNet CD for more information on the following topics: Active Directory, domain controllers, domains, tree, forest, trusts, sites, Global Catalog Server, Operation Masters, DNS, TCP/IP, and LDAP.

Installing
Windows 2000 Server

. . . .

Terms you'll need to understand:

✓ Setup Wizard

✓ Licensing mode

✓ Distribution server

✓ Setup Manager

✓ UDF

✓ Unattended.txt

✓ Disk duplication

✓ Domain controller

✓ DCPROMO

Techniques you'll need to master:

✓ Understanding the hardware and software requirements for Windows 2000 Server, Advanced Server, and Datacenter

✓ Installing Windows 2000 Server from the CD-ROM

✓ Installing Windows 2000 Server from a network drive

✓ Installing Windows 2000 Server from Setup Manager

✓ Installing Windows 2000 Server from disk duplication

✓ Using the DCPROMO utility

✓ Upgrading from NT 4.0 Server to Windows 2000 Server

✓ Upgrading from NT 3.51 Server to Windows 2000 Server

✓ Upgrading from NT 3.5 Server to Windows 2000 Server

✓ Promoting a member server to a domain controller

This chapter discusses the installation of Windows 2000 Server. Installation is a topic that needs to be fully understood by any person taking the Windows 2000 Server exam. Questions about installation could possibly comprise up to 10 percent of the exam. The exam may focus on attended and unattended installations. The exam also may ask a few questions about the winnt.exe and the winnt32.exe switches. You need to be able to perform multiple installations and to understand the upgrade process. You also may be tested on your knowledge of upgrading different Microsoft operating systems to Windows 2000 Server.

Windows 2000 Server Requirements

The requirements for Windows 2000 Server are higher than other Microsoft operating systems. Windows 2000 is an advanced product that needs memory and hard drive space to function adequately. You see the best performance of Windows 2000 is on those systems that exceed the minimal server requirements. Windows 2000 Server encompasses three different operating systems: Windows 2000 Server, Windows 2000 Advanced Server, and Windows 2000 Datacenter. Windows 2000 Server is the standard Microsoft operating system; whereas Advanced Server and Datacenter are operating systems built to function with large amounts of memory and multiple processors.

Minimum Windows 2000 Server Requirements

These requirements are for Windows 2000 Server and Windows 2000 Advanced Server:

➤ Minimum memory of 128MB

➤ Hard drive space minimum is 1GB, with 2GB recommended

➤ Processor speed should be 133MHz or faster

➤ A minimum of a VGA monitor

➤ A keyboard

➤ A mouse

➤ A floppy drive, unless a CD-ROM or network can be used as an alternative

➤ CD-ROM drive (12X or faster is recommended)

➤ Network interface card (NIC)

You should always consult the *Hardware Compatibility List* (*HCL*) before starting an installation. Microsoft provides this list as a reference for hardware that is supported by Windows 2000 Server. Use the HCL to verify that the hardware is compatible with Windows 2000 Server. Microsoft has implemented a new technique called *driver signing*. This technique verifies driver compatibility before it is installed onto a Windows 2000 Server. We will discuss driver signing further in Chapter 4. To access the HCL, go to **www.microsoft.com/hcl**. If the hardware you are using is not on the HCL, you should address the driver and compatibility problems before you try to install the operating system.

Maximum Windows 2000 Server Requirements

Windows 2000 Server is limited in the hardware that it can support. If a Windows 2000 Server exceeds the maximum requirements, it is recommended that Advanced Server or Datacenter be purchased instead. During network planning, you should investigate the server requirements. The following are the maximum requirements, which cannot be exceeded:

➤ Maximum of 4GB of memory for Windows 2000 Server

➤ Maximum of four processors for Windows 2000 Server

➤ Maximum of 8GB of memory for Windows 2000 Advanced Server

➤ Maximum of eight processors for Windows 2000 Advanced Server

➤ Maximum of 64GB of memory for Windows 2000 Datacenter

➤ Maximum of 32 processors for Windows 2000 Datacenter

Windows 2000 Server Installations

You can install Windows 2000 Server in at least four different ways: A CD-ROM installation, a network installation, an automatic installation using Setup Manager, and an automated installation using disk duplication.

Windows 2000 Server CD-ROM Installation

One of the easiest ways to install Windows 2000 is from a CD-ROM. Installation is ready to begin after you check the HCL, verify the minimum requirements for 2000 Server, and purchase the 2000 Server CD-ROM. Install Windows 2000 Server as follows:

1. Insert the CD-ROM or the first of the four setup boot floppies.

To create four setup boot floppies, insert the Windows 2000 CD-ROM and at the command prompt type: *<DRIVE>*:/bootdisk/makeboot a:.

2. You can start the CD-ROM installation in three ways:

   ➤ If the hardware supports bootable CD-ROMs, simply boot the computer to start the installation.

   ➤ Start the Setup program by typing "<*DRIVE*>:/I386/winnt.exe" at the command prompt.

   ➤ If the four boot floppies are being used, insert the first floppy and start the computer.

3. Press Enter at the Welcome Screen to install Windows 2000.

4. Press F8 to accept the licensing agreement.

5. Select a partition on which to install Windows 2000 Server and press Enter.

Note: If you have a device with a Hardware Abstraction Layer (HAL) that is supplied by the vendor, there will be a line at the bottom of the screen early in the setup process that tells you to press F5 to supply a HAL.

6. Select the file system to format the partition. File systems are discussed more in Chapter 8. The two file system choices are NT File System (NTFS) or File Allocation Table (FAT).

Note: Remember that NTFS is the only file system supported by Windows 2000 that offers security features.

If you choose to format a new file system with a partition size larger than 2GB, Windows 2000 will automatically format it in FAT32.

The hard drive is now formatted, and the installation files are copied to the drive.

The computer restarts into a Graphical User Interface (GUI) interface. This interface is referred to as the Setup Wizard.

Do not confuse the Setup Wizard with the Setup Manager. Setup Manager is discussed in more detail later in this chapter. Setup Wizard is used for attended installations and Setup Manager is used for unattended installations.

7. Press Enter at the Window 2000 Server Setup screen, or wait and the installation continues without intervention.

8. Click one of the Customize buttons to change the regional options or keyboard layout. Then click Next.

9. Type your name and the organization or company name. Click Next.

10. Enter the product key from the back of your CD-ROM case. Click Next.

11. Choose a licensing mode. Per Server is the number of client connections to this server. Per Seat is the number of clients, regardless of how many servers they access. *Client Access Licenses (CAL)* must be purchased for the number of clients and the licensing mode that is chosen. Click Next.

Note: Client Access Licenses are not required for Internet Information Server (IIS), Telnet connections, or File Transfer Protocol (FTP) connections.

12. Type the computer name.

13. Type the administrator password and confirm the password. Click Next.

14. Choose any optional components to install. See Table 3.1 for an explanation of the optional components.

 You also can configure these options after the setup is complete by using the Add/Remove Programs icon in Control Panel.

 The exam may focus on IIS, Network Services, Network File and Print Services, Remote Installation Services, and Terminal Services. Before taking the exam, the tester should be able to recognize all of the optional components.

15. Adjust the computer time and date fields. Click Next.

Note: The time and date are critical on a server that will become a domain controller. If the time and the date are inaccurate, domain replication may not occur.

16. Choose the Network Interface Card (NIC) drivers and define the NIC settings.

 NIC and protocol settings may be covered on the exam. Be prepared for TCP/IP questions, which are discussed more in Chapter 5.

Files are then copied, configurations are applied, temporary files are deleted, and the system restarts with Windows 2000 Server installed.

Table 3.1 Windows 2000 Server Optional Components.	
Component	**Description**
Accessories	Contains options for vision, hearing, mobility needs, games, mouse pointers, WordPad, Chat, Hyper Terminal, Phone Dialer, and multimedia
Certificate Server	Installs the public key certificate authority application
Cluster Server	This option is only available on Advanced Server and Datacenter. It allows servers to work together, even during hardware failures
Index Server	Installs full text-searching capabilities
Internet Information Server (IIS)	Installs IIS 5.0 for Web and FTP services
Management and Monitoring Tools	Adds tools for improving network performance
Message Queuing Service	Installs a network communication service
Networking Services	Installs services such as DNS, DHCP, TCP/IP, Site Server, WINS, Control Services, Internet Authentication Service, and Internet Proxy Service
Network File and Print Services	Installs file services for Macintosh and print services for Macintosh and Unix
Remote Installation Services	Allows remote installation of Windows 2000
Remote Storage	Installs a tool to store files on other media types
Script Debugger	Enables programmers to find errors in scripts
Terminal Services	Installs a service to access Windows programs from remote computers
Terminal Services Licensing	Installs a service to keep track of Terminal Services' users
Windows Media Services	Allows streaming multimedia

Windows 2000 Server Network Installation

The network installation of Windows 2000 uses a mapped network drive on a distribution server. Administrators prefer this installation because the files are located on the network, and there is no need to keep track of a CD-ROM. The initial setup for a network installation is more complex than the CD-ROM installation. It requires a preconfigured network connection before installation can begin. A distribution server must be set up and available on the network. The distribution server contains a shared folder that is available to administrators on the network. The distribution server folder needs to have a copy of the I386 directory that is located on the Windows 2000 Server CD-ROM.

After the I386 directory is copied, the distribution server folder has the files needed to install Windows 2000 Server. You can access the server installation by starting the programs winnt.exe or winnt32.exe.

Winnt.exe Switches

The *winnt.exe* command should be executed to install Windows 2000 Server on Windows 3.x or DOS operating systems. You also can issue this command from a command prompt on any 16-bit operating platform.

When installing Windows 2000, it is sometimes necessary to change the installation process. Using switches allows for a pre-defined installation process to execute. Table 3.2 examines the winnt.exe switches and their functions.

Winnt32.exe Switches

If a version of Windows 95, Windows 98, Windows NT Server 4.0, Windows NT Server 3.51, or Windows 2000 is already installed, winnt32.exe can be executed. The *winnt32.exe* is the upgrade command for Windows 2000 Server. An upgrade saves the current operating system settings; therefore they do not have to be reconfigured. Winnt32.exe defines switches that allow pre-defined processes to be executed. Table 3.3 examines the winnt32.exe switches and their functions.

The exam may cover winnt.exe and winnt32.exe command switches, so you should understand this subject area thoroughly.

The steps for installing Windows 2000 Server over the network are as follows:

1. Boot the machine that will be used to install Windows 2000 Server.

2. Map a network drive to the distribution server.

3. Run the winnt.exe or winnt32.exe program from the distribution server folder.

4. The remaining steps are identical to the CD-ROM installation steps 3 through 16.

Automatic Installation Using Setup Manager

Setup Manager is a new tool provided in the Windows 2000 Resource Kit or on the Windows 2000 Server CD-ROM. It is used to automatically install Windows 2000 Professional and Windows 2000 Server. It assists you in creating scripting files for automatically installing Windows 2000 operating systems.

Unattended installation using Setup Manager may be covered on the exam. You need to be familiar with the process of implementing an unattended installation using an unattended file and a UDF file.

Table 3.2 Winnt.exe Switches and Functions	
Winnt.exe Switch	**Function of the Switch**
/a	Allows the accessibility options to be used during an upgrade
/e:command	Executes a command before the end of the Setup program
/i:file	Defines the location of the setup information file
/r:folder	Adds a folder to the systemroot folder
/rx:folder	Copies a folder to the systemroot folder
/s:path	Specifies the source of the installation files
/t:drive	Specifies where to put the temporary setup files
/u:file	Defines the location of an answer file that is used for unattended installations
/udf:file	Specifies a Uniqueness Definition File (UDF) to answer installation questions

Table 3.3 Winnt32.exe Switches and Functions	
Winnt32.exe Switch	**Function of the Switch**
/copydir:folder	Adds a folder to the systemroot folder
/cmd:command	Executes a command before the end of the Setup program
/cmdcons	Adds files for a recovery or repair console
/debug level:file	Debugs programs at a given level and logs information to a file
/s:path	Defines the location of the installation files
/syspart:drive	Marks a partition active so it is bootable in the event that the hard drive will be moved to another system
/tempdrive:drive	Defines the location of where to put the temporary installation files
/unattend:file	Defines the location of an unattended install with an answer file
/udf:file	Specifies a Uniqueness Definition File (UDF) to answer installation questions

The benefits of the Setup Manager are as follows:

➤ It provides a GUI interface to create and modify answer files and *Uniqueness Definition Files (UDF)*. Unlike NT 4.0 cryptic text file configuration, it provides a GUI question and answer interface.

➤ The *answer file* is used to give specific answers to general questions during installation.

➤ The *UDF* provides answers to questions that are unique to the individual computer being installed.

Note: Answer files and UDFs that had to be manual configured in NT 4.0 were difficult to use because of the complicated file syntax.

➤ It uses the GUI interface to ask installation questions and creates a file from your responses. There is no confusion about cryptic syntax in files.

➤ Multiple computers with different computer names can be automatically installed for you. This setup also can assign each machine with its own IP address and configuration information.

➤ You can load Original Equipment Manufacturer (OEM) programs, add additional files, and execute additional commands by simply specifying the location in Setup Manager.

➤ You can create storage devices and install network printers.

➤ You can customize Internet Explorer.

➤ It automatically creates a distribution folder for the installation.

➤ You can save your answer file to a floppy disk. The floppy disk enables you to perform an automatic setup to occur from a CD-ROM installation. The CD-ROM loads the operating system, and the floppy supplies the answer files.

Note: When saving the answer file to a floppy disk, the file should be saved as a:\winnt.sif. The winnt.exe program on the CD-ROM searches for this file when it boots.

To run Setup Manager, follow these steps:

1. Install the Windows 2000 Resource Kit or the Setup Manager from the Windows 2000 Server CD.

2. Start Setup Manager.

3. Click Next at the welcome screen. Figure 3.1 shows the welcome screen.

4. Specify whether you want to create a new answer file, create an answer file that duplicates this computer's configuration, or modify an existing answer file.

The rest of Setup Manager walks step by step through all the questions asked during installation. These answers are then put into an unattended.txt file. If you specified unique information, a UDF is also created. This information is then put into a shared distribution folder. If you specify, the Setup Manager adds the files needed to install Windows 2000 into the shared folder. The unattended.txt and the UDF can then be accessed from the shared folder or can be copied onto a disk for individual setups.

Figure 3.1 The welcome screen for Setup Manager.

Automated Installation Using Disk Duplication

Disk duplication capabilities have been added to Windows 2000. This option allows one installation to be duplicated to other computers. During the duplication process a program called *System Preparation Tool* is used, also referred to as the Sysprep.

Sysprep is run on a test computer that has Windows 2000 installed, but is not a member of a domain. It prepares the hard drive to be duplicated for another computer. Sysprep runs a program on the hard drive to be duplicated that deletes the *Security Identifiers (SID)* and other computer specific information. After the hard drive is prepared, a third party disk utility is used to copy the duplication to other computers.

Note: Only run Sysprep on a test computer. If you run it on a production computer, all of the original SIDs are deleted. Changing the original SIDs on a production computer, especially a server, can lead to undesired results.

The following steps must be completed to automate an installation using disk duplication:

1. Install Windows 2000 Server on a test computer to be duplicated.

2. Install any additional information that you want to be duplicated, including applications, files, or folders.

3. On the test computer to be duplicated, at the command prompt type "sysprep" to run the System Preparation Tool.

Figure 3.2   The warning screen before the test computer is prepared for duplication and the SIDs are deleted.

A warning screen such as the one in Figure 3.2 appears. This security-warning screen provides the last place to Cancel before the SIDs on the test machine are deleted.

The computer automatically shuts down.

4. Use a third party imaging utility to copy the duplicated test computer.

5. Install the image and the setupcl.exe program onto the computer or computers that require the duplicated image.

6. When the computer is started setupcl.exe will regenerate new SIDs for the computer and start the Mini-Setup Wizard. The Mini-Setup Wizard asks any questions that were not answered by the image and then completes the installation.

Domain Controller Installation

You can deploy Windows 2000 server as a member server or as a domain controller. A domain controller has the domain information, including the Active Directory database. A member server does not have domain information and does not take part in the Active Directory replication and security, although it is part of Active Directory. At any time you can upgrade a member server to a domain controller by using the **DCPROMO** command.

The *DCPROMO* command promotes a Windows 2000 member server to a Windows 2000 domain controller. Before this promotion can take place, the member server must meet the following requirements:

➤ The computer must be a Windows 2000 Server, Windows 2000 Advanced Server, or Windows 2000 Datacenter.

Note: If you run DCPROMO on a domain controller rather than a member server, the DCPROMO program will uninstall the domain controller and all of its Active Directory information. DCPROMO will then have to be run again to reinstall a fresh copy of the Active Directory.

➤ TCP/IP must be installed.

➤ The correct time and time zone must be configured.

Note: Because of the Active Directory replication, timing is critical to all domain controllers.

➤ A DNS server that supports *Service Resource Records* (SRV) must be on the network. If one is not available, the new domain controller you are installing can be configured to be the Domain Name System (DNS) server.

 If a DNS server is not available on the network, DCPROMO asks you to install this computer as the DNS server. If no DNS server is on the network, you must install DNS on the first domain controller. If a DNS server is temporarily unavailable, quit DCPROMO until you can locate the DNS on the network.

➤ One of the volumes must be formatted in NTFS for the Active Directory.

➤ The only person who can install a new domain controller is an administrator with rights to add a domain controller.

After these requirements are met, the **DCPROMO** command can be executed. The administrator is asked a series of questions to determine where this new domain controller will fit into the organization. Figure 3.3 shows the screen that contains the two questions. You are asked whether this is a new domain, or an additional domain controller for an existing domain.

1. Do you want to add a new domain controller to a new domain?

    Yes: Continue to questions A and B.

    No: Continue to step 2.

  A. Will this domain controller be a new domain tree?

    Yes: Continue to questions a or b.

    No: Continue to step B.

    a. Will this be a new forest?

    b. Will this domain controller be joining an existing forest?

  B. Will this domain controller be a child domain in an existing tree?

2. Do you want to add an additional domain controller for an existing domain?

After the DCPROMO wizard is completed, the Active Directory is installed, and the server becomes a domain controller.

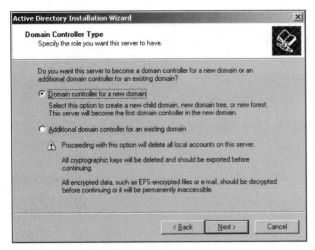

Figure 3.3 The Domain Controller Type screen. The options you see after this screen vary depending on your choice.

Upgrade Paths for Windows 2000

Designated paths are followed for upgrading computers to Windows 2000. The order of upgrading servers is important for the success of an upgrade. There are certain ways to upgrade NT networks to Windows 2000, and there are certain ways to upgrade depending on the function of the computer being upgraded. The following paragraphs describe different server upgrades.

 Knowing how to upgrade to Windows 2000 is an important topic that may be on the exam. You should know how to upgrade the different operating systems and what order to upgrade them.

Order of Upgrading Domain Controllers

The primary domain controller (PDC) should be the first server that you upgrade to Windows 2000. Upgrading the PDC to a Windows 2000 domain migrates the security accounts database from NT to the Active Directory database. This process saves administrators the time of having to input or reconfigure account information.

You can upgrade the backup domain controllers (BDC) at any time after you upgrade the PDC. It is recommended that one BDC be taken offline to remain as an NT computer until the decision to migrate all domain controllers to Windows 2000 has been made, keeping a BDC as a backup in case you decide to revert to an NT 4.0 domain. The BDC has the NT account database information. You can promote the BDC to a PDC to restore the NT domain if necessary.

Order of Upgrading Member Servers

You can upgrade Windows NT member servers to Windows 2000 servers at any time. The member servers do not hold security or account information for the domain. There is no conflict between the accounts database or domain information.

Windows 2000 Member Servers to Windows 2000 Domain Controllers

You can upgrade Windows 2000 member servers to domain controllers at any time. Member servers do not hold domain security information, and do not affect the domain security. To upgrade a Windows 2000 member server to a Windows 2000 domain controller, use the **DCPROMO** command.

Upgrading NT 4.0 Servers to Windows 2000 Servers

If an organization has NT 4.0 PDCs, BDCs, and member servers, you can upgrade these computers directly to Windows 2000. The PDC should be the first server in an NT 4.0 domain to be upgraded.

Upgrading NT 3.51 Servers to Windows 2000 Servers

Windows NT 3.51 servers can be upgraded to Windows 2000 Servers.

Note: NT 3.51 computers on 2000 domains are not recommended. Authenticaion is a problem because of two-way transitive trusts. In addition, NT 3.51 does not understand user accounts moved to a Windows 2000 domain.

Upgrading NT 3.1-3.5 Servers to Windows 2000 Servers

A server running Windows NT 3.1 or Windows 3.5 needs to be upgraded to a Windows NT 3.51 Server or Windows NT 4.0 Server and then upgraded to a Windows 2000 Server. The PDC should be upgraded to Windows 2000 and then the BDCs can be upgraded.

Mixed Mode and Native Mode

Windows 2000 Server and the Active Directory can function in mixed mode or native mode. Mixed mode defines the presence of NT and Windows 2000 domain controllers in an organization, whereas native mode defines the presence of only Windows 2000 domain controllers in an organization. There are benefits to both mixed mode and native mode.

Mixed Mode

A domain that is running in mixed mode is a network that contains Windows 2000 domain controllers and Windows NT domain controllers. Mixed mode provides support for domain controllers that are not Windows 2000. A network can remain in mixed mode indefinitely.

One of the advantages of mixed mode is that the domain can be reverted to an NT domain. Mixed mode also allows for a slow migration to Windows 2000. Migrations can take place as time allows. If all of the domain controllers in a domain are Windows 2000 servers, that domain can then be switched to native mode.

Native Mode

A switch to native mode is completed because all of the domain controllers in the domain are Windows 2000 Servers. In native mode, only domain controllers need to be Windows 2000; member servers and client computers can be running any operating system. Switching to native mode adds advanced security features such as nested groups and a new Universal Group. These features are discussed in later chapters.

To switch a domain to native mode, follow these steps:

1. Go to the Active Directory Domains and Trusts.

2. Right-click the domain you want to switch.

3. Go to Properties.

4. On the General tab, click the Change Mode box.

Note: Switching from mixed mode to native mode is a one-way process. You cannot switch a domain back to mixed mode.

Troubleshooting

During installation an administrator can have many different kinds of problems. Problems can stem from hardware, software, media, or incorrect typing. The following sections cover different types of problems that could occur during installation.

Hardware Problems

If the computer does not or cannot load Windows 2000, you may have hardware problems. Check the following items:

➤ Verify that all the hardware is supported on the HCL.

➤ Verify that there is at least 128MB of RAM in the server.

➤ Verify that the floppy drive and CD-ROM drive are functioning properly.

➤ If an error exists, check with the hardware vender or check Microsoft's TechNet.

Hard Drive Problems

If the hard drive does not boot, you may be experiencing problems with the hard drive. Check the following items:

➤ Verify that the hard drive is on the HCL.

➤ Verify that there is an operating system on the drive. Has the hard drive crashed or failed? If so, the hard drive needs to be replaced.

➤ Is the drive spinning up? If it is not spinning, it needs to be replaced.

If you cannot load Windows 2000 on the hard drive, check the following items:

➤ Verify that enough space exists on the drive. You may have to delete the operating system that is on the drive to free up enough space to load a new version of Windows 2000.

➤ When setting up partitions, verify that the partition has enough free space.

➤ Purchase a new hard drive with enough free space.

Media Problems

If the CD-ROM does not boot, you may be experiencing media problems. Check the following items:

➤ Verify that the hardware supports a bootable CD-ROM.

➤ Verify that the CD-ROM is not damaged.

➤ Configure a distribution server, and install Windows 2000 from a network drive.

➤ Create the four setup boot floppies to start the Windows 2000 installation.

Services Not Starting

If the message "One or more services failed to start" appears, check the following items:

➤ Check the Event Viewer to isolate the error. Take the Event ID, and use TechNet to find a fix for the problem.

➤ Verify that the network card is functioning.

➤ Check the network card drivers and settings.

➤ Verify that there is not a computer with the same name on the network.

DCPROMO Problems

If DCPROMO failed to run or a domain could not be created, check the following items:

➤ Verify that the domain name, tree name, and forest name are spelled correctly.

➤ Verify that a DNS server that supports Service Resource Records (SRV) records is functioning and available on the network.

➤ Verify in DNS that the computer domain name, fully qualified domain name, and IP address are correct.

➤ Verify that in the DCPROMO wizard that the computer name, domain name, and DNS name are spelled correctly.

If your domain is behaving erratically after running DCPROMO, check the following:

➤ If the computer was already a domain controller and you completed the DCPROMO setup, then this computer is no longer a domain controller for that domain. The domain controller information has been erased. DCPROMO must be run again to make the computer a domain controller.

Practice Questions

Question 1

> Winnt.exe setup is run using the **/e** and **/s** options. What function do these commands provide? [Check all correct answers]
>
> ❑ a. Windows 2000 is being installed.
> ❑ b. Windows 2000 is being upgraded.
> ❑ c. A program is being encrypted after installation.
> ❑ d. A program is being executed after installation.
> ❑ e. A program is being deleted after installation.
> ❑ f. The Setup file location is being specified.
> ❑ g. The Setup files are being deleted after installation.

Answers a, d, and f are correct. Answer b is incorrect because winnt32.exe is used for an upgrade. Answer c is incorrect because Encrypted File Systems (EFS) cannot be implemented until after installation. Answer e is incorrect because there is not a switch for deleting a program after installation. Answer g is incorrect because the Setup files are automatically deleted after installation.

Question 2

> You have a small domain with two Windows 2000 domain controllers, 50 Windows 2000 Professional computers, and 25 Windows NT 4.0 Workstations. You run the DCPROMO wizard on one domain controller. Two days pass and your event log is full of replication errors. What has occurred?
>
> ○ a. The **DCPROMO** command only changed the correct system time. You need to run the command again.
> ○ b. The **DCPROMO** command deleted the domain controller.
> ○ c. The **DCPROMO** command uninstalled the network card for the domain controller.
> ○ d. The **DCPROMO** command ran, and now the DNS server cannot be located.

Answer b is correct. Answer a is incorrect because DCPROMO does not change the system time, and running it again would reinstall it again. Answer c is incorrect because the network card must be functioning for DCPROMO to work. It does not uninstall the network card. Answer d is incorrect because you cannot complete the DCPROMO wizard without a DNS server being available.

Question 3

You need to create an unattended answer file for the installation of 20 new Windows 2000 Servers. Choose all the tasks that need to be completed. [Check all correct answers]

❑ a. Run the Setup Manager.

❑ b. Run the Setup Wizard.

❑ c. Run the Sysprep tool.

❑ d. Install a test computer with Windows 2000 Server.

❑ e. Create a distribution folder and make it available on the network.

❑ f. Make sure to add the number 20 to the box labeled Number Of Computers Being Installed.

Answer a is the only correct answer. Answer b is incorrect because the Setup Wizard is the same as the Installation Wizard used to install Windows 2000. Answer c is incorrect because Sysprep is used for the disk duplication process. Answer d is incorrect because you do not need a test computer to run Setup Manager. Answer e is incorrect because Setup Manager creates a shared distribution folder for you. Answer f is incorrect because there is not a box labeled Number Of Computers Being Installed.

Question 4

You are thinking about installing Windows 2000 Server. What are the minimum specifications the hardware must have? [Check all correct answers]

❑ a. 64MB of memory

❑ b. 128MB of memory

❑ c. 192MB of memory

❑ d. 850MB of hard drive space

❑ e. 1GB of hard drive space

❑ f. 2GB of hard drive space

Answers b and e are correct. Windows 2000 Server requires a minimum of 128MB of memory and 1GB of hard drive space.

Question 5

> After installing Windows 2000 Server, you log on and receive the following message:
>
> A service has failed to start.
>
> What is likely the problem?
>
> ○ a. The server could not log you on.
>
> ○ b. The server didn't correctly load Windows 2000.
>
> ○ c. The server has a video card problem.
>
> ○ d. The server is okay; this is a noncritical error.
>
> ○ e. The server has a problem with its internal clock.
>
> ○ f. The server has a network card problem.

Answer f is correct. Answer a is incorrect because this is not a logon or lock out error. Answer b is incorrect because the operating system booted to the logon screen. Answer c is incorrect because you can see the error message. Answer d is incorrect because you got the error message. Answer e is incorrect because an internal clock error would be given at bootup.

Question 6

> Where can you locate a copy of Setup Manager? [Check all correct answers]
>
> ❑ a. The Windows 2000 Server Resource Kit
>
> ❑ b. The Windows 2000 Server CD-ROM
>
> ❑ c. The Windows NT 4.0 Server Resource Kit
>
> ❑ d. The Windows NT 4.0 CD-ROM
>
> ❑ e. It is installed on the server by default

Answers a and b are correct. Answers c and d are incorrect because Setup Manager is a new product for Windows 2000. Answer e is incorrect because Setup Manager is an add-on product only found in the Windows 2000 Server Resource Kit and the Windows 2000 CD-ROM.

Question 7

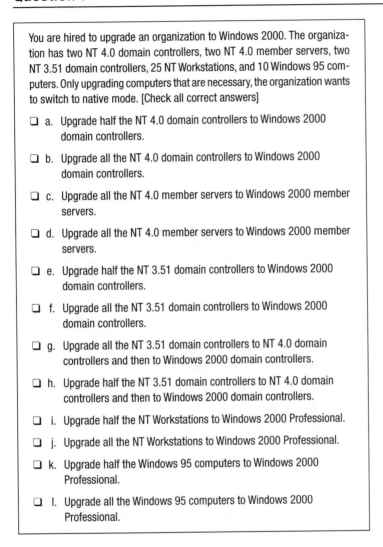

You are hired to upgrade an organization to Windows 2000. The organization has two NT 4.0 domain controllers, two NT 4.0 member servers, two NT 3.51 domain controllers, 25 NT Workstations, and 10 Windows 95 computers. Only upgrading computers that are necessary, the organization wants to switch to native mode. [Check all correct answers]

- ❑ a. Upgrade half the NT 4.0 domain controllers to Windows 2000 domain controllers.

- ❑ b. Upgrade all the NT 4.0 domain controllers to Windows 2000 domain controllers.

- ❑ c. Upgrade all the NT 4.0 member servers to Windows 2000 member servers.

- ❑ d. Upgrade all the NT 4.0 member servers to Windows 2000 member servers.

- ❑ e. Upgrade half the NT 3.51 domain controllers to Windows 2000 domain controllers.

- ❑ f. Upgrade all the NT 3.51 domain controllers to Windows 2000 domain controllers.

- ❑ g. Upgrade all the NT 3.51 domain controllers to NT 4.0 domain controllers and then to Windows 2000 domain controllers.

- ❑ h. Upgrade half the NT 3.51 domain controllers to NT 4.0 domain controllers and then to Windows 2000 domain controllers.

- ❑ i. Upgrade half the NT Workstations to Windows 2000 Professional.

- ❑ j. Upgrade all the NT Workstations to Windows 2000 Professional.

- ❑ k. Upgrade half the Windows 95 computers to Windows 2000 Professional.

- ❑ l. Upgrade all the Windows 95 computers to Windows 2000 Professional.

Answers b and f are correct. Answers a and e are incorrect because switching to native mode requires that all of the domain controllers in the domain are Windows 2000 domain controllers. Answers c and d are incorrect because only domain controllers have to operate Windows 2000 to switch to native mode. Answers g and h are incorrect because you can upgrade NT 3.51 to Windows 2000. NT 3.5 and NT 3.1 must be upgraded to NT 4.0 or NT 3.51 and then upgraded to Windows 2000. Answers i, j, k, and l are all incorrect because only domain controllers have to be Windows 2000. Desktop operating systems do not have to have Windows 2000 Professional installed to switch to native mode.

Question 8

> With which operating systems would you use the **winnt.exe** command?
> [Check all correct answers]
>
> ❑ a. DOS.
>
> ❑ b. Windows 3.1x
>
> ❑ c. Windows 95
>
> ❑ d. Windows 98
>
> ❑ e. Windows NT 3.5
>
> ❑ f. Windows NT 3.51
>
> ❑ g. Windows NT 4.0

Answers a and b are correct. Answers c, d, e, f, and g are incorrect because winnt.exe is the Windows 2000 upgrade for 16-bit operating system platforms.

Question 9

> You are setting up a distribution server to install five Windows 2000 servers. What needs to be available from a distribution server?
>
> ○ a. The i386 directory from the Windows 2000 Server CD.
>
> ○ b. The i386 directory from the Windows 2000 Professional CD.
>
> ○ c. The i486 directory from the Windows 2000 Server CD.
>
> ○ d. The i486 directory from the Windows 2000 Professional CD.

Answer a is correct. Answer b is incorrect because you are installing Windows 2000 Servers not Windows 2000 Professional. Answers c and d are incorrect because there is not a directory called i486.

Question 10

What command is used to create the four setup floppies?

○ a. **setup /ox**

○ b. **setup /b**

○ c. **makeboot**

○ d. **winboot**

Answer c is correct. Answers a and b are incorrect because these commands are Windows NT 4.0 setup switches. Answer d is incorrect because it is a made-up command.

Need to Know More?

Russel, Charlie, and Sharon Crawford: *Microsoft Windows 2000 Server Administrator's Companion*. Microsoft Press, Redmond, Washington, 2000. ISBN 1-57231-819-8. This is a valuable resource from which to learn more about installing and upgrading Windows 2000.

Search TechNet on the Internet at **www.microsoft.com/technet/default.asp** or the TechNet CD for information on: Setup Manager, Setup Wizard, Sysprep, Mini-Setup Wizard. setupcl.exe, licensing mode, distribution server, winnt.sif, disk duplication, and DCPROMO.

Search the Hardware Compatibility List (HCL) at **www.microsoft.com/hwtest/hcl**.

For more information on the following terminology and implementation of that terminology, refer to Microsoft Windows 2000 Help. To access this resource, click on Start and then click on Help. Terms and technologies to search for include: winnt.exe, winnt32.exe, Setup Manager, Setup Wizard, DCPROMO, upgrading, promoting, installation, and installing Active Directory.

Hardware Devices and System Optimization

Terms you'll need to understand:

✓ Drivers

✓ Driver signing or code signing

✓ Device Manager

✓ Windows Update

✓ Performance tool

✓ System Monitor

✓ Performance logs and alerts

✓ Objects and counters

✓ Task Manager

✓ Application server

✓ Web server

✓ File and print server

Techniques you'll need to master:

✓ Installing non-Plug and Play devices

✓ Updating device drivers using Device Manager

✓ Defining the correct IRQ settings for a manually configured device

✓ Setting up and configuring multiple hardware profiles

✓ Setting up and configuring multiple monitors

✓ Monitoring system performance with the Performance tool

✓ Monitoring the main performance counters and understanding their functions

This chapter covers hardware devices and system optimization. It is necessary for you to understand and be able to install, update, and optimize hardware that supports your Windows 2000 Server. Reviewing system hardware, plug-and-play devices, system performance, and the way to update drivers is important because these topics relate to the exam objectives. The troubleshooting section of the exam will be easier if you are familiar with system hardware configuration and server optimization.

Hardware Devices

A *hardware device* is a piece of equipment that is physically connected to a computer. Whether you start with great hardware when you installed Windows 2000 or you have added new hardware to your system, you need to know how to maintain it. Before you purchase new hardware, check the Hardware Compatibility List (HCL) at **www.microsoft.com/hwtest/hcl**. Microsoft only supports hardware that appears on this list. It provides this list as a reference for hardware that is supported by Windows 2000.

> The exam may cover hardware devices including IRQ settings, BIOS settings, and Device Manager configuration. You should be familiar with changing and implementing these different settings and configurations.

Plug and Play

Plug and Play is the program that automatically detects, installs, and loads the correct drivers for a device. Any device that is on the Hardware Compatibility List (HCL) automatically uses Plug and Play. You can use the Add/Remove Hardware Wizard in the Control Panel to add non-Plug and Play devices to a system. Manually configuring devices can take time and effort.

Note: To use the Add/Remove Hardware Wizard, you must be a member of the Administrators group. You also must not be restricted by any system policy that prevents you from installing new devices.

IRQ

If you manually install a device with the Add/Remove Hardware Wizard, you may be asked to specify the IRQ for the device. An *interrupt request (IRQ)* is a specific hardware channel that is used to send signals to the processor. Each device has its own unique IRQ that is a number from 0 to 15. If two devices have the same IRQ, a conflict message appears, and the device is disabled. Table 4.1 lists common devices and their corresponding IRQs.

Table 4.1 Common devices and their IRQs.	
Device	IRQ
System timer	0
Keyboard	1
Secondary IRQ controller or video adapter	2
COM 2 or COM 4	3
COM 1 or COM 3	4
LPT2 or sound card	5
Floppy disk controller	6
LPT1	7
Realtime clock	8
Unassigned	9
Unassigned or primary SCSI controller	10
Unassigned or secondary SCSI controller	11
PS/2 mouse	12
Unassigned	13
Primary hard drive controller	14
Unassigned or secondary hard drive controller	15

BIOS Settings

Basic Input Output System (BIOS) is the initial software program that tests hardware and transfers data to hardware devices. Windows 2000 supports the following BIOS standards: Advanced Configuration and Power Interface (ACPI), Advanced Power Management (APM), and Plug and Play. If your server is not using a Windows 2000-compliant BIOS, the setting can interfere with hardware configurations and setup. A noncompliant BIOS halts the computer at startup and displays instructions on how to fix the problem. If instructions do not appear, contact the hardware manufacturer.

 If you are using an Industry Standard Architecture (ISA) device that is not supported by Plug and Play, set the BIOS to reserve all IRQs currently in use by these devices. This procedure may alleviate errors when you reboot.

Device Manager

Device Manager supplies information about installed system devices, configurations, drivers, and their status. With Device Manager, you can check hardware status and update drivers. Figure 4.1 displays the Device Manager screen, which

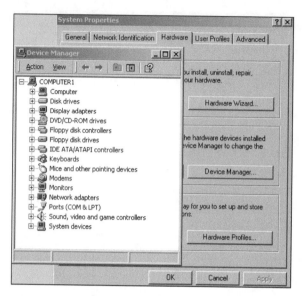

Figure 4.1 The Device Manager.

you access through the System icon in Control Panel. On the Hardware tab, click the Device Manager button.

Hardware Profiles

A *hardware profile* tells the computer which devices to load when the computer starts. You can have multiple hardware profiles for different computer configurations. You can set up one profile for the network and another profile for non-network activity. Only the profile that is on the network loads the network interface card (NIC) and its settings.

Configure hardware profiles by going to Control Panel and selecting the System icon. On the Hardware tab, click the Hardware Profiles button. Highlight Profile One, click Copy, and name the new profile. The two profiles listed in the box now are available choices when you restart the system. An administrator can use the hardware profile screen to select which profile should be started as the default and how long to wait before loading it. After a profile is created and selected at startup, you can use Device Manager to enable and disable devices for that profile.

Multiple Monitors

One of the new technologies in Windows 2000 is the support of multiple monitors, which spreads the desktop interface across 1 to 10 monitors. Multiple monitors require an additional PCI or AGP video adapter. When you restart the computer, Plug and Play detects and installs the additional monitors. In Control Panel, select the Display icon, and choose the Settings tab. Two options are available: Use This

Device As The Primary Monitor or Extend My Windows Desktop Onto This Monitor. These options give you the ability to have multiple monitors and to control which monitor displays which portion of the desktop.

Operating System Settings

Operating system settings control the way in which the system starts, displays information, and organizes information. The system settings are found in Control Panel. Table 4.2 lists some of the operating system settings, their location, and their function.

Drivers

A *driver* is software that binds a hardware device to the operating system. There are thousands of drivers that come with Windows 2000. The following sections discuss updating drivers and driver signing.

Updating Drivers

You can update drivers in Windows 2000 one at a time or all at once. To update a driver, use the System icon in Control Panel. On the Hardware tab, select Device

Table 4.2 Operating system settings.		
Operating System Setting	**Location in Control Panel**	**Function**
Startup And Recovery Options	System|Advanced	Controls the default operating system, the time to wait before the operating system starts, and what to do during a system failure.
Environment Variables	System|Advanced	Controls user variables such as the location of the Temp directory and system variables such as operating system information.
Regional Options	Regional Options	Controls the default language and keyboard layout.
Accessibility Options	Accessibility Options	Controls options such as screen magnification and keyboard speed.
Power Options	Power Options	Controls different schemes for power and uninterruptible power supply (UPS) settings.
Display Options	Display Options	Controls options such as monitor settings, appearance, and desktop schemes.

Manager. Choose the hardware device you want to update, select the Driver tab, and click the Update Driver button to start the Update Driver Wizard. To update all of the drivers on the server, go to the Start button and select Windows Update. Windows Update scans your computer for outdated files and drivers and then accesses the Microsoft Web site to automatically replace them with the most current versions.

 You should be familiar with installing and updating drivers.

Driver Signing

Driver signing, sometimes referred to as code signing, is another new technology in Windows 2000. *Driver signing* verifies that a digital signature was added to the drivers or operating system files by Microsoft. The digital signature assures you that the drivers and system files have been tested by Microsoft and are in their original condition. Driver Signing Options are reached via the System icon in the Control Panel on the Hardware tab. Figure 4.2 displays the options available for driver signing implementation.

The options include:

➤ *Ignore*—Installs all files regardless of which digital signature is used.

➤ *Warn*—Alerts the user before the operating system installs an unsigned, unverified file.

➤ *Block*—Prevents installation of unsigned or unverified files.

Figure 4.2   Driver Signing Options dialog box.

Driver signing may appear on the exam. You should be familiar with driver signing and signing options.

Three additional components enhance driver signing:

➤ *Windows File Protection*—Prevents system files from being replaced by files that are not digitally signed by Microsoft. Protected files have extensions such as .sys, .dll, .exe, .ocx, .ttf, and .fon. Windows File Protection monitors system files, verifies the digital signatures, and replaces non-Microsoft files with the original copies that are backed up in the Dllcache folder.

➤ *System File Checker*—A command line utility, sfc.exe, that verifies the correct system files versions is in use. It detects incorrect file versions and replaces them with a correct copy from the Dllcache folder.

➤ *File Signature Verification*—A wizard that is initiated by the **sigverify** command. It scans Windows 2000 and starts a log file that reports which files are signed, which files are unsigned, the modified date, and the version of each file.

System Performance

Many factors contribute to overall system performance: server function, hardware, and optimization. This section looks at ways to monitor a server for optimized performance.

Monitoring System Peformance

Monitoring and optimizing system performance can be a large task for any administrator. An administrator can use two tools to monitor system resources: the Performance tool and Task Manager. The Performance tool enables an administrator to log system performance counters to a file. The administrator then uses the data that is collected to analyze and optimize the server. Task Manager gives an overview of the system's performance and enables an administrator to stop processes that are slowing down the server.

Performance Tool

Windows NT 4.0 Performance Monitor has been replaced by a more powerful program called the Performance tool. It is used to monitor, collect, and store information about local and remote servers. The data that is collected can be used to optimize and troubleshoot the server. Data that is collected over time is helpful in finding server slowdowns or bottlenecks. Bottlenecks can sometimes be easily fixed by adding more memory or another processor, or they can be complex problems that take hours of research.

Table 4.3	The components of Performance Tool.
Component	**Function of the Component**
System Monitor	An administrator adds performance counters to be charted, logged, or reported. The system performance information is displayed in realtime and can be saved to a log file. Important objects and counters are displayed in Table 4.4.
Counter Logs	Record and collect data about specified counts and log the information to a file. The defined set of counters can be scheduled to run at specific time intervals.
Trace Logs	Record and collect data about the operating system and programs to a file. Collected data can be scheduled to run at specific time intervals.
Alerts	Notify the administrator when a defined counter falls above or below a specified range.

In front of each log there is a colored icon. A green icon indicates that the log is running, and a red icon indicates that the log has stopped.

The Performance tool consists of System Monitor and Performance Logs And Alerts. Table 4.3 defines the different components of the Performance tool. You can access the Performance tool through the Administrative tools by clicking Performance, as displayed in Figure 4.3.

Note: Log files can be exported to spreadsheets for further analysis.

Objects are main divisions of tracking system performance. The most frequently monitored objects are cache, memory, objects, paging file, physical disk, process, processor, server, system, and thread. *Counters* are the data associated with an

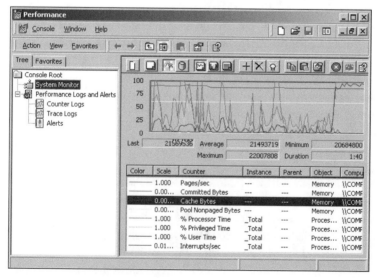

Figure 4.3 The Performance tool.

object's performance. The Performance tool has the capability to track thousands of performance counters. Some of the main objects to monitor are memory, process, disk, and network. As you add Microsoft programs, more counters may be added to the Performance tool to assist in monitoring the new programs. Table 4.4 lists common objects, counters, and what they monitor.

The exam may cover objects and counters used in the Performance tool. You should be familiar with counters, the range of normal values, and understand what it means when a counter is higher or lower than expected. For example, if the Memory|Pages/sec is high, excessive paging is occurring between the page file and RAM. In this case an administrator would know to add more memory.

The **diskperf -y** command must be executed and the system must be rebooted before disk counters can collect data.

Task Manager

Task Manager is a tool used to monitor programs, track system performance, and maintain processes. It can also be used to stop processes that are not responding and monitor which processes are using up system resources. You can access Task Manager by right-clicking on the Taskbar and selecting Task Manager. Figure 4.4 displays the Task Manager interface.

Image Name	PID	CPU	CPU Time	Mem Usage
System Idle Process	0	00	2:02:50	16 K
System	8	00	0:00:17	212 K
smss.exe	176	00	0:00:01	344 K
csrss.exe	204	01	0:00:18	472 K
winlogon.exe	224	00	0:00:09	2,816 K
services.exe	252	00	0:00:09	4,488 K
lsass.exe	264	00	0:00:25	10,420 K
svchost.exe	460	00	0:00:00	2,180 K
SPOOLSV.EXE	500	00	0:00:00	1,724 K
hh.exe	604	00	0:00:58	7,792 K
cmd.exe	648	00	0:00:00	40 K
msdtc.exe	688	00	0:00:00	2,284 K
dfssvc.exe	804	00	0:00:01	2,108 K
tcpsvcs.exe	816	00	0:00:02	3,368 K
svchost.exe	848	00	0:00:01	3,792 K
ismserv.exe	860	00	0:00:00	2,240 K
mdm.exe	892	00	0:00:00	1,932 K
llssrv.exe	900	00	0:00:02	3,364 K
ntfrs.exe	932	00	0:00:05	680 K

End Process

Processes: 30   CPU Usage: 100%   Mem Usage: 95776K / 210028K

Figure 4.4 Task Manager.

Table 4.4	Counters to watch out for.	
Object	**Counter**	**What It Monitors**
Memory	Available Bytes	Records the available physical memory.
Memory	Committed Bytes	Records the virtual memory committed.
Memory	Pages/sec	Records hard page faults per second.
Memory	Pool Non-Paged Bytes	Records the number of bytes in the nonpaged pool.
Processor	% Processor Time	Records the time for threads to process.
Processor	% Privilege Time	Records the time spent on processing threads.
Processor	% User Time	Records the time spent on processing users threads.
Processor	Interrupts/sec	Records the number of hardware interrupts the processor receives per second.
Physical Disk	% Disk Time	Records the time a disk spends working.
Physical Disk	Avg. Disk Bytes/Transfer	Records the number of bytes transferred to and from a disk.
Physical Disk	Disk Bytes/sec	Records the rate of bytes being transferred.
Physical Disk	Current Disk Queue Length	Records the number of requests that require processing.
Network Interface	Bytes Total/sec	Records the bytes sent and received per second.
Network Interface	Current Bandwidth	Records the estimated bits per second.
Network Interface	Bytes Sent/sec	Records the bytes sent per second.

Task Manager has three tabs that you can use to track system resources:

➤ The Applications tab displays the currently running programs and their status. Right-clicking on a program enables you to switch to that task and end the task. The Applications tab is mainly used to stop programs that are not responding by ending the task.

➤ The Processes tab displays the current processes that are running, process ID (PID), Central Processing Unit (CPU) percentage, CPU time, and memory usage. The Processes tab is mainly used to end processes and set process priority. To change the priority of a process, right-click it, select Set Priority, and click the new priority. Processes can be set to Realtime, High, Above Normal, or Low. The default process starts at Normal, but an administrator should know how to change a process's priority and what priority to change it to.

Note: Setting a priority of Realtime makes all the other processes on the server halt because the server spends all of its processing on the Realtime process.

➤ The Performance tab displays the CPU usage, memory usage, and statistics on memory and processor information. This tab gives an overview of the system and is only for viewing.

Optimizing System Performance

Optimizing a system's performance takes time and effort on the part of an administrator. You can use the Performance tool to set up and track counters on a daily or hourly schedule. The log files can be used to track changes over time and find system bottlenecks. The two most common bottlenecks are lack of memory and processing power.

 You should be familiar with the Performance tool and its functions. The exam may cover different counters and their meanings, tracking individual processes, or counters that need to be monitored to achieve a baseline result.

The exam may include questions regarding servers that function with specific roles in the network. These roles include an application server, a Web server, and a file and print server. You monitor different performance counters depending on the type of role you are trying to monitor and optimize. The following types of servers can be optimized by focusing on the most used resources of the server.

Application Server

An *application server*'s function is to provide applications to the users on the network. Examples of an application server include a dedicated Terminal Server or a server that runs a broad range of applications in a client/server environment. If you are trying to optimize an application server, focus on the processor and memory counters. Application servers tend to use processor and memory system resources, while not heavily utilizing the available network and disk resources. Chapters 9 and 10 address different application server services and how to install them.

Web Server

A *Web server*'s function is to provide Web services, file transfer protocol (FTP) services, Network News Transfer Protocol (NNTP), and Simple Mail Transfer Protocol (SMTP) to clients. If you are trying to optimize a Web server, analyze the memory and network performance counters. A Web server tends to use more memory and network system resources than other servers, but depending on the size of the Web server, it can use extensive processor and disk resources. Chapter 9 focuses on Web server setup and maintenance.

File and Print Server

A *file and print server* supports file storage, while still providing access to net-worked printers. If you are trying to optimize a file and print server, focus on the memory and disk counters. A file and print server tends to use more memory than any of the other system resources. Processor and network resources are only lightly used by this type of server, but the disk may be more heavily used. Chapter 9 focuses more on setting up and maintaining a file and print server environment.

Practice Questions

Question 1

> You are using the Performance Tool System Monitor to log the following counters. What is most likely needed to optimize this server's performance over the long term?
>
> | Counter | Value |
> |---|---|
> | Available Bytes | Medium |
> | Pages/Sec | High |
> | % User Time | Low |
> | % Processor Time | Low |
> | % Disk Time | High |
>
> ○ a. Add more memory
> ○ b. Add another processor
> ○ c. Add another hard drive
> ○ d. Reboot the system
> ○ e. Restrict users to system resources

Answer a is correct. Answer b is incorrect because the processor counter is low. Answer c in incorrect because the high usage of the disk is probably due to excessive paging from RAM to virtual memory. Answer d is incorrect because rebooting the system clears the page file, but does not fix the long term problem. Answer e is incorrect because the user time on the system is low.

Question 2

> You are using the Performance Tool System Monitor to create a baseline of a new server. The disk counters that you are monitoring are not displaying data. What should you do? [Check all correct answers]
>
> ❑ a. Restart the computer
> ❑ b. Reload the Performance Tool
> ❑ c. Run Diskperf -y
> ❑ d. Run Diskperf -u
> ❑ e. Stop and restart the System Monitor

Answers a and c are correct. You will need to run Diskperf -y and then restart the computer to activate the disk counters. Answer b is incorrect because reloading the Performance Tool does not activate the disk counters. Answer d is incorrect because Diskperf -u is a nonexistent switch. Answer e is incorrect because System Monitor does not have the option to stop and restart. In addition, stopping and starting this tool does not activate the disk counters.

Question 3

> What tool would an administrator use to update all of a server's system files?
>
> O a. Performance Tool
>
> O b. Plug and Play
>
> O c. Task Manager
>
> O d. Update Driver Wizard
>
> O e. Windows Update

Answer e is correct. Answer a is incorrect because the Performance tool is used to monitor system performance, not to update drivers. Answer b is incorrect because Plug and Play is a program that executes when new hardware devices are installed, and it does not update system files. Answer c is incorrect because Task Manager is used to monitor system performance and stop programs that are not responding. Answer d is incorrect because the Update Driver Wizard is used to update a driver for a particular hardware device.

Question 4

> Which of the following tools can you use to monitor system hardware? [Check all correct answers]
>
> ❏ a. Device Manager
>
> ❏ b. Task Manager
>
> ❏ c. Hardware Monitor
>
> ❏ d. Performance Tool
>
> ❏ e. The BIOS
>
> ❏ f. Plug and Play
>
> ❏ g. Explorer

Answers a, b, and d are the correct answers. Answer c is incorrect because it is a non-existent program. Answer e is incorrect because the BIOS does not monitor system hardware. Answer f is incorrect because Plug and Play is a program that detects and installs new hardware; it does not monitor the hardware. Answer g is incorrect because Explorer is not used to monitor system hardware.

Question 5

You are using the Performance Tool System Monitor to track the following counters. What is most likely needed to optimize the server's performance over the long term?

Counter	Value
Available Bytes	Medium
Pages/Sec	Medium
% User Time	High
% Processor Time	High
% Disk Time	Low

○ a. Add more memory

○ b. Add another processor

○ c. Add another hard drive

○ d. Reboot the system

Answer b is correct. Answer a is incorrect because the processor is high, but the memory usage and the page file are still midrange. Answer c is incorrect because the disk time is low, which also helps rule out adding more memory. Answer d is incorrect because rebooting does not fix the long-term problem.

Question 6

> You installed a new modem onto a server's COM 1 port. Plug and Play did not work to detect the modem. You start the Add/Remove Hardware program, and the wizard asks you to define the IRQ. What IRQ setting should you use?
>
> ○ a. IRQ 2
>
> ○ b. IRQ 3
>
> ○ c. IRQ 4
>
> ○ d. IRQ 6
>
> ○ e. IRQ 7
>
> ○ f. IRQ 8

Answer c is correct. Answer a is incorrect because the secondary IRQ controller or video adapter uses IRQ 2. Answer b is incorrect because COM 2 or COM 4 uses IRQ 3. Answer d is incorrect because the floppy disk controller uses IRQ 6. Answer e is incorrect because LPT1 uses IRQ 7. Answer f is incorrect because the realtime clock uses IRQ 8.

Question 7

> When monitoring a server you detect that a process in running that needs a higher priority. You want to change the priority of the process to Above Normal. What program do you use to change the priority?
>
> ○ a. Device Manger
>
> ○ b. Task Manager
>
> ○ c. Hardware Monitor
>
> ○ d. Performance Tool
>
> ○ e. Plug and Play
>
> ○ f. Explorer

Answer b is correct. Answer a is incorrect because Device Manager is used to monitor and update hardware. Answer c is incorrect because there is no program called Hardware Monitor. Answer d is incorrect because Performance Tool is a monitoring tool and does not allow for changing process priority. Answer e is incorrect because Plug and Play is used to detect and add new hardware. Answer f is incorrect because Explorer is not used to set process priority.

Question 8

A heavily used application server is running on the network. You are asked to assess the server and report to corporate on the status. Before you start to monitor the server, which two objects do you suspect have the most usage? [Check all correct answers]

❏ a. Memory

❏ b. Process

❏ c. Processor

❏ d. Network

❏ e. Disk

❏ f. Cache

Answers a and c are correct. Answer b is incorrect because Process is a counter used to track individual processes on a server. Answer d is incorrect because although the network is utilized, it is normally not as heavily used as the memory and processor. Answer e is incorrect because an application server normally does not use a lot of disk resources, although it should also be monitored. Answer f is incorrect because the cache is not as heavily used as the memory and processor.

Need to Know More?

 Search the Hardware Compatibility List (HCL) for hardware that is supported by Windows 2000 at **www.microsoft.com/hwtest/hcl**.

 Search TechNet on the Internet at **www.microsoft.com/technet/ default.asp** or the TechNet CD for information on: code signing, hardware profiles, Plug and Play, multiple monitors, BIOS, Windows Update, Device Manager, Task Manager, Performance tool, System Monitor, objects, and counters.

 For more information on the following terminology and implementation of the terminology refer to Microsoft Windows 2000 Help. To access this resource, select Help from the Start menu. Terms and technologies to search for include: code signing in Windows 2000, hardware overview, hardware profiles overview, Performance tool overview, Plug and Play device driver support, setting up a monitoring configuration, understanding ACPI BIOS, updating your system files using Windows Update, using Device Manager, using Windows Task Manager.

Networking Services

Terms you'll need to understand:

- ✓ Network adapters
- ✓ HCL
- ✓ Plug and play
- ✓ Protocol
- ✓ Services
- ✓ Client Services For Microsoft
- ✓ TCP/IP address
- ✓ Subnet mask
- ✓ Default gateway

- ✓ DHCP
- ✓ Automatic IP addressing
- ✓ NWLink
- ✓ Frame type
- ✓ Network number
- ✓ Internal network number
- ✓ Client Services For NetWare
- ✓ Gateway Services For NetWare

Techniques you'll need to master:

- ✓ Installing a network card
- ✓ Installing and configuring TCP/IP manually
- ✓ Installing and configuring DCHP
- ✓ Installing and configuring NWLink

- ✓ Installing and configuring Gateway Services For NetWare
- ✓ Installing and configuring a modem

In this chapter we will look at the Windows 2000 Server networking services. These services provide access to resources on a network and enable data communication between computers. Installation and configuration of these services are critical to understanding the Windows 2000 Server.

Networking Services

Networking services include all of the components required to communicate with other computers on a network. The following hardware and software are needed to connect a computer to the network: an adapter, adapter drivers, a protocol, and services.

➤ An *adapter* is a hardware device inserted into the computer to allow input and output of network communication. Examples of adapters include a network interface card (NIC) and a modem.

➤ *Drivers* are the software programs that allow a hardware device to communicate with an operating system.

➤ A *protocol* is a standard that is used to send information to other computers on the network. Examples of protocols include TCP/IP and NWLink.

➤ A *Client Service* is the software that assists in communication with computer systems. Examples of services include Client Services For Microsoft, Client Services For NetWare, and Gateway Services For NetWare.

Network communication can occur with an adapter after the adapter drivers are loaded and a protocol is bound to the adapter. In addition, a service may be bound to the protocol to help in communicating with different types of operating systems. The networking services work together to provide communication among different computers and operating systems.

Network Adapters and Drivers

A *network interface card (NIC)* is the most popular type of network adapter used in servers running Windows 2000. NICs are available in many varieties depending on the network architecture. An Ethernet network uses an Ethernet NIC, whereas a token ring network uses a token ring NIC. After you define the architecture, refer to the *Hardware Compatibility List (HCL)* to verify Microsoft supports the NIC. If the NIC is not on the HCL, Microsoft does not guarantee its functionality. If the NIC is on the HCL, Windows 2000 automatically detects and configures the NIC when it is installed.

Windows 2000 is a plug-and-play operating system. *Plug and play* refers to the operating system's capability to automatically detect a new piece of hardware and install the hardware. A Windows 2000 computer initiates the plug-and-play pro-cedure when you physically install a new network adapter. Plug and play detects the new adapter, loads the drivers for the adapter, and configures the adapter. The installation of new hardware is seamless in Windows 2000. Default configura-tions are used, and no questions are asked of the user. An administrator can reconfigure or set up additional components at any time.

Note: If your computer supports hot swap hardware, or has the ability to add hardware without shutting off the computer, Windows 2000 will support hot swap plug and play. Windows 2000 detects a change in hardware while the computer is operating, and automatically installs the new hardware.

Software drivers allow communication between the operating system and the network adapter. The HCL is important because it lists the hardware that is supported by Windows 2000. When plug and play initiates, it installs the Win-dows 2000 software drivers for the network adapter.

Protocols and Services

A *protocol* is a standard that regulates the transmission of data between comput-ers. The two main protocol suites for Windows 2000 are TCP/IP and NWLink. The TCP/IP protocol is bound to a network card by default when plug and play detects it.

NWLink is commonly used to communicate with Novell's NetWare servers that are operating with IPX/SPX. NWLink is a protocol that can be bound to a net-work card, but it is not installed by default. The other protocols supported by Windows 2000 are AppleTalk, DLC, and NetBEUI.

A client service is a program that allows communication between computer op-erating systems. The networking services automatically installed with a new NIC are Client Services For Microsoft Networks, and File And Print Sharing For Microsoft Networks. *Client Services For Microsoft Networks* provides communi-cation with Microsoft networks. *File And Print Sharing For Microsoft Networks* provide access to files and printers on Microsoft networks.

Microsoft also has services that facilitate network communication in a networked environment. These networking services are provided with Windows 2000 Server to enable network resources for all clients on the network. The Windows 2000 networking services are described in Table 5.1.

Follow these instructions to install Microsoft services on a Windows 2000 Server:

1. In the Control Panel, double-click the Add/Remove Programs icon.

2. Click Add/Remove Windows Components.

Table 5.1	Microsoft services for Windows 2000.
Networking Service	**Function**
COM Internet Service Proxy	Enables the Distributed Component Object Model (DCOM) to integrate with HTTP.
Domain Name System (DNS)	Enables computer and domain name resolution to IP address.
Dynamic Host Configuration Protocol	Enables automatic assigning of IP addresses to computers.
Internet Authentication Service	Enables authentication and accounting of Virtual Private Networks and dial in users.
QoS Admission Control Service	Enables control of network connections on a subnet, and bandwidth priority.
Simple TCP/IP Services	Enables features such as the Quote Of The Day and the **echo** command.
Site Server ILS Service	Enables the use of TCP/IP for updating site server directories.
Windows Internet Name Service (WINS)	Enables the resolution of IP addresses to NetBIOS names.

3. Scroll down the components list and highlight the Networking Services item.

4. Click Details.

5. Select the Networking Services you want to install. Refer to Figure 5.1 for more details.

6. Click OK to install the selected components.

Normally you do not need to reboot the server when new services are installed.

TCP/IP

TCP/IP is the default protocol for Windows 2000. It is a suite of protocols that provides reliable transmission of data between computers. If two computers are to be able to communicate and transfer data, they must both be using the same protocol. TCP/IP is the most widely used protocol in the world. To communicate on the same subnet by using TCP/IP, the computer must have an IP address, and a subnet mask. To communicate with computers outside of the local subnet the computer must have an IP address, a subnet mask, and a default gateway.

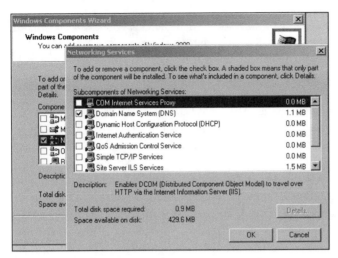

Figure 5.1   The available Windows 2000 Networking Services.

IP Address

An *IP address* is a unique 32-bit number that identifies a computer. This number must be unique. Network errors occur if duplicate IP addresses are assigned. An IP address is divided into 4 different octets that make a number such as 122.222.132.14.

Note: You must contact an administrator if you do not know the IP address for your computer . If you are the administrator who is responsible for assigning IP addresses, you must contact a company such as InterNIC to be assigned a specific IP range. It is important to verify that all IP addressess on your network are registered with an authorized IP provider.

IP addresses are also divided into different address classes. An address class is a predefined subdivision of IP ranges based on the number of hosts that the network can support. A Class A address is defined by the first octet ranging from 1 to 126; this enables each network to have 16 million hosts. A Class B address is defined by the first octet ranging from 128 to 191; this enables each network to have 65,534 hosts. A Class C address is defined by the first octet ranging from 192 to 223; this enables each network to have 254 hosts. Table 5.2 lists the different address classes, their IP ranges, and the default subnet mask.

Remember that the IP address 127.0.0.1 is reserved for the loop back address for the network card. IP addresses that start with 127.X.Y.Z are invalid on the network.

Table 5.2   Address class, IP range, and default subnet mask.

Address Class	IP Range	Default Subnet Mask	Binary Subnet Mask
A	1-126.X.Y.Z	255.0.0.0	11111111.00000000.00000000.00000000
B	128-191.X.Y.Z	255.255.0.0	11111111.11111111.00000000.00000000
C	192-223.X.Y.Z	255.255.255.0	11111111.11111111.11111111.00000000

An IP address can be assigned and configured manually by an administrator or dynamically through the Dynamic Host Configuration Protocol (DHCP) service. If the IP address, subnet mask, and default gateway are manually entered into the TCP/IP properties box, the computer has static TCP/IP properties. It is recommended that a server have manually configured static TCP/IP properties. Manual configuration of TCP/IP properties requires dedicated administrative overhead because each computer must have the properties inserted manually. To decrease the overhead, client computers can have a DHCP service dynamically assign IP addresses, subnet masks, and default gateways every time the information is needed. Dynamically assigning IP addresses is discussed later in this chapter.

Note: When plug and play is used to install a NIC, TCP/IP is configured to automatically look for a DHCP Server service.

Subnet Mask

A *subnet mask* is a 32-bit number that identifies the segment of the network where the computer is located. Subnet masks are numbers in the form of 255.255.255.0, or 255.255.255.224. Converting the subnet mask to binary makes it easy to determine if two computers are on the same subnet. The consecutive 1s in the binary form of the subnet mask is the network ID. The rest of the subnet mask, signified by 0s, is the number of host IDs, or the IPs for the network ID. The process to determine whether two computers are on the same subnet is called *ANDing*. Use the ANDing process in the following steps to determine whether two computers are on the same subnet:

1. Convert the two numeric IP addresses into binary.

2. Switch the numeric subnet masks into binary.

3. Subtract the subnet mask binary number from its prospective IP address. See Table 5.3 for an example of the ANDing process.

Table 5.3	The ANDing Process
An example of the ANDing process used to identify whether two computers are on the same network.	
Computer 1	
IP Address	126.55.2.62
Subnet Mask	255.255.255.224
Binary IP	11111110.00110111.00000010.00111110
Binary Subnet	11111111.11111111.11111111.11100000
ANDing Result	11111110.00110111.00000010.**00100000**
Computer 2	
IP Address	126.55.2.94
Subnet Mask	255.255.255.224
Binary IP	11111110.00110111.00000010.01011110
Binary Subnet	11111111.11111111.11111111.11100000
ANDing Result	11111110.00110111.00000010.**01000000**

Binary counting is different from normal addition or subtraction. Remember the following binary math ANDing operations:

0 + 0 = 0

0 + 1 = 0

1 + 1 = 1

It can be concluded from the ANDing process that Computer 1 and Computer 2 are not on the same subnet.

Default Gateway

A *default gateway* is the IP address of a computer or piece of hardware that routes the TCP/IP packets between subnets. The default gateway is the 32-bit IP address of the hardware designated to be the default gateway.

Manual Configuring TCP/IP

Follow these steps to manually configure TCP/IP after you install a network interface card:

1. Right-click on My Network Places.

2. Click the Properties menu.

3. Double-click the Local Area Connection icon. This icon provides the configuration information for the newly installed NIC.

4. Highlight the Internet Protocol (TCP/IP) component, and then click the Properties button.

5. Click Use The Following IP Address. Enabling this option disables the Obtain An IP Address Automatically option. Obtaining An IP Address Automatically requires a DHCP service to request an IP address. Refer to Figure 5.2 for more information.

6. Enter an IP address in the IP Address field.

7. Enter a subnet mask in the Subnet Mask field.

8. Enter the default gateway in the Default Gateway field.

Note: For a nonrouted network, a default gateway is not necessary. Non-routed computers only require a IP address and a subnet mask.

9. Click OK.

10. Click OK to close and save the changes.

DHCP

Dynamic Host Configuration Protocol (DHCP) is a networking service that dynamically assigns TCP/IP addresses to client computers. DHCP is configured by an administrator with a range of valid IP addresses for the network. These IP addresses are then leased to client computers requesting one. DHCP in Win-

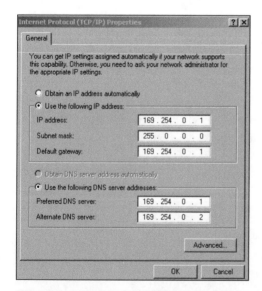

Figure 5.2 Internet Protocol (TCP/IP) Properties box used to manually configure TCP/IP.

dows 2000 can be configured with different IP ranges. These different IP ranges are referred to as a *scope*. Each IP scope can support different *scope options*. The scope options allow other services, besides the IP address and subnet mask, to be assigned to client computers. The scope options can include DNS servers, a WINS server, a default gateway address, and many more options.

When a DHCP client computer first boots, it automatically looks for a DHCP server to acquire an IP address, subnet mask, and any additional scope options. If a DHCP service is available, it assigns the client all the necessary information.

If a Windows 2000 client computer does not have a manual IP address, and it cannot find a DHCP server to fill its request, *Automatic Private IP Addressing (APIPA)* is initiated. APIPA is a new feature for Windows 2000 operating systems. If an IP address cannot be obtained, the Windows 2000 operating system automatically assigns itself an IP address. The assigned IP address is in a range of IPs from 169.254.0.1 to 169.254.255.254, with a subnet mask of 255.255.0.0. Automatic Private IP Addressing is used so that Windows 2000 computers can communicate when a DHCP server is unavailable or has ran out of IP addresses. Because only an IP address and subnet mask are assigned to the computer, it can only communicate with other APIPA computers.

Note: Automatic Private IP Addressing computers query the network every five minutes looking for an available DHCP server.

DHCP Setup and Configuration

To install the DHCP service, follow these steps:

1. Select Control Panel|Add/Remove Programs|Add/Remove Windows Components|Networking Services|DHCP and click OK.

Note: Normally you do not need to reboot Windows 2000 after you add Networking Services. Only reboot Windows 2000 if you are instructed to do so.

2. Open MMC and add the DHCP snap-in.

3. Note that DHCP should be configured and active. The DHCP service is active if the icon next to the computer name displays a green arrow. The service is stopped or paused if the arrow is red. Right-click on the computer name.

4. Click New Scope.

Note: A scope is the defined IP range and subnet mask that will be leased by the DHCP service to clients.

5. Type the appropriate information for the new scope in the Name and the Description fields and click Next.

6. Enter the Start IP address, the End IP address, the Subnet Mask. Click Next.

7. Enter the IP address of any address you want to exclude from the scope and click Next.

 It is recommended that you exclude all of the IP addresses that you manually assigned to computers on the network from the DHCP scope. If an IP address is not excluded, DHCP leases that IP address to a client computer, which causes IP conflicts on the network and incapacitates the computers involved.

8. Enter the amount of time the IP will be leased to a computer and click Next.

9. Click No and Next to finish configuration. Figure 5.3 displays the newly created scope that is inactive. Inactive scopes cannot release IP addresses to DHCP clients. When completed, notice that the scope is not active. The red arrow indicates that the service is stopped. After all configurations are complete, right-click, and click Activate to enable the DHCP server to start releasing IP addresses.

 The activation of a DHCP service may be on an exam, so be careful to watch out for which services are started and stopped. Also be careful of routers that do not support DHCP/BOOTP; DHCP traffic cannot cross a router without it. If BOOTP is not supported, a DHCP/BOOTP Relay Agent must be installed.

10. Right-click Scope Options.

11. Click Configure Options.

12. Configure any additional options. If additional options are configured, they are then passed onto the computer that leases an IP address. The following options are recommended if they apply to your network:

➤ Use 003 Router to configure the default gateway.

➤ Use 006 DNS Server to configure the DNS Server.

➤ Use 044 WINS/NBNS Server to configure the WINS Server.

➤ Use 046 WINS/NBT Node Type to activate different types of broadcast resolution for WINS information.

13. Click OK after you configure the scope options.

14. Right-click the new scope.

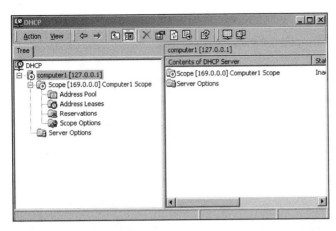

Figure 5.3   An inactive DHCP scope.

15. Click Activate to activate the scope. The red arrow disappears to indicate that the scope is active. The DHCP server is now ready to start leasing IP addresses to DCHP clients.

Domain Name System (DNS)

The Domain Name System (DNS) is a service that provides TCP/IP clients with resolution of computer and domain names to IP addresses. You can install this service through Control Panel. Select the Add/Remove Programs icon, Add/Remove Windows Components, and Networking Services. A snap-in, as shown in Figure 5.4, can be added to an MMC console for easy administration.

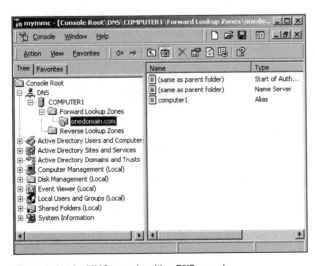

Figure 5.4   An MMC console with a DNS snap-in.

When the service is installed, the DNS wizard will walk through the setup and configuration. Remember that DNS names must be registered with a domain name authority if your DNS is resolving Internet requests.

As discussed in Chapter 3, a DNS server that supports SRV records must be implemented on the network to install Active Directory. Active Directory can implement different types of DNS servers, as long as they support SRV records and are RFC compliant. The Windows 2000 Server DNS service is RFC compliant and offers increased functionality, including:

➤ *Dynamically updating DNS records*—Dynamic updating enables Windows 2000 computers and DHCP to automatically update their resource records in DNS. This decreases the manual configuration of DNS by an administrator.

➤ *Active Directory Integrated Zones*—This enables Active Directory to replicate DNS information throughout the domain increasing the fault tolerance of DNS information. This ensures that DNS information will always be available to client requests.

➤ *Improved interface and a command prompt utility*—The improved DNS MMC interface is easier to configure and is supplied with Wizards to make tasks easier for administrators. The command prompt utility (dnscmd.exe) can be used to perform most of the GUI DNS tasks.

➤ *Full zone transfer and incremental zone transfer*—A full zone transfer sends all of the zone data information to receiving servers. An incremental zone transfer sends only zone data that has changed; this helps reduce zone transfer traffic.

 You should be familiar with how multiple DHCP and DNS function in a large environment. Security, fault tolerance, and successful access of resources with multiple DHCP and DNS servers should be understood.

NWLink

NWLink is a protocol that can be used to connect to any system using IPX/SPX. This protocol has less system overhead than TCP/IP, but is not commonly used outside of NetWare. NWLink is the Microsoft version of Novell's *Internetwork Packet Exchange/ Sequence Packet Exchange (IPX/SPX) Protocol*.

The three main NWLink components that need to be configured are as follows:

➤ *Frame type*—This component is the format in which the packets are sent. Computers that need to communicate must have the same frame type. Computers with different frame types cannot transmit data between themselves. The frame types that are available with NWLink are Ethernet 802.2, Ethernet 802.3, Ethernet II, and Ethernet SNAP.

▶ *Network number*—This component is the number associated with the network that is broadcasting data. It is similar to the subnet portion of an IP subnet; it dictates where the traffic is segmented. All computers that need to communicate must have the same network number.

▶ *Internal network number*—This component is a unique eight-digit hexadecimal identifier that distinguishes a NetWare server. The NetWare administrator assigns this number to a server.

If NWLink is installed, it automatically detects the frame type and network number. If an internal network number is used on the NetWare network, it must be assigned after NWLink is installed.

NWLink Configuration

NWLink needs to be installed in an environment where NetWare servers use IPX/SPX. Follow these steps to install NWLink:

1. Right-click Network Neighborhood and select the Properties menu.

2. Double-click the network connection icon on which you want to install NWLink.

3. Click Install on the General tab.

4. Double-click Protocol on the Select Network Component Type box.

5. Double-click the NWLink IPX/SPX/NetBIOS Compatible Transport Protocol. Then click Add.

Note: The NWLink NetBIOS and NWLink IPX/SPX/NetBIOS Compatible Transport Protocol will be added to the list of components. NWLink NetBIOS does not have configurable properties.

6. Highlight NWLink IPX/SPX/NetBIOS Compatible Transport Protocol and click Properties.

7. Select Manual Frame Type Detection and click Add. This screen lists the Frame Types and Network Number. Refer to Figure 5.5 for further details. Click OK.

8. Click Close to close the Local Area Connection Properties box.

Gateway Services For NetWare (GSNW)

Microsoft provides two services that assist in accessing NetWare servers. These services help with file and printer access to NetWare servers. The two services and their functions are as follows:

▶ *Client Services For NetWare (CSNW)*—This service allows Microsoft clients to connect and authenticate to file and print resources of a NetWare server.

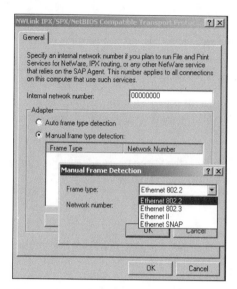

Figure 5.5 The NWLink Manual Frame Detection box.

CSNW is recommended for clients that frequently need to access a NetWare server. If clients rarely use the NetWare servers, the GSNW may be a better service to install.

➤ *Gateway Services For NetWare (GSNW)*—This service acts as a gateway for Microsoft clients and servers to access and authenticate to a NetWare file and print server. GSNW is installed on a server to provide a gateway for clients who rarely access the NetWare servers. A bottleneck can occur if one server is heavily used as a gateway for all access to NetWare servers.

 You should be familiar with implementing, administering, and trouble-shooting domains with CSNW and GSNW installed. This includes the ability to configure and troubleshoot the NWLinkIPX/SPX/NetBIOS Compatible Transport Protocol.

When GSNW is installed, CSNW and NWLink are automatically installed. It is recommended that you install NWLink before GSNW to avoid the automatic installation.

 Gateway Services For NetWare automatically installs NWLink and CSNW.

Gateway Services For NetWare Configuration

Follow these steps to install and configure Gateway Services For NetWare:

1. Right-click Network Neighborhood and select the Properties menu.

2. Double-click the network connection on which you want to install GSNW.

3. Click Install on the General tab.

4. Double-click the Client icon on the Select Network Component Type box.

5. Highlight Gateway (And Client) Services For NetWare and click OK.

6. Enter a Preferred Server or a Default Tree And Context. Click OK.

7. Click Close to exit the Local Area Connection Properties box.

You access the Properties screen for the GSNW through Control Panel GSNW. Refer to Figure 5.6 for more screen details.

To configure the gateway account, click the Gateway button on the Gateway Services For NetWare configuration box. The Configuration Gateway screen allows an administrator to enable the Gateway account. A gateway account must be configured on both NetWare and Microsoft servers. After the account is authenticated, shares and permissions can be configured.

Modems

You can use modems in Windows 2000 to dial directly to other computers over a telephone line or to an Internet Service Provider (ISP). Modems are mainly used

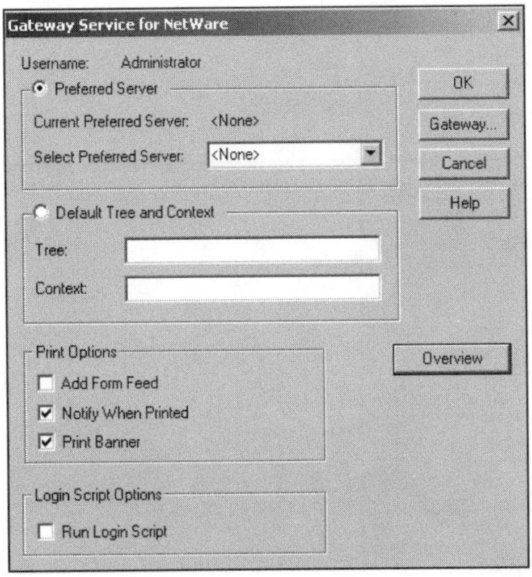

Figure 5.6 The Gateway Services For NetWare Properties screen accessed through the Control Panel.

with Windows 2000 Server for Remote Access Services (RAS), which is discussed further in Chapter 10.

Modem Configuration

Installing a modem is as easy as installing a NIC. If the modem is on the HCL, then Windows 2000 automatically detects it with Plug and Play. Plug and Play installs the modem and the software drivers. If a modem is not on the HCL, you may have difficulty getting it installed.

Follow these steps to confirm proper installation and configuration of a modem:

1. In the Control Panel, double-click the Phone And Modem icon.

2. Click the Modems tab.

3. Choose the modem you want to configure, and then click Properties.

4. Click the Diagnostics tab. Refer to Figure 5.7 for more information.

5. Choose Query Modem to confirm that the modem was correctly installed and configured.

6. Click OK to close the Modem screen.

7. Click OK to close the Phone And Modem Options screen.

Follow these steps to configure a new dialing location:

1. Right-click My Network Places.

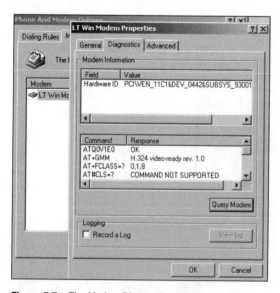

Figure 5.7   The Modem Diagnostics screen.

2. Click Properties.

3. Double-click Make New Connection.

4. Click Next at the Network Connection Wizard welcome screen.

5. Click the type of connection you are trying to make with the modem.

6. Enter the telephone number of where you are dialing. Click Next.

7. Choose to Create This Connection: For All Users Or Only For Yourself. Click Next.

8. If you want Internet sharing, select the checkbox to enable Internet Connection Sharing for this computer. Click Next.

9. Type a name of the new connection, and select the checkbox to add a shortcut to the desktop. Click Finish.

10. Type a user name and password. Then click Dial to test the new connection.

Troubleshooting Networking Services

There are many things that can go wrong when you are trying to set up or maintain a network. This section will give some helpful troubleshooting techniques. The exam will more than likely cover troubleshooting networking services.

Network Adapter and Driver Troubleshooting

The best tool for troubleshooting network adapters and drivers is *Device Manager*. You access the Device Manager through Control Panel. Click the System icon, and click the Device Manager button on the Hardware tab. Device Manager lists hardware devices and their current status. To access more information, double-click on the hardware icon and choose a device. A screen similar to that shown in Figure 5.8 displays.

Device Manager Property screens display the status of the device, the drivers used, the resource settings, and advanced properties. These screens enable you to configure and troubleshoot hardware devices and drivers.

Network Interface Card Troubleshooting

Troubleshooting a NIC should first be done through Device Manager so that you can verify the configuration and installation of the NIC. The following list of items helps identify where and when the NIC failed. This list may assist you in locating the problem:

➤ Verify that the device is functioning properly through Device Manager.

➤ Is the cable plugged into the NIC?

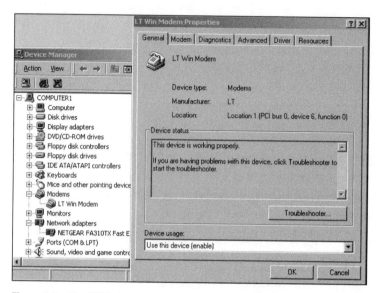

Figure 5.8 The LT Win Modem Properties screen accessed through Device Manager.

➤ Has this NIC ever worked before?

➤ Does the NIC have lights on it? If it does, can you see connection lights?

➤ Is this the only computer with the problem, or is the problem more global? If the problem is global, the NIC for this machine may be fine. Look to other sources for a fix.

➤ When did the problem first occur? The time frame can give you a better idea of what the problem might be.

➤ Has the user reconfigured something on the machine or loaded any new software?

➤ Follow the TCP/IP Troubleshooting steps to identify other problems.

If this list did not help locate the problem, continue on to the next sections. The problem may be with the protocols or services.

TCP/IP Troubleshooting

Troubleshooting a TCP/IP problem can become very tedious and time consuming. One of the most typical errors in setting up TCP/IP is typing the wrong numbers. At the command prompt, type the following commands to help identify problems:

➤ **ipconfig /all**—This screen enables you to verify that all the numbers were typed correctly, and that the settings are right for this machine.

➤ **ping 127.0.0.1**—This loopback address for all computer NICs verifies that the NIC is functioning properly.

➤ **ping** *[the computer's IP address]*—Pinging the computer IP address verifies that the correct IP is being used.

➤ **ping** *[another computer on the same subnet]*—Pinging a computer on the same subnet verifies that the subnet mask is correct.

➤ **ping** *[the default gateway]*—Pinging the default gateway verifies that the gateway is functioning, and that this computer should be able to access remote domains.

➤ **ping** *[a remote IP address]*—Pinging a remote IP address verifies that you did not really have a problem in the first place.

DHCP Troubleshooting

If DHCP clients are not receiving IP addresses, check the following list:

➤ Is the DHCP server up and operational?

If it is not, then restart the service or reboot the machine. After the server is operational, it is capable of filling IP requests.

➤ Is the DHCP scope activated?

If the scope has been deactivated, activate it. After the scope is activated, the server can fill IP requests.

➤ Does the DHCP server have IPs left in its IP scope?

When the server runs out of IP addresses, the rest of the client requests cannot be fulfilled. Acquire a larger pool of addresses for the server, or change to a shorter lease period of IP addresses to resolve the problem.

DNS Troubleshooting

If you can ping a computer by IP address but not by the computer or domain name, check the following list:

➤ Ping the DNS IP address.

Pinging verifies that the problem computer can reach the DNS server.

➤ Check the DNS server and make sure it is operational.

Checking the DNS server reassures you that the DNS server is working.

➤ Check the records that the problem computer is having trouble accessing.

Checking records reassures you that the DNS records are correct.

➤ Ping the DNS computer name or domain name.

Pinging the DNS computer name or domain name verifies that the problem computer can reach the DNS server using a computer or domain name

NWLink Troubleshooting

If you have just installed NWLink and are having problems, check the following items:

➤ Check that the frame type is the same as the NetWare servers on your network.

➤ Check that the network number is the same as your NetWare servers on your network.

Gateway Services For NetWare (GSNW) Troubleshooting

To test the function of GSNW connection to a NetWare server, map a network drive, view the server through Windows Explorer, or browse to the resource using My Network Places. One of these methods can verify that the GSNW is installed correctly. The following steps can help you troubleshoot if the preceding steps failed:

➤ At the command prompt, type **net view /network:nw**.

This command lists all of the NetWare servers on your network.

➤ Check the gateway account through the GSNW icon in the Control Panel.

This step verifies that the gateway account is correctly configured and also enables you to assign shared resources and set permissions.

➤ Check the Windows 2000 Server gateway account and the NetWare gateway account for configuration errors or a locked out account.

➤ Checking both gateway accounts rules out the possibility that one of the accounts is locked out or was set up incorrectly.

Modem Troubleshooting

One of the best resources for troubleshooting modems is Device Manager. Use Device Manager to verify that the modem is functioning, the correct drivers are installed, and there are no resource conflicts.

The next step is to verify that the modem is initializing. The Phone and Modem Options icon in the Control Panel assists you in testing the modem. Access the Modems tab, go to the properties of the modem, and click the Diagnostics tab. The Query Modem button tests the modem's communication.

Practice Questions

Question 1

You receive a call from a concerned user. The user's computer is not able to access the onedomain.com. You go to the computer and at the command prompt you type "ipconfig /all" to get computer IP information. Given the following information, what is the problem?

- Hostname: Computer1
- DNS: 111.111.111.2
- Default Gateway:
- IP address: 169.254.0.50
- Description: Netgear Fast Ethernet Adapter
- Physical Address: 00-A0-CC-5F-73-91

○ a. The computer name is duplicated on the network.

○ b. The DNS is unavailable.

○ c. The DNS is not resolving the onedomain.com.

○ d. The IP address is duplicated.

○ e. The IP address is an Automatic Private IP Address.

○ f. The physical address is duplicated.

Answer e is correct. When Automatic Private IP Addressing is used, scope options are not applied to the computer. Automatic Private IP Addressing only configures an IP address and a subnet mask, which makes the DNS service unreachable. A static DNS address can be assigned in Windows 2000 even if the computer is using Automatic Private IP Addressing. Answers a, d, and f are incorrect because they would flag an error message and are logged in Event Viewer. Answers b and c are incorrect because the DNS is available, but this particular computer cannot reach it because of Automatic Private IP Addressing.

Question 2

Which command should be used to verify that GSNW is correctly configured?

○ a. **net view /netware**

○ b. **net view /network**

○ c. **net view /network:nw**

○ d. **net view /network:gsnw**

○ e. **net view /gsnw**

Answer c is the correct answer. The rest of the answers contain fake switches.

Question 3

Over the past seven days all of your company's DHCP clients have become unable to connect to any resources that are on the network. What is likely the problem?

○ a. The DHCP server address pool is not activated.

○ b. The DHCP server scope is not enabled.

○ c. The DHCP server address pool options were not configured.

○ d. The DHCP server scope options were not configured.

○ e. The DHCP server is out of reservations.

Answer b is correct. Answer a is incorrect because the address pool cannot be activated or deactivated. Answer c is incorrect because there are no address pool configurations options after the IP range and exclusion ranges are configured. Answer d is incorrect because scope options are additional components to the IP address that is given; they do not affect the distribution of IP addresses. Answer e is incorrect because reservations are reserved for specific computers and do not effect the distribution of normal client IP addresses.

Question 4

A Windows NT Workstation user cannot get on the network. You can ping the loopback address at the user's command prompt, but you cannot successfully ping anything else on the network. What could be the problem or problems? [Check all correct answers]

❏ a. An incorrect IP address.

❏ b. An incorrect subnet mask.

❏ c. An incorrect or unavailable DNS service.

❏ d. An incorrect or unavailable DHCP service.

❏ e. An incorrect or unavailable default gateway.

❏ f. An incorrect driver was installed.

Answers a, b, and d are correct. Answer a is correct because an incorrect IP address leads to communication problems. Answer b is correct because the wrong subnet mask makes communications to other subnets impossible. Answer d is correct because if an NT Workstation cannot access a DHCP service, it registers a 0.0.0.0 IP address and communication does not occur. Answer c is incorrect because a machine uses DNS for computer name to IP resolution; the computer should still be able to ping by IP. Answer e is incorrect because the default gateway is used to access remote networks. This computer cannot even access resources on its own network. Answer f is incorrect because you can ping the loopback address; therefore all drivers and the NIC are working properly.

Question 5

To which address class does the IP address 126.11.4.3 belong?

○ a. Class A.

○ b. Class B.

○ c. Class C.

○ d. None; it is the loopback address.

Answer a is correct. Class A IP's range from 1-126.X.Y.Z, Class B IP's range from 128-191.X.Y.Z, Class C IP's range from 192-223.X.Y.Z. The IP address 127.0.0.1 is the loopback address.

Question 6

> Which of the following computers are on the same subnet? See Figure 5.9. [Check all correct answers]
>
>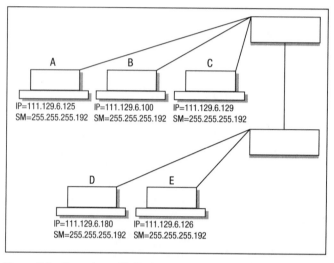
>
> **Figure 5.9** Computers with IP addresses and subnet masks.
>
> ❑ a. Computers A, B, and C are on the same subnet.
>
> ❑ b. Computer A, B, and D are on the same subnet.
>
> ❑ c. Computer A, B, and E are on the same subnet.
>
> ❑ d. Computers A and D are on the same subnet.
>
> ❑ e. Computers B and D are on the same subnet.
>
> ❑ f. Computers C and D are on the same subnet.
>
> ❑ g. Computers E and D are on the same subnet.

Answers c and f are correct. Calculations follow in Table 5.4.

Computers A, B, and E are on the same subnet and computers C and D are on a different subnet.

Table 5.4	Calculations explaining Question 5.	
Computer A Binary Information		
IP =	01101111.10000001.00000110.01111101	111.129.6.125
SM =	11111111.11111111.11111111.11000000	255.255.255.192
ANDing =	01101111.10000001.00000110.**01000000**	
Computer B Binary Information		
IP =	01101111.10000001.00000110.01100100	111.129.6.100
SM =	11111111.11111111.11111111.11000000	255.255.255.192
ANDing =	01101111.10000001.00000110.**01000000**	
Computer C Binary Information		
IP =	01101111.10000001.00000110.10000001	111.129.6.129
SM =	11111111.11111111.11111111.11000000	255.255.255.192
ANDing =	01101111.10000001.00000110.**10000000**	
Computer D Binary Information		
IP =	01101111.10000001.00000110.10110100	111.129.6.180
SM =	11111111.11111111.11111111.11000000	255.255.255.192
ANDing =	01101111.10000001.00000110.**10000000**	
Computer E Binary Information		
IP =	01101111.10000001.00000110.01111110	111.129.6.126
SM =	11111111.11111111.11111111.11000000	255.255.255.192
ANDing =	01101111.10000001.00000110.**01000000**	

Question 7

The following two computers are trying to communicate. Why are they not able to communicate?

	Computer 1	Computer 2
Internal Network Number	00000000	00000000
Frame Type	802.2 and 802.3	802.5
Network Number	11	11

○ a. Wrong internal network number

○ b. Wrong frame type

○ c. The computers are on different subnets

○ d. One computer cannot have more than one frame type

Answer b is correct. Computers that do not have the same frame type cannot communicate. Answer a is incorrect because Computer 1 and Computer 2 have the same internal network number. Answer c is incorrect because NWLink does not define subnets. Answer d is incorrect because one network card can have more than one frame type assigned.

Question 8

Using all of the commands in the following list, put these NIC troubleshooting steps in the correct order.

ping another computer on the same subnet

ping a remote IP address

ping 127.0.0.1

ping the computer's IP address

ping the default gateway

ipconfig /all

Answer is as follows:

ipconfig /all

ping 127.0.0.1

ping the computer's IP address

ping another computer on the same subnet

ping the default gateway

ping a remote IP address

Need to Know More?

 Russel, Charlie, and Sharon Crawford: *Microsoft Windows 2000 Server Administrator's Companion*. Microsoft Press, Redmond, Washington, 2000. ISBN 1-57231-819-8. This book is a valuable resource for information about setting up network services and troubleshooting.

 Tittel, Ed, Kurt Hudson, and James Michael Stewart: *MCSE TCP/IP Exam Cram*. The Coriolis Group, Scottsdale, AZ, 1998. ISBN 1-57610-195-9. For a quick reference of TCP/IP subnetting, ANDing, and subdividing a network, refer to Chapters 4 and 5.

 Search TechNet on the Internet at **www.microsoft.com/technet/ default.asp** or the TechNet CD for information on: Network adapters, protocols, services, HCL, Plug and Play, TCP/IP addresses, subnet masks, default gateway, DHCP, Automatic IP Addressing, NWLink, frame type, network number, internal network number, Client Services For Microsoft, Client Services For NetWare, Gateway Services For NetWare.

Organizational Units and Objects

Terms you'll need to understand:

- ✓ MMC
- ✓ Active Directory Users And Computers
- ✓ Objects
- ✓ Users
- ✓ Groups
- ✓ User profile
- ✓ Security groups
- ✓ Distribution groups
- ✓ Domain local group
- ✓ Global group
- ✓ Universal group
- ✓ Native mode
- ✓ Mixed mode
- ✓ GPO
- ✓ Override inheritance
- ✓ Block Policy inheritance

Techniques you'll need to master:

- ✓ Administering the MMC snap-in Active Directory Users And Computers
- ✓ Adding objects and OUs in Active Directory
- ✓ Administering objects and OUs in Active Directory
- ✓ Configuring and implementing user profiles
- ✓ Configuring and implementing group policies
- ✓ Blocking inheritance
- ✓ Overriding inheritance
- ✓ Disabling a GPO without deleting it

This chapter addresses administrating objects in Windows 2000 Server. We will look at how MMC is used to administer these objects, and then we will address administration of users, computers, groups, OUs, and group policies.

The MMC

You use MMC for administrating the Active Directory in Windows 2000 Server. You can configure the MMC by adding snap-ins, as seen in Chapter 2. MMC can be defined for different modes and levels of administration. These console modes include Author Mode, User Mode-Full Access, User Mode-Limited Access Multiple Window, and User Mode-Limited Access Single Window. To access the MMC options, go to the Console menu item and choose Options, as seen in Figure 6.1.

The MMC snap-in *Active Directory Users And Computers* is used for administrating organizational units (OU), users, groups, computers, and objects. Figure 6.2 shows the MMC console with the Windows 2000 Server default configuration. These default containers and OUs are discussed in the following sections.

The Default Active Directory Users And Computers

After you install the first domain controller, Active Directory is set up with a default configuration. Figure 6.2 shows the default configuration, and Table 6.1 defines the default containers and OUs.

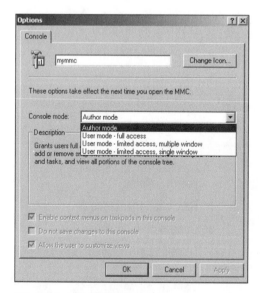

Figure 6.1   The MMC options.

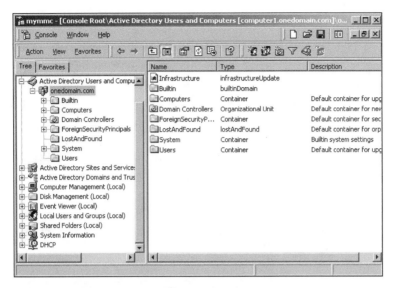

Figure 6.2   The MMC snap-in for Active Directory Users And Computers.

Table 6.1 Active Directory Users And Computers default settings.		
Container or OU	**Type of Container or OU**	**Description of Container or OU**
Builtin	builtinDomain	Contains the default built-in local security groups
Computers	Container	Contains upgraded computer accounts
Domain Controllers	Organizational Unit	Contains the new Windows 2000 domain controllers with a list of all the domain controllers for the domain
ForeignSecurity Principals	Container	Contains security identifiers (SIDs) associated with objects from external, trusted domains
LostAndFound	lostAndFound	Contains orphaned objects
System	Container	Contains system settings for policies, IP security Dfs configuration, RAS, and other system items
Users	Container	Contains upgraded user accounts

Note: You can only view LostAndFound and System containers by implementing the advanced features. To implement these features, right-click on the domain name. Select the View option and click Advanced Features.

Two main items make up the Active Directory Users And Computers: objects and Organizational Units (OUs). These items are discussed in the following sections.

Objects

An *object* is a single item in the Active Directory database, including printers, users, folders, files, or groups. Every object has its own unique set of attributes. The remainder of this section looks at user, group, and computer objects. Chapter 9 addresses printer objects, and Chapter 8 discusses file and folder objects.

User Objects

The default user accounts for Active Directory are set up in the Users container under the domain. Table 6.2 defines the default user accounts.

To export information in Active Directory, right-click the container and click Export List. This technique enables you to save the comma or tab delimited information to a file.

To add a user to the container, right-click on the container, go to New, and then click User. Follow the on screen instructions to add the user. To configure a user, double-click on it to access the user's Properties screen. Table 6.3 defines the Properties tabs, and Figure 6.3 shows a user's Properties screen.

Note: All members of the Administrators group have permissions to create OUs anywhere in the domain.

You also can perform special actions on a user or group of users. You can access these actions by right-clicking the object. The quick actions for a user's object include resetting the password, disabling the account, moving the account, copying the account, sending mail to the user, and adding the user to a group.

Table 6.2	Default users in the Users container of Active Directory Users And Computers.
Name	**Description**
Administrator	The account used to administer the computer and the domain
Guest	The account used for guest access to the computer and the domain
krbtgt	The account used for the Key Distribution Center Service
TsInternetUser	The account used by Terminal Services

Table 6.3 The User Properties tabs.	
Property Tab	**Description of the Property Tab**
General	Informational fields for first name, last name, telephone number, email, and Web page.
Address	Informational fields for street, P.O. Box, city, state, zip, and country.
Account	Informational fields for user logon name, user domain, restricting logon hours, restricting logging on computers, setting account options, dictating a password change, disabling an account, and account expiration.
Profile	Informational fields for the profile path, logon script, and home folder.
Telephones	Informational fields for the home phone number, pager, mobile, fax, IP phone, and any extra notes.
Organization	Informational fields for the title, department, company, manager name, and to whom the user reports.
Published Certificates	A list of X.509 certificates for the user.
Member Of	A list of groups to which this user is a member and the primary group.
Dial-in	Informational fields for remote access permissions (dial-in or VPN), callback options, static IP addresses, and static routing. (Note that the default setting is to control dial-in access through the Remote Access Policy.)
Object	Informational fields with the user's fully qualified domain name, the created date, the modified date, and the Update Sequence Numbers (USN).
Security	Informational fields on user and group permissions, general account permissions, and inherited permissions.
Environment	Informational fields to configure programs to start and connect client devices.
Sessions	Informational fields to control the Terminal Services. The fields define when to disconnect a session, active session limits, and the policy on allowing reconnections.
Remote Control	Informational fields to configure Terminal Services for remote control settings. The fields available include enabling remote control, a user's permission for remote control, and the level of remote control. As the default setting, remote control is enabled and the user's permission is required.
Terminal Services Profile	Informational fields to configure the Terminal Services user profile, home directory, and permission to log on to a terminal server. (The default is to allow all users logon access to the Terminal Services.)

The Domain Users group is the default group for all users.

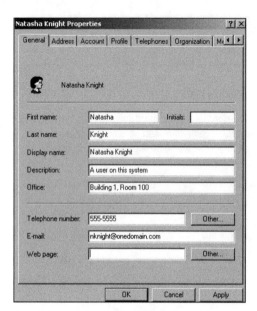

Figure 6.3 A User Properties screen.

Note: To access the Object and Security tabs, the Advanced Features must be enabled.

User Profiles

A *user profile* is created the first time a user logs on to a computer. A profile stores the user's settings such as desktop configurations, background settings, and printer configurations. The profiles are located in the Documents And Settings folder. The profile is in the folder with the user's logon name. User profiles can be stored on the local machine or on a server. If the profile is stored on the server, the user can access the profile from anywhere the user logs on. To save a specific profile to the server, copy the whole folder to the server location, and make sure there is a file called ntuser.dat in the folder. If a machine has been upgraded from NT 4.0, the profile is located in the system root profiles folder.

The exam may cover user profiles. You should be familiar with how to implement and configure the different types of profiles.

There are three different types of profiles: local user profiles, roaming user profiles, and mandatory user profiles. The three types are described as follows:

➤ A *local user profile* is created the first time a user logs on to a specific computer. This profile is stored on the local computer and can only be accessed from that computer.

➤ A *roaming user profile* is stored on the server and is available to users whenever and wherever they log in. When changes to a roaming profile are made, the changes are updated and stored on the server.

➤ A *mandatory user profile* is a roaming profile that the user cannot update. When users try to change a mandatory profile, the changes are not updated on the server; they continue to get the same stored mandatory profile.

Note: To make a profile mandatory, the profile must be stored on the server and the extension must be changed from .dat to .man.

Follow these steps to implement a roaming user profile:

1. Create a user, log in as that user, arrange the desktop settings as desired, and then log off.

2. Log on as an administrator. In Active Directory Users And Computers, right-click the user who will be assigned the roaming profile, and click Properties.

3. Go to the Profile tab and type in the share name of where the profile will be located; click OK. Figure 6.4 displays the User Properties Profile screen.

To customize the roaming profile, these additional steps need to be taken:

4. Click the System icon in Control Panel and choose the User Profiles tab.

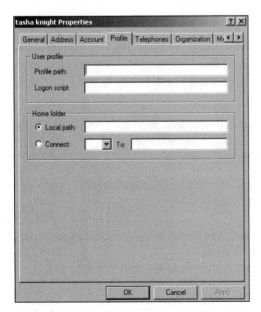

Figure 6.4 The User Properties Profile screen.

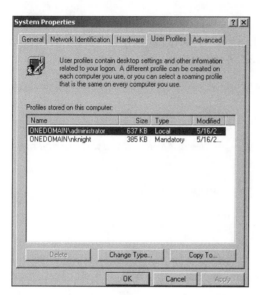

Figure 6.5   The System Properties User Profiles screen.

5. Click the Copy To button, and type or browse to the share on which the profile is located. Figure 6.5 displays the System Properties User Profiles screen after a profile has been added.

Group Objects

Groups are used in Windows 2000 to combine common users for the purpose of organizing and assigning permissions. There are two different types of groups: security groups and distribution groups, described as follows:

➤ *Security groups* are used for security purposes. The members of a security group are listed in the *Discretionary Access Control List (DACL)*. The DACL is a list of permissions that allows or denies users access to resources. Security groups can also be used as email distribution lists.

➤ *Distribution groups* are used only for email distribution. These groups are not associated with security or permissions.

 The exam is likely to cover the different group types and group scopes. You should be able to use the groups in the appropriate situations. It is also important to know which groups to add to other groups so that users get the appropriate access to resources.

Each of the two groups contains three group scopes. A *group scope* defines who can be in the group and where the group is implemented in a forest. The three group scopes are domain local, global, and universal:

➤ The *domain local group scope* can have users from any domain in the forest, but the users can only access resources in the local domain.

➤ The *global group scope* can only have users from the local domain, but they can access resources in any domain in the forest.

➤ The *universal group scope* can have users from any domain in the forest, and they can access resources in any domain in the forest.

The group scope membership is defined by the forest's mode. If the forest is in mixed mode, the group membership is more refined, as seen in Table 6.4. Remember that in mixed mode the universal group cannot be accessed.

If the forest is in native mode, the group membership is more diverse, as seen in Table 6.5. Remember that in native mode the universal group can be implemented and that groups can be nested.

To add a new group, right-click on a container, go to New, and click Group. Figure 6.6 shows the New Object - Group screen.

To access the Properties screen, double-click the group. Figure 6.7 shows a Group Properties screen.

Windows 2000 has default built-in groups located in the Built-in container of Active Directory Users And Computers. The default *Built-in Local Groups* are defined in Table 6.6.

Note: You cannot add the Built-in container to other groups.

Table 6.4	Mixed mode group membership.
Group	**Membership**
Domain local	Can contain users and global groups from any domain in the forest.
Global	Can contain only users from the local domain.
Universal	Does not apply for mixed mode.

Table 6.5	Native mode group membership.
Group	**Membership**
Domain local	Can contain users, global groups, and universal groups from any domain in the forest. It can also contain domain local groups from the same domain.
Global	Can contain users and global groups for the local domain.
Universal	Can contain users, global groups, and other universal groups from any domain in the forest.

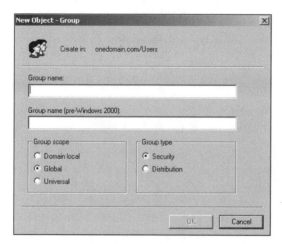

Figure 6.6 The New Object - Group screen.

Table 6.6 Built-in Local Security Groups.	
Local Group	**Membership**
Account Operators	The members can administer domain users and group accounts.
Administrators	The members have complete and unrestricted access to the computer/domain.
Backup Operators	The members can override security restrictions for the purpose of backing up or restoring files.
Guests	The members have limited access. The Guest account is disabled by default.
Pre-Windows2000 Compatible Access	The members are from a backward compatibility group, which allows read access on all users and groups in the domain.
Print Operators	The members can administer domain printers.
Replicator	The members support file replication in a domain.
Server Operators	The members can administer domain servers.
Users	The members are prevented from making accidental or intentional system-wide changes. They can run certified applications but not most legacy applications.

Windows 2000 also defines default domain local groups, global groups, and universal groups as shown in Table 6.7. These groups are located in the Users container under Active Directory Users And Computers.

Group Membership

You can add users to groups in many different ways by using MMC. Two of the ways to add users to groups are as follows:

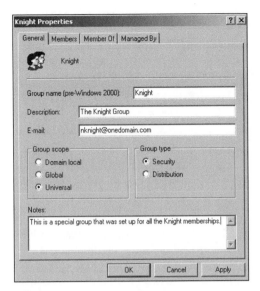

Figure 6.7   A Group Properties screen.

➤ Highlight the users you want to add to the group. Right-click, select Add Members to a Group, and double-click the group. Figure 6.8 displays the Select Group screen.

➤ On the Users Properties screen, choose the Member Of tab, then click Add, and select the group.

Computer Objects

The default Computers container is used to organize *computer accounts* which accounts uniquely identify computers in the domain. To create a computer account, right-click a container, select New, and click Computer. Figure 6.9 displays the New Object - Computer screen.

Contact Objects

Contact objects are used for information and email purposes only. To add a contact, right-click the container, select New, and click Contact. To define the properties of a contact, right-click the contact and select Properties. Figure 6.10 shows the Contact Properties screen.

Organizational Units

Organizational Units are used to group objects together. An OU is the lowest level container that you can assign group policies and the delegation of control.

Table 6.7   The Default groups in the Users container.

Group	Type of Group	Membership
DHCP Administrators	Security Group - Domain Local	The members have administrative access to the DHCP service.
DHCP Users	Security Group - Domain Local	The members have view-only access to the DHCP service.
DnsAdmins	Security Group - Domain Local	The members can administer DNS.
RAS and IAS Servers	Security Group - Domain Local	The members can administer remote access properties of users.
Cert Publishers	Security Group - Global	The members are Enterprise certification and renewal agents.
DnsUpdateProxy	Security Group - Global	The members are permitted to perform dynamic updates on behalf of other clients like DHCP servers.
Domain Admins	Security Group - Global	The members can administer the domain.
Domain Computers	Security Group - Global	The members are workstations and servers that join the domain.
Domain Controllers	Security Group - Global	The members are domain controllers.
Domain Guests	Security Group - Global	The members are domain guests.
Domain Users	Security Group - Global	The members are domain users.
Enterprise Admins	Security Group - Global	The members are designated administrators of the enterprise.
Group Policy Creator Owners	Security Group - Global	The members can modify group policy for the domain.
Schema Admins	Security Group - Global	The members are designated administrators of the schema.

Figure 6.8   The Select Group screen.

Figure 6.9 The New Object - Computer screen

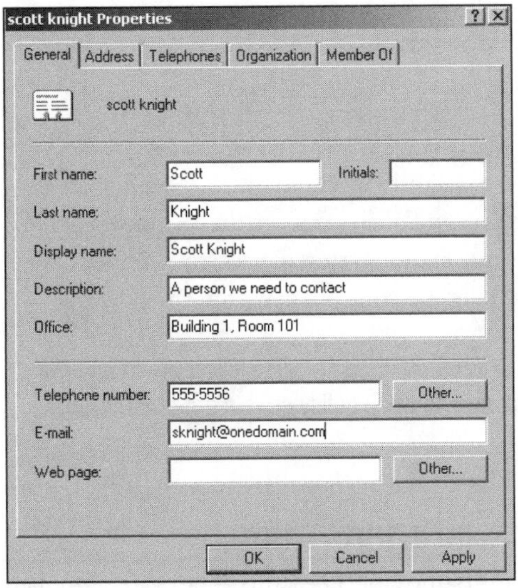

Figure 6.10 The Contact Properties screen.

Figure 6.11 shows an OU's Properties screen. The Properties screen defines a general information tab, a management tab, and the tab to apply group policies.

Containers

Containers are also Organizational Units that group objects together. The main difference between containers and OUs is that containers cannot have group policies applied to them, but the delegation of control can still be assigned. If you go to the Properties screen of a container, there are no additional tabs to configure.

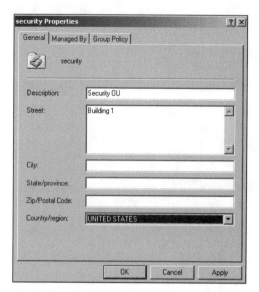

Figure 6.11 An Organizational Unit's Properties screen.

Group Policies

Group Policies allow for user and group security in Windows 2000. They are flexible, secure, and easy to administer. Group Policies replace the Windows NT 4.0 System Policy Editor. Group policy information is stored in a Group Policy Object or GPO. GPOs are replicated to all domain controllers within the domain.

 You should know how to implement and block GPOs, how to use the inheritance feature, and how to set a policy so it is not overridden.

The Addition of GPOs to an Organization

Policies can be applied at different levels of Active Directory. They can be applied at a site, a domain, an OU, or a computer. Table 6.8 shows the different levels where GPOs can be applied and how they are applied at those levels.

The Implementation Order of GPOs

You should establish the order of implementing GOPs so that an administrator knows which policies are being implemented or overridden. GPOs are applied to the user and computer in the following order:

➤ The Windows NT system policies

➤ The local group policy

Table 6.8	How to apply GPO levels.
GPO Level	**How to Apply the GPO**
A site	Using Active Directory Sites And Services, right-click on the default site, go to the Properties menu, and access the Group Policy tab.
A domain	Using Active Directory Users Aand Computers, right click on the domain, go to the Properties menu, and access the Group Policy tab.
An OU	Using Active Directory Users And Computers, right-click on the OU, go to the Properties menu, and access the Group Policy tab.
A computer	In MMC, add a snap-in for a Group Policy by browsing to the appropriate computer.
A local computer	In MMC, add a snap-in for a Group Policy and leave the default as the local computer.

➤ The site policy

➤ The domain policy

➤ The OU policy

➤ The child OU policy

 The exam may cover the implementation order of GPOs. If you are planning on taking the exam, you should know how GPOs are implemented, overridden, and inherited.

The Inheritance of GPOs

By default, GPOs are inherited throughout a forest. If a GPO is applied to a parent OU, that GPO is applied to all of the child OUs. If the child OU has another GPO that contradicts the parent GPO, the child's GPO overrides the parent's GPO.

Overriding Inheritance

The default inheritance can be overridden in Windows 2000. The *No Override* option can be enabled so that a child GPO does not override a parent GPO. Figure 6.12 shows the No Override option, and the following steps show how to apply the option:

1. On the Group Policy tab, right-click on the policy that you do not want overridden.

2. Choose the No Override option, as seen in Figure 6.12.

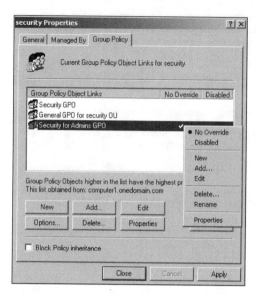

Figure 6.12   Group Policy's No Override feature.

You can disable GPOs in the same manner as you override them.

Blocking Inheritance

You also can block GPO inheritance from child OUs, thus preventing child OUs from inheriting the parents GPOs. To block inheritance, check the Block Policy Inheritance box. Refer to Figure 6.12 for more details.

Configuring GPOs

You can configure GPOs by clicking the Properties button. The Properties screen displays the GPO values that can be configured. Figure 6.13 displays the GPO Properties screen.

There are two types of objects that can be configured in a GPO: Computer Configuration and User Configuration. These two configurations allow an administrator to control almost every aspect of a computer and a user. There are so many configuration options in a GPO that they cannot all be addressed in this section. It is recommended that you spend some time with the GPO Properties screen to familiarize yourself with the available options.

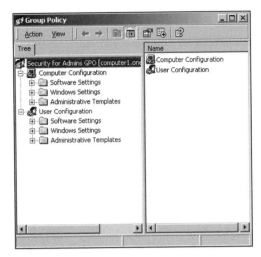

Figure 6.13   The GPO Properties screen.

Implementing GPOs

GPOs are configured by default to be implemented by each authenticated user. If a GPO is configured at a site level, then all authenticated users of that site will implement the group policy. To change and administer the security of a GPO, follow these steps:

1. Highlight the GPO that needs to have the security settings checked.

2. Click the Properties button and choose the Security tab.

3. Highlight a group in the Name box and check the associated permissions in the Permissions box.

   ➤ Allow applies the permissions.

   ➤ Deny specifically does not apply the permissions.

4. Use the Add and Remove buttons to associate other groups with this GPO.

Note: A group must have Read And Apply Group Policy for the GPO to be implemented for that group.

After you configure the GPO using the GPO Properties and the Security Properties, the last component is the priority order. If there are multiple GPOs implemented in the GPO box, the top-most GPO has the highest priority. You can use the Up and Down buttons to reconfigure the GPO priorities.

Refreshing GPOs

Policy changes are recorded immediately, but these changes are not automatically passed on to the users or computers. The following is a list of the times when policies are updated:

➤ When a computer starts

➤ When a user logs on

➤ When a user requests an update

 To request a refresh, type: **secedit /refreshpolicy machine_policy**.

➤ When an application requests a policy refresh

➤ When a policy interval has been reached

Note: The policy refresh interval is not implemented by default; it must be configured. To do so, go to the GPO, to the Computer Configuration\ Administrative Templates\ Group Policies, and edit the Group Policy Refresh Interval For The Computers option.

Practice Questions

Question 1

List the following steps in the order in which you would provide a new user with a mandatory roaming profile.

A. Rename the file ntuser.dat to ntuser.man.

B. Log on as an administrator. In Active Directory Users And Computers, right-click on the user that will be assigned the profile, and choose Properties. Go to the Profile tab and type the share name of the location where the profile will be located. Then click OK.

C. Open the System icon in Control Panel, and click on the User Profiles tab. Click on the Copy To button and type or browse to the share where the profile is located.

D. Have the user log on and test the profile.

E. Create a user, log in as that user, arrange the desktop settings as desired.

○ a. E, B, C, A, D

○ b. E, A, C, B, D

○ c. A, E, B, C, D

○ d. A, D, E, C, B

Answer a is correct. Answer b is incorrect because the profile has not been copied to the server, which makes it a local mandatory profile, not a roaming mandatory profile. Answers c and d are incorrect because there is no profile to rename if the user has not logged on for the first time.

Question 2

Zoe and Tim have been working for the Onedomain.com corporation for many years. They have both excelled in sales and marketing. Tim has had more success in marketing than Zoe, and he has more permissions on the network. Tim is a member of more groups in the forest than Zoe. Zoe is content with her job, but because the domain has moved to native mode she wants to know more about the forest structure. Their group memberships follow. What are Zoe and Tim's local domains? [Check all correct answers]

- Zoe and Tim are both members of the Domain Local Group sales in domain sales.onedomain.com.

- Zoe and Tim are both members of the Domain Local Group marketing in sales.onedomain.com.

- Zoe is a member of the Global Group salesg in marketing.onedomain.com.

- Zoe is a member of the Global Group salesh in marketing.onedomain.com.

- Tim is a member of the Domain Local Group corp in sales.onedomain.com.

- ❑ a. Zoe's local domain is sales.onedomain.com.
- ❑ b. Zoe's local domain is marketing.onedomain.com.
- ❑ c. Tim's local domain is sales.onedomain.com.
- ❑ d. Tim's local domain is marketing.onedomain.com.
- ❑ e. There is not enough information to define Zoe's local domain.
- ❑ f. There is not enough information to define Tim's local domain.

Answers b and f are correct. Answers a, c, and d are all incorrect because domain membership cannot be defined by a domain local group. A domain local group can have users from any domain in the forest, but they can only access resources in the local domain. Answer e is incorrect because Zoe is a user in the Global Group salesg and salesh in the marketing.onedomain.com. Because global groups can only have users from the local domain, they can access resources in any domain in the forest, which means that Zoe is a member of the local domain marketing.onedomain.com.

Question 3

GPOs have been implemented on the OU shown in Figure 6.14. What information is passed on to Marketing group for the child OUs? [Check all correct answers]

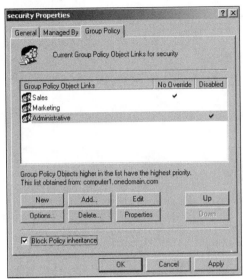

Figure 6.14   Security Properties Group Policy screen.

☐ a. The child OU will inherit permissions of the Marketing group.

☐ b. The child OU will not inherit permissions of the Marketing group.

☐ c. The child OU GPO will not override the Marketing group GPO.

☐ d. The child OU GPO will override the Marketing group GPO.

Answers b and d are correct. Answer a is incorrect because the Block Inheritance box has a checkmark, so the GPO is not inherited to the child OU. Answer c is incorrect because there is not a check in the No Override box so the child OU can override the Marketing GPO, although the GPO information is not inherited.

Question 4

GPOs have been implemented to an OU, as shown in Figure 6.15. What information is passed on to the child OUs of the Marketing GPO? [Check all correct answers]

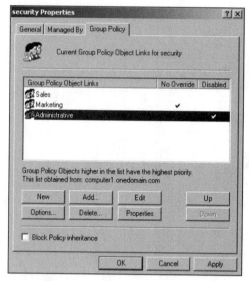

Figure 6.15   Security Properties Group Policy screen.

❑ a. The child OU will inherit permissions of the Marketing group.

❑ b. The child OU will not inherit permissions of the Marketing group.

❑ c. The child OU GPO will not override the Marketing group GPO.

❑ d. The child OU GPO will override the Marketing group GPO.

Answers a and c are correct. Answer b is incorrect because the box to block inheritance is not checked, so GPOs are inherited. Answer d is incorrect because the No Override box is checked, which means that the child OU will not override the parent OU.

Question 5

Tim is a member of the Global Group sales. He is concerned that he cannot access a resource that he needs because the domain has been switched to native mode. Tim calls you wanting to know why he cannot access the sales and marketing report. The sales and marketing report is located in the sales.onedomain.com and the report group has permission to access it. Which of the following statements are true? [Check all correct answers]

Group	Type of Group	Members of the Group
sales	Global Group for sales.onedomain.com	Tim, Administrators, Sales Administrators
marketing	Domain Local Group for marketing. onedomain.com	Sales Administrators, Marketing Administrators, Tim
reports	Global Group for sales.onedomain.com	Administrators, and the sales group

☐ a. Tim is a member of the correct global group.

☐ b. Tim is a member of the correct domain local group.

☐ c. Tim cannot access remote domains.

☐ d. Tim cannot access his local domain.

☐ e. Tim does not have permissions to access the resources.

☐ f. Tim has all the access he needs to the resource; he just does not know how to access it.

☐ g. Tim needs to be assigned Administrative privileges.

Answers a and f are correct. Answer b is incorrect because Tim does not need to be a member of a domain local group to access the reports. Answer c is incorrect because Tim can access remote domains; a global group scope can only have users from the local domain, but they can access resources in any domain in the forest. Answer d is incorrect because Tim has access to his local domain. Answer e is incorrect because Tim does have access to the resources because global groups can contain users and global groups for the local domain. Tim is a member of the sales group and that group has permissions to the reports folder. Answer g is incorrect because Tim already has access to the resources; there is no reason to assign him unnecessary privileges.

Question 6

In this native mode forest, the following GPOs exist.

There is a GPO for Domain1 in Site2.

There is a GPO for OU9 in OU6.

There is a GPO for Site2.

There is a GPO for OU6 in Domain1.

Which GPO will be the last to apply to a user that is a member of all the GPOs?

○ a. OU9

○ b. OU6

○ c. Domain1

○ d. Site2

Answer a is correct. Answers b, c, and d are incorrect because the order of implementing OUs is site, domain, OU, and child OUs. OU9 is a child of OU6 located in Domain1 which is in Site2. The GPOs would be applied to the user in the following order: Site2, Domain1, OU6, OU9.

Question 7

Put the following list in order that the GPOs are applied, starting with the first GPO to be applied.

The child OU policy

The domain policy

The local group policy

The OU policy

The site policy

The Windows NT system solicies

Answer:

The Windows NT System Policies

The Local Group Policy

The Site Policy

The Domain Policy

The OU Policy

The Child OU Policy

Question 8

Match the group with the correct definition.

Group:

Domain local group

Global group

Universal group

Definition:

Can only have users from the local domain, but they can access resources in any domain in the forest.

Can have users from any domain in the forest, and they can access resources in any domain in the forest.

Can have users from any domain in the forest, but they can only access resources in the local domain.

Answers:

The domain local group can have users from any domain in the forest, but they can only access resources in the local domain.

The global group can only have users from the local domain, but they can access resources in any domain in the forest.

The universal group can have users from any domain in the forest, and they can access resources in any domain in the forest.

Need to Know More?

 Russel, Charlie, and Sharon Crawford: *Microsoft Windows 2000 Server Administrator's Companion*. Microsoft Press, Redmond, Washington, 2000. ISBN 1-57231-819-8. This book is a valuable resource for information about implementing GPOs and user policies.

 Search TechNet on the Internet at **www.microsoft.com/technet/default.asp** or the TechNet CD for information on: Active Directory Users And Computers, user profile, profiles, security groups, distribution groups, domain local group, global group, universal group, native mode, mixed mode, GPO, block policy inheritance, inheritance, override inheritance.

 For more information on the following terminology and implementation of that terminology, refer to Microsoft Windows 2000 Help. To access this resource, click on Start and then click on Help. Terms and technologies to search for include: group policy overview, group policy software settings, group policy computer settings, group policy vs. system policy, group policy and MMC, user profiles, user profile editing, user profile mandatory, user profile roaming.

Managing Storage

Terms you'll need to understand:

✓ Basic storage

✓ Dynamic storage

✓ Disk Management

✓ Volumes

✓ Partitions

✓ Mirrored volumes

✓ Mirrored sets

✓ Striped volumes

✓ Striped sets

✓ Striped volumes with parity

✓ Striped sets with parity

✓ RAID 1 and RAID 5

✓ Mounted volumes

Techniques you'll need to master:

✓ Adding volumes, spanned volumes, mirrored volumes, striped volumes, and striped volumes with parity

✓ Changing from basic storage to dynamic storage and vice versa

✓ Extending spanned volumes

✓ Repairing basic storage partitions, mirrored sets, striped sets, and striped sets with parity

✓ Repairing dynamic storage volumes, spanned volumes, mirrored volumes, striped volumes, and striped volumes with parity

✓ Recovering from disk failures

✓ Identifying error messages from dynamic disks and fixing the error

Windows 2000 Server provides a new tool for administering storage devices called Disk Management, and two new types of storage. Windows 2000 terminology has changed from NT 4.0. In this chapter, we will look at the Disk Management tool, the two ways Microsoft defines the storage devices, and the new Windows 2000 terminology. The exam is likely to cover most of these topics in addition to configuration, interpreting error messages, and repairing different kinds of volumes. Managing and implementing storage could make up as much as 10 percent of the exam.

Disk Management Using MMC

You use the Microsoft Management Console's (MMC) Disk Management snap-in tool to manage storage in Windows 2000. This tool is used for all disk management in Windows 2000. By using the Disk Management tool, you can convert, add, create, extend, mount, and delete hard drives from the local computer system or from a remote system halfway around the world, if you have the correct permission. The snap-in Disk Management tool can be seen in Figure 7.1.

Introduction to Windows 2000 Storage

Windows 2000 Server has two types of storage: basic and dynamic. When you add a new hard drive to a Windows 2000 Server, the hard drive by default is a basic storage device. Basic storage devices have limited capabilities in Windows 2000. Thus, Microsoft's preferred option to basic storage is dynamic storage. Dynamic storage allows for volumes, spanned volumes, mirrored volumes, striped volumes, and striped volumes with parity, commonly referred to as RAID 5, all of

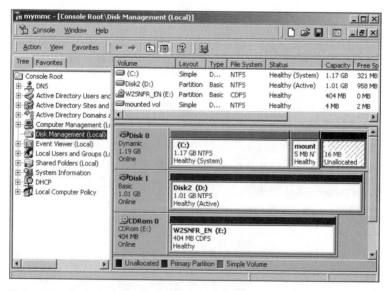

Figure 7.1 The Disk Management snap-in tool in MMC.

which are discussed in this chapter. Before we cover both of these storage devices in more detail, it is important to keep in mind the following information:

➤ Basic and dynamic storage devices can be formatted in NTFS, FAT, or FAT32.

➤ NTFS is the only file system that allows for disk security.

➤ NTFS is the only file system that supports extending volumes that are on dynamic storage.

➤ A hard drive cannot contain multiple storage types; the device is either all basic storage or all dynamic storage.

➤ A basic disk can be converted at any time to a dynamic disk without the loss of data.

➤ Converting a dynamic disk to a basic disk can only occur by restoring data from a backup.

➤ Removable media and hard drives on laptops cannot be converted to dynamic storage.

Basic Storage

Basic storage in Windows 2000 is the same as NT 4.0 storage. Basic storage can use either four primary partitions or three primary partitions with extended partitions as space allows. When a new hard drive is added to a Windows 2000 system, it is a basic disk by default. Basic disks are used for disk partitioning and extended partitioning.

Note: 1MB of unallocated space must be available on a disk so that it can be converted to a dynamic disk.

Remember these points about basic storage disks:

➤ The number of primary partitions on a basic disk is limited to four.

➤ Only a primary partition on a basic disk is bootable.

➤ Partitions cannot be extended to use free space from another disk.

➤ Basics disks are not capable of creating new volumes, new mirrored volumes, or new striped volumes.

➤ The partitions, mirrored sets, and striped sets from NT 4.0 function normally in Windows 2000 Server, and they will be defined as basic disks.

Dynamic Storage

Dynamic storage is Microsoft's preferred storage system. *Dynamic storage* enables you to create volumes, spanned volumes, mirrored volumes, striped volumes, and striped volumes with parity, commonly referred to as RAID 5. It was developed to expand storage, increase fault tolerance in the storage, and improve your ability to recover damaged storage. Dynamic storage allows for options not available with a basic disk, and it extends the capability to repair, regenerate, and resynchronize a volume. Dynamic storage has many advantages over basic storage:

➤ You are not limited to the number of volumes you can create on a disk.

➤ You can extend volumes by using free space on other dynamic disks.

➤ To extend dynamic volumes, the volumes must be formatted in NTFS.

➤ New volumes, new mirrored volumes, new striped volumes, and new RAID 5 volumes can be created only on dynamic disks.

➤ You can repair, regenerate, and resynchronize a volume that is on a dynamic disk.

➤ You can perform disk management without rebooting the computer.

Storage Fault Tolerance

Windows 2000 supports three levels of fault tolerance, which is known as redundant array of independent disks (RAID). Explanations of RAID 0, RAID 1, and RAID 5 are as follows:

➤ RAID 0, also referred to as disk striping, is the process of evenly writing data across the participating drives. RAID 0 requires between 2 and 32 hard drives. There is a low disk overhead for RAID 0 because all of the drive space is used. If one drive fails, however, all of the data is lost. The main reason to implement RAID 0 is to increase the read and write or input and output performance of your hardware.

➤ RAID 1, also referred to as disk mirroring, occurs when two physical disks have replicas of one set of data. RAID 1 requires two hard drives—one for the original data and the other to hold a copy of the original data. There is a 50 percent disk overhead for RAID 1 because one drive holds a copy of the information. If one disk in a mirror fails, a copy of the data is available on the other disk in the mirror.

➤ RAID 5, also referred to as disk striping with parity, is the process of data being written evenly across each of the drives in the array. RAID 5 is like a striped volume, but parity information is stored as fault tolerance. Parity is a calculation that can be used to reconstruct the data in case of a failure. RAID 5 requires at least three hard drives and has a proportional overhead to the amount of hard drives used. If three drives are used, there is a one-third disk overhead for the parity information.

Configuring Volumes on Dynamic Disks

Volumes, spanned volumes, striped volumes, and RAID 5 are all configured in the same way. Use the following steps to configure volumes on dynamic disks:

1. In Disk Management, right-click on the unallocated space that will be used for the volume.

2. Select Create Volume, and click Next.

3. Choose the type of volume you are configuring and click Next. Figure 7.2 shows the options that are available when you use the Create Volume Wizard.

4. Select the dynamic disks that will be used, the size of the volume, and click Next. Figure 7.3 shows the Disk and the Size Option screen.

5. Assign a drive letter to the new volume, and click Next.

6. Choose the format of the file system, the allocated unit size, and the volume label. Click Next.

7. Click Finish to complete the Create Volume Wizard.

A volume that is formatted in NTFS can be extended to use unallocated free space on dynamic disks. The following steps describe how to extend volumes:

1. In Disk Management, right-click on the volume you want to extend.

2. Select Extend Volume, and click Next.

3. Select the dynamic disk that will be used to extend the volume, the size of the volume, and click Next.

4. Click Finish to extend the volume.

 You cannot extend a system or boot volume.

A Simple Volume on a Dynamic Disk

A *simple volume* consists of the space used from one dynamic disk. A disk can contain one or multiple simple volumes. The file systems that can be used for a simple volume are NTFS, FAT, or FAT32.

Note: There is no fault tolerance implemented with simple volumes. If a simple volume fails, the data must be recovered from a backup.

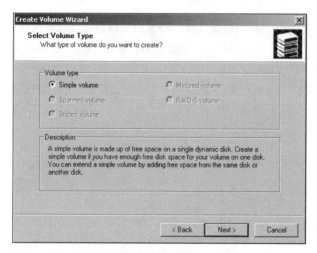

Figure 7.2   The Create Volume Wizard Volume Type screen.

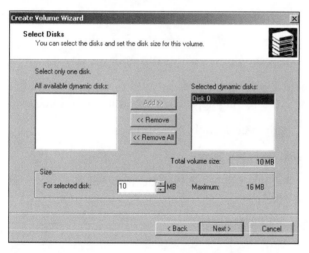

Figure 7.3   Configuring the disk and size of the new volume.

Spanned Volumes on Dynamic Disks

A *spanned volume* consists of space from at least 2 dynamic disks, but is limited to 32 dynamic disks. The file systems that can be used for a simple volume are NTFS, FAT, or FAT32. A spanned volume writes data to one disk in the volume until that disk is full. Then the space on the next disk is used.

Note: There is no recovery built into a spanned volume. If any disk in the spanned volume is damaged, the whole volume is lost and the data must be recovered from a backup.

Mirrored Volumes on Dynamic Disks

A *mirrored volume* is one disk volume that has an exact copy of its data on another disk. It is also referred to as RAID 1 because of the built-in fault tolerance. The fault tolerance consists of two different hard drives with the same information; therefore, if one of the disks is damaged, a copy of the data still exists on the other volume of the mirror. New mirrors in Windows 2000 can only be created on dynamic disks.

Configuring a Mirrored Volume on Dynamic Disks

Follow these steps to configure a mirrored volume:

1. Using the Disk Management tool, right-click on the volume you want to mirror.

2. Select Add Mirror.

3. Specify the location of the second volume in the mirror.

After you create the mirrored volume, the volume should have a Healthy status.

Extending a Mirrored Volume

Mirrored volumes that use basic storage cannot be extended because Windows 2000 does not enable the capability. Therefore, a mirrored volume cannot be extended.

Recovering from a Mirrored Volume Failure

If part of a mirrored volume fails, the volume displays a Failed Redundancy status. One of the volumes registers an Offline, Missing, or Online (Errors) status. Follow these steps to repair the mirror:

1. Using the Disk Management tool, right-click on the disk that has errors.

2. Select Reactivate Disk. The status should return to Healthy.

If the status still acknowledges an error, the disk may be damaged and needs replacement. In this case, the mirror must be broken. Follow these steps to repair the volume:

1. Using the Disk Management tool, right-click on the volume.

2. Select Remove Mirror.

3. Replace the damaged disk with a new disk.

4. Click Add Mirror, and use the other disk to reestablish the mirror.

If disk recovery appears on the exam, be alert to the following items:

➤ Are the disks basic or dynamic?

➤ Do disks need to be replaced? If so, how many? And should they be basic or dynamic?

➤ Does data need to be restored from a backup or can the repair take place without a restore?

Striped Volumes on Dynamic Disks

Striped volumes are similar to spanned volumes, except that they write data across all of the disks evenly. A striped volume can be formatted in NTFS, FAT, or FAT32 and requires at least two or more hard drives. The main reason for using a striped volume is to increase the speed of the data read and write performance.

Extending a Striped Volume

A striped volume cannot be extended. The data on all the disks is written sequentially, which makes it impossible to add free space into the volume. For the same reason, the striped volume cannot be mirrored.

Recovering from a Striped Volume Failure on Dynamic Disks

There is no fault tolerance built into a striped volume. If one of the disks in the volume fails, all of the data for the whole striped volume is lost. In this case, the data must be restored from a backup.

RAID 5 Volumes on Dynamic Disks

A *striped volume with parity*, also referred to as RAID 5, consists of three or more hard drives. A striped volume with parity allows one disk in the volume to fail without data loss and still allows access to the volume. If more than one disk fails in the volume, however, all the data in the striped volume with parity must be recovered from a backup. Striped volumes with parity can only be implemented on dynamic disks.

Extending a Striped Volume

A striped volume with parity cannot be extended. The data on all the disks is written sequentially, which makes it impossible to add free space into the volume. For the same reason, the striped volume with parity cannot be mirrored.

Recovering from a RAID 5 Volume Failure on Dynamic Disks

There are two ways a striped volume with parity can be recovered. You can Reactivate The Disk, or Repair The Volume. The following section discusses the two methods.

If a volume has a status of Offline, Missing, or Online (Errors), follow these steps to reactivate the volume:

1. Using the Disk Management tool, right-click on the disk that you want to reactivate.

2. Select Reactivate Disk, and the status should return to Healthy.

If a volume's status does not return to Healthy, the disk must be repaired. To repair a striped volume with parity, replace the failed disk and follow these steps:

1. Right-click on the failed disk.

2. Select Repair Volume.

3. In the Repair Volume box, select the new disk.

 Repairing failed volumes is a topic that may appear on the exam. Keep the following tips in mind when you repair volumes on dynamic disks:

➤ To repair a failed mirror volume, the option to employ is Reactivate Mirror.

➤ To repair a failed striped volume with parity, the options are Reactivate Disk and Repair Volume.

➤ A volume, spanned volume, or striped volume cannot be repaired. The data must be recovered from a backup.

Partitions on Basic Disks

A *partition* is a section of the hard drive that is used to store data that is accessible by a drive letter. Partitions are legacy storage from NT 4.0. A new partition can be created on an existing hard drive in Windows 2000. The only way to repair a damaged partition is to restore the data from a backup.

Mirrored Sets on Basic Disks

Mirrored sets that were upgraded from NT 4.0 Servers to Windows 2000 remain mirrored sets on basic disks. A new mirrored set cannot be created by using basic disks; instead, a new mirrored volume must be created by using dynamic disks.

Configuring a Mirrored Set on Basic Disks

Mirrored sets cannot be configured on basic disks with Windows 2000 Server. Instead, new mirrored volumes must be created on dynamic disks.

Recovering from a Mirrored Set Failure on Basic Disks

When one part of a mirrored set fails, the set displays a status of Failed Redundancy in Disk Management. The mirror is still available, but the bad part of the mirror needs to be repaired. To recover a mirrored partition on basic disks, there must be another basic disk available with the required free space. Follow these steps to recover a mirrored set:

1. In Disk Management, right-click on the mirror you want to repair.

2. Select Repair Volume, and then follow the steps in the Repair Volume Wizard.

The status should return to Healthy. If the status does not return to Healthy, follow these steps:

3. Right-click on the set.

4. Select Resynchronize Mirror.

Striped Sets on Basic Disks

A striped set on basic disks is a legacy from NT 4.0 Server. If a striped set on NT 4.0 Server is upgraded to Windows 2000 Server, the striped set remains a striped set on a basic disk. A striped set requires at least two hard drives, and all of the data is striped evenly across each of the drives. There is no fault tolerance in a striped set. A new striped set cannot be created on basic disks; instead, a new striped volume is created on dynamic disks.

RAID 5 Sets on Basic Disks

After you upgrade to a Windows 2000 Server from an NT 4.0 Server, the striped sets with parity or RAID 5 sets are migrated to basic disks. The disks can be repaired or regenerated, but a new striped set cannot be added; instead, a new striped volume with parity is created using dynamic disks.

Recovering from a Striped Set with Parity Failure on Basic Disks

If a disk fails that is part of a striped set with parity, the set has a status of Failed Redundancy in Disk Management. The data on the set is still accessible, but the set must be repaired. Another basic disk must be available to repair the set. After you install a basic disk that has available space, follow these steps to make repairs:

1. In Disk Management, right-click on the set.

2. Select Repair Volume, and then follow the steps in the Repair Volume Wizard.

The status of the set should return to Healthy. If the status does not return to Healthy, follow these steps:

3. Right-click on the set.

4. Select Regenerate Parity to recalculate the parity information with the rest of the set.

Repairing failed sets may appear on an exam. Keep the following tips in mind when making repairs to sets on basic disks:

➤ To repair a failed mirrored set, the options are Repair Volume and Resynchronize Mirror.

➤ To repair a failed striped set with parity or RAID 5 set, the options are Repair Volume and Regenerate Parity.

➤ A partition or striped set cannot be repaired. The data must be recovered from a backup.

Mounting Volumes

Microsoft has added the capability to mount volumes that are NTFS as folders in Windows 2000 Server. The mounted volume then represents a folder in an existing directory. This feature can be implemented when a drive letter is not available or desirable. A newly mounted volume can be used to add more space to an existing hierarchy.

Configuring Mounted Volumes

Follow these steps to configure a mounted volume:

1. In Disk Management, right-click on unallocated free space.

2. Select Create Volume in the Create Volume Wizard.

3. Select Simple Volume.

4. Select the disk and the size of the new volume.

5. Click Mount This Volume At An Empty Folder That Supports Drive Paths and then click Browse. Figure 7.4 shows the mounted volume path screen.

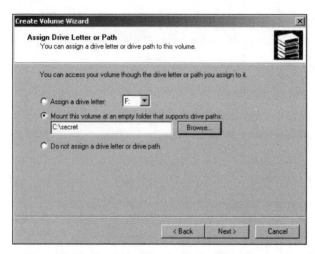

Figure 7.4 A new volume mounted on the C: drive in an empty folder called \secret.

6. Browse to the location of the new mount point on an NTFS volume. If a folder does not exist, you can create it by clicking on the New Folder button.

7. Designate the type of file system, assign a volume label, and complete the Wizard's steps.

Extending a Mounted Volume

To extend a mounted volume, you must format it in NTFS. To extend a mounted volume, follow these steps:

1. In Disk Management, right-click on the mounted volume you want to extend.

2. Select Extend Volume.

3. Designate the amount of space you want to add to the mounted volume.

4. Click Next, and then click OK.

Disk Management of Storage

Disk Management is used for all administration of Windows 2000 Server disks. Administration includes upgrading disks to deleting disks. Some management operations are discussed in the following sections.

Upgrading Basic Disks to Dynamic Disks

You can upgrade basic disks to dynamic disks at any time without data loss. Any disk you upgrade must have 1MB of unallocated free space for the conversion. It is recommended that a backup be performed before an upgrade. Table 7.1 shows the conversion process from basic disks to dynamic disks.

Note: Upgrading to a dynamic storage makes the disk unreadable to operating systems other than Windows 2000.

To upgrade a basic disk to a dynamic disk, follow these steps:

1. In Disk Management, right-click on the disk you want to upgrade. Figure 7.5 displays a drive being upgraded from a basic disk to a dynamic disk.

2. Select Upgrade To Dynamic Disk. Figure 7.6 displays the warning screen received when you upgrade a disk.

3. The system may have to be rebooted before the update takes place.

Table 7.1 The Conversion Process from a Basic to a Dynamic Disk.	
Original Basic Disk	**After the Conversion to Dynamic Disk**
System partition	Simple volume
Boot partition	Simple volume
Free space	Free space
Logical drive	Simple volume
Volume sets	Spanned volumes
Mirrored sets	Mirrored volumes
Striped sets	Striped volumes
Striped sets with parity (RAID 5 set)	Striped volumes with parity (RAID 5 volume)

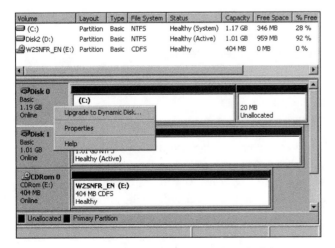

Figure 7.5   A basic disk being upgraded to a dynamic disk.

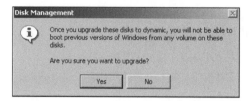

Figure 7.6 A dynamic disk warning screen.

Reverting from a Dynamic Disk to a Basic Disk

Reverting to a basic disk is a more difficult task. To revert to a basic disk, follow these steps:

1. Back up all of the data on the dynamic disk.

2. Delete the dynamic disk. All information on the disk will be lost.

3. Right-click on the disk, and select Revert Back To Basic Disk.

4. Restore the data from the backup onto the new basic disk.

Deleting Volumes and Sets

All volumes and sets, regardless if they are basic or dynamic, can be deleted. After you delete a volume or set, all of the information is lost. Follow these steps to delete a partition, volume, or set:

1. In Disk Management, right-click on the partition or volume you want to delete.

2. Select Delete Partition or Delete Volume.

3. Click Yes to confirm that the partition or volume should be deleted.

Breaking a Mirrored Volume or Mirrored Set

To break a mirrored set, right-click on it and select Break Mirror. This option makes the two disks independent of each other, but no data will be lost.

Updating Disk Management Storage Information

You use Disk Management to update storage information and to verify that the correct information is displayed. After information is changed or disks are added, right-click on Disk Management, and select Rescan or Refresh. Rescan looks at all of the drives associated with the system and updates the information in Disk Management, whereas Refresh updates all of the Disk Management information including type of disks, drive letters, and file systems.

Drive Letters

You can use Disk Management to change and assign drive letters. Alphabetic letters can be used from A through Z, although A and B are reserved for floppy drives. An administrator should be careful not to change letters that may be linked in the Registry to a particular drive letter. To change a drive letter for a storage device, follow these steps:

1. In Disk Management, right-click on the device that needs a different drive letter.

2. Select Change Drive Letter And Path option.

3. Choose Edit to change the drive letter.

4. In the Assign A Drive Letter box, choose the new drive letter and click OK.

Adding Storage

Adding new storage devices to Windows 2000 can be done in two ways. One way is to shut down the machine and install the new device. When the computer is restarted, Windows 2000 Server acknowledges the new device, installs it, and the device appears in Disk Management. The second way is only supported if the computer has hot swap hardware. In this case, after the disk is installed, use the Disk Management tool by selecting the Action menu and choosing Rescan Disks.

Adding a Storage Device from Another Computer

Windows 2000 Server can support storage devices from other computers. When a storage device is moved from one computer to another, Windows 2000 automatically detects the device, activates it, and marks it ready for use.

In rare instances, a storage device from another computer displays a Foreign status. In this case, follow these steps to import the device from the other computer:

1. In Disk Management, right-click on the disk that displays a Foreign status.

2. Select Import Foreign Disk.

3. Select the disk that you want to add.

4. Choose Select Disk.

Errors in Adding Storage from Another Computer

There are two types of errors that may be received when trying to import storage from another computer: Failed: Incomplete Volume and Failed Redundancy, described below:

➤ *Failed: Incomplete Volume*—Appears if the disks being imported are an incomplete part of a spanned volume, striped volume, or RAID. This error occurs when the whole volume is not imported to the machine. The rest of the volume must be imported before the data on the disks can be recovered.

➤ *Failed Redundancy*—Appears if the disks being imported were part of a mirrored volume or RAID 5 volume with one part of the volume missing. In this case, the data can be accessed, but there is no redundancy in the imported volume.

Error Checking Storage

You can check storage for errors by using the Error-Checking tool provided in Windows 2000. This tool checks a disk for file system errors, attempts to fix errors, and tries to recover bad sectors. To run the Error-Checking tool, follow these steps:

1. In Windows Explorer or Disk Management, right-click on the disk you want to check for errors.

2. Select Properties, and select the Tools tab.

3. Choose the Check Now button in the Error-Checking section.

4. Place checkmarks in the boxes labeled Automatically Fix File System Errors and Scan For And Attempt Recovery Of Bad Sectors.

5. Choose Start.

If exclusive access cannot be obtained by the Error-Checking, it attempts to schedule the task next time the system is rebooted.

Disk Defragmentating

Windows 2000 has supplied a disk defragmenter program that can increase the performance of a server's hard drives. The program scans the hard drive for data that is fragmented and tries to relocate the data to contiguous space for better read/write performance.

Note: Depending on the size of the hard drive, defragmenting can take several hours.

You can start the disk defragmenter in the following way:

1. In Windows Explorer, right-click the disk you want to analyze.

2. Select Properties, and then select the Tools tab.

3. Choose the Defragment Now button.

4. Click Analyze to see whether the disk is fragmented.

5. If fragmentation seems to be a problem, click Defragment.

 It is important to know when to use the Disk Defragmenter tool on Windows 2000 server.

Practice Questions

Question 1

A Windows 2000 Server has a mirrored volume, a spanned volume, a primary partition, and a striped set with parity. One of the disks that is part of the striped set with parity fails. What are the two best options for the administrator of this server? [Check the two best answers]

❏ a. Restore the data from a backup

❏ b. Create a new striped set with parity

❏ c. Create a new striped volume with parity

❏ d. Replace the failed disk and Repair Volume

❏ e. Reactivate Volume

❏ f. Regenerate Parity

Answers d and f are correct. Answer a is incorrect because a striped set with parity continues to function if one disk is lost. Answers b and c are incorrect because the striped set with parity still functions, so creating a new set is unnecessary. Answer e is incorrect because only striped volumes with parity can be reactivated.

Question 2

A Windows 2000 Server has a mirrored volume, a spanned volume, a primary partition, and a striped volume with parity. One of the disks that is part of the RAID 5 volume fails. What are the two best options for the administrator of this server? [Check the two best answers]

❏ a. Restore the data from a backup

❏ b. Create a new striped set with parity

❏ c. Create a new striped volume with parity

❏ d. Replace the failed disk and Repair Volume

❏ e. Reactivate the Volume

❏ f. Regenerate Parity

Answers d and e are correct. Answer a is incorrect because a striped volume with parity continues to function if one disk is lost. Answers b and c are incorrect because the striped volume with parity is still functioning, so creating a new volume is unnecessary. Answer f is incorrect because only striped sets with parity can be regenerated.

Question 3

A Windows 2000 Server has a mirrored volume, a spanned volume, a primary partition, and a striped volume. One of the disks that is part of the striped volume fails. What are the two best options for the administrator? [Check the two best answers]

- ❑ a. Restore the data from a backup
- ❑ b. Create a new striped set
- ❑ c. Create a new striped volume
- ❑ d. Replace the failed disk and Repair Volume
- ❑ e. Reactivate Volume
- ❑ f. Regenerate Parity

Answers a and c are correct. Answer b is incorrect because you cannot create a new striped set; you must create a new volume. Answers d, e, and f are incorrect because there is no fault tolerance in a striped volume. The information cannot be repaired if one disk of a striped volume fails.

Question 4

A Windows 2000 Server has a mirrored volume, a spanned volume, a primary partition, and a striped volume. One of the disks that is part of the mirrored volume fails. What is the best option for the administrator?

- ○ a. Restore the data from a backup
- ○ b. Create a new mirrored set
- ○ c. Create a new mirrored volume
- ○ d. Replace the failed disk and Repair Volume
- ○ e. Resynchronize
- ○ f. Reactivate Disk

Answer f is correct. Answers a, b, and c are incorrect because if one disk of the mirror failed there is still another disk with a copy of the data. The mirror does not need to be restored, and a new mirror does not need to be created. Answers d and e are incorrect because Repair Volume and Resynchronize are options for mirrored sets on basic disks.

Question 5

A Windows 2000 Server has a mirrored set, a spanned volume, a primary partition, and a striped volume. The two disks that are part of the mirrored set fail. What are the best options for the administrator? [Check all correct answers]

❑ a. Restore the data from a backup

❑ b. Create a new mirrored set

❑ c. Create a new mirrored volume

❑ d. Replace the failed disk and Repair Volume

❑ e. Replace the failed disk and Resynchronize

❑ f. Replace the failed disk and Reactivate Disk

Answers a and c are correct. Answer b is incorrect because a new mirrored set cannot be created; instead a new mirrored volume must be created on dynamic storage. Answers d, e, and f are incorrect because both disks in the mirror have failed. There are no disks in the mirror to repair, resynchronize, or reactivate.

Question 6

An administrator must extend a spanned volume. The hard drives on the system are dynamic storage, formatted in FAT32, and have free space. What is the correct option for the administrator?

○ a. Add more free space and extend

○ b. Convert the disks to basic disks

○ c. Convert the disks to dynamic disks

○ d. Highlight the volume and click Extend

○ e. The disk cannot be extended

Answer e is correct because only NTFS volumes can be extended. Answer a is incorrect because the question specifies that there is free space available. Answer b is incorrect because extending a volume requires dynamic disks. Answer c is incorrect because the disks are already dynamic disks. Answer d is incorrect because a FAT32 volume cannot be extended, only NTFS volumes can be extended.

Question 7

Figure 7.7 represents a Windows 2000 Server. The administrator is having trouble converting from basic storage to dynamic storage. What seems to be the problem?

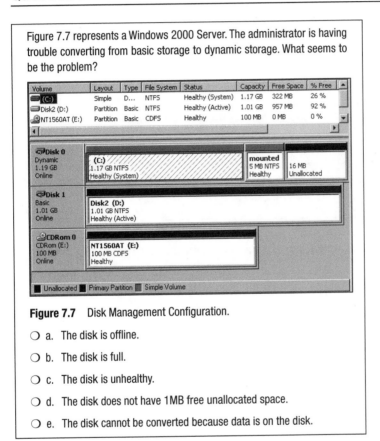

Figure 7.7 Disk Management Configuration.

○ a. The disk is offline.

○ b. The disk is full.

○ c. The disk is unhealthy.

○ d. The disk does not have 1MB free unallocated space.

○ e. The disk cannot be converted because data is on the disk.

Answer d is correct. Answer a is incorrect because all of the disks are online. Answer b is incorrect because it does not matter how full the disk is as long as 1MB of free unallocated space is available for the conversion. In addition, the disk has 92 percent free space. Answer c is incorrect because all of the disks are healthy. Answer e is incorrect because you can convert a disk with data on it, and no data will be lost.

Question 8

For what reasons would an administrator convert a basic disk to a dynamic disk? [Check all correct answers]

❑ a. To add a new volume

❑ b. To add a new striped set

❑ c. To add a new striped volume with parity

❑ d. To add a new striped set with parity

❑ e. To add a new mirrored volume

❑ f. To add a new mirrored set

Answers a, c, and e are correct. Answers b, d, and f are incorrect because new sets cannot be created on basic disks. New volumes must be created on dynamic disks.

Question 9

Put the correct items in the correct order to convert a dynamic disk to a basic disk.

Restore the data

Delete one volume on the disk

Delete the disk

Revert To Basic Disk option

Revert To Dynamic Disk option

Back up data

Answer:

Back up data

Delete the disk

Revert Back To Basic Disk option

Restore the data

Question 10

The following screen, shown in Figure 7.8, represents the default Create Volume Wizard screen. Choose the option that enables you to create a striped volume with parity.

Create Volume Wizard ☒

Select Volume Type
What type of volume do you want to create?

Volume type
- ⦿ Simple volume
- ○ Spanned volume
- ○ Striped volume
- ○ Mirrored volume
- ○ RAID-5 volume

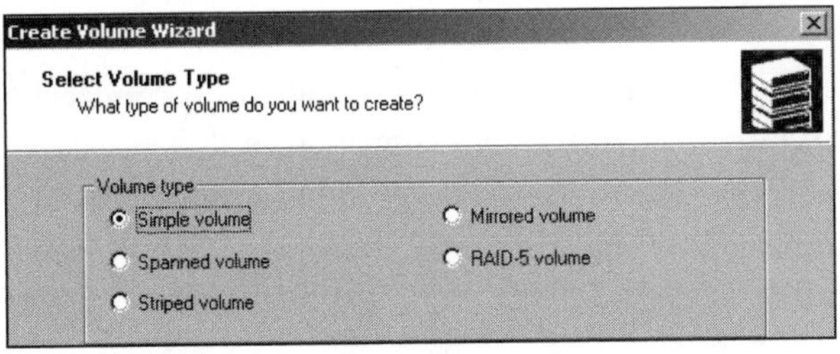

Figure 7.8   Default Create Volume Wizard.

Answer: A striped volume with parity is the same as RAID 5 volume. Figure 7.9 displays the Create Volume Wizard for creating a striped volume with parity.

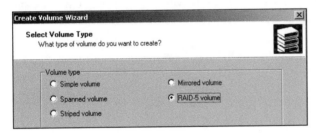

Figure 7.9   Create Volume Wizard set to create a striped volume with parity.

Need to Know More?

 Russel, Charlie, and Sharon Crawford: *Microsoft Windows 2000 Server Administrator's Companion.* Microsoft Press, Redmond, Washington, 2000. ISBN 1-57231-819-8. This is a valuable resource from which to learn more about implementing storage.

 Search TechNet on the Internet at **www.microsoft.com/technet/default.asp** or the TechNet CD for information on: disk management, Windows 2000 storage, mirrored sets, mirrored volumes, striped sets, striped volume, striped sets with parity, RAID 5, RAID 1, RAID 0, repair volumes, defragmentation, mounted volumes, drive letters, and deleting volumes.

 For more information on the following terminology and implementation of that terminology refer to Microsoft Windows 2000 Help. To access this resource, click on Start and then click on Help. Terms and technologies to search for include: mounting volumes overview, RAID, RAID 5, striped sets, striped sets with parity, dynamic disks, basic disk, repairing disk resources, and repairing RAID 5 volumes.

Files and Folders in Windows 2000

Terms you'll need to understand:

✓ FAT

✓ FAT32

✓ NTFS 5.0

✓ Permissions

✓ Share permissions

✓ Security permissions

✓ NTFS permissions

✓ Compression

✓ Disk quotas

Techniques you'll need to master:

✓ Calculating a user's share permissions and security permissions

✓ Calculating inheritance of share permissions and security permissions

✓ Establishing and maintaining shares on a network

✓ Troubleshooting permission problems

✓ Compressing and uncompressing data

✓ Configuring and implementing disk quotas

✓ Troubleshooting disk quotas

This chapter addresses files and folders in Windows 2000. NTFS, FAT, FAT32, and the different permissions that are available are discussed. Administrative tools for compression and implementing disk quotas also are addressed. This chapter emphasizes the importance of permissions in Windows 2000 and how to administer the system for security. The exam will likely cover share and NTFS permissions, how to calculate permissions for users, and how to administer and troubleshoot disk quotas.

Windows 2000 Server File Systems

Windows 2000 Server supports three different files systems: FAT, FAT32, and NTFS. FAT and FAT32 support legacy products, and NTFS provides operating system security. The following section provides a brief overview of the file systems and includes facts you should consider before implementing a file system.

FAT

FAT or *File Allocation Table* is a table that maintains the segment status for storage on a hard drive. The table holds information about files including file names and file attributes. It uses 16-bit pointers to reference the table and supports 16-bit applications. FAT implements 8.3 file names, using eight characters for the file name and three letters for the file extension.

You should keep in mind the following facts when choosing FAT for your Windows 2000 file system:

➤ The maximum volume size is 4GB.

➤ The maximum file size is 2GB.

➤ FAT can be used to dual boot other operating systems.

➤ FAT can access MS-DOS, all Windows operating systems, all NT operating systems, and Windows 2000.

➤ FAT does not allow for file or folder security.

➤ FAT can be used to format a floppy disk.

Only Windows 2000 and Windows NT can view FAT partitions that are larger than 2GB.

FAT32

FAT32, first introduced with Windows 95 Service Release 2, is similar to FAT except that it can support larger files, larger disk sizes, and uses space more efficiently. FAT32 supports native 32-bit programs, and also exceeds the 512 root directory limitations of FAT.

You should keep in mind the following facts when choosing FAT32 for your Windows 2000 file system:

➤ The maximum volume size is 32GB.

➤ The maximum file size is 4GB.

➤ FAT32 can be used to dual boot other operating systems.

➤ FAT32 can access Windows 95 with OSR2, Windows 98, and Windows 2000.

➤ FAT32 does not allow for file or folder security.

➤ FAT32 can be used to format a floppy disk.

NTFS 5.0

NTFS 5.0, introduced and designed for Windows NT, is the preferred file system for Windows 2000 Server because of its reliability, fault tolerance, and security. NTFS has built in recoverability and has the capability to secure items at the local machine level. Security permissions can be implemented with NTFS, as discussed later in this chapter.

You should keep in mind the following facts when choosing NTFS 5.0 for your Windows 2000 file system:

➤ The maximum volume size is 2TB.

➤ The maximum file size is limited by the volume size.

➤ The minimum volume size is 10MB.

➤ NTFS 5.0 is recommended for any volume larger than 32GB.

➤ NTFS 5.0 cannot be used to dual boot other operating systems. The exception is Windows NT 4.0 with Service Pack 4 or later.

➤ There is no access for non-NTFS 5.0 file systems.

➤ There is file and folder security.

➤ NTFS 5.0 cannot be used to format a floppy disk.

NTFS 5.0 has some advanced features that allow Windows 2000 to be implemented securely. Some of the new features include disk quotas, encryption, and the addition of Active Directory. NTFS 5.0 features provide security for Windows 2000.

NTFS 5.0 features are as follows:

➤ It provides file and folder security.

➤ It is required for domain controllers and Active Directory.

➤ It can be used to store encrypted data. The data is then automatically encrypted and decrypted as it is written or read.

➤ It allows for disk quotas so that the amount of data users can store is limited.

➤ It implements an Update Sequence Number (USN) journal that keeps a log of all the changes to the file system.

➤ It implements reparsed points that can trap and redirect file input and output. This feature makes it possible to mount volumes.

➤ It can sparse files to permit large files to use only the space they need, only as they need it.

Converting to NTFS

FAT and FAT32 can be converted to NTFS 5.0 without any data loss. This conversion is a one-way process and cannot be reversed. If a server does not need to dual boot to another operating system, then consider converting it to NTFS. Converting to NTFS enables you to take advantage of the Windows 2000 security features. You must run the following command to convert a drive to NTFS 5.0 at a command prompt; there is not a GUI version. After the command is executed, the conversion will take place. If the operating system cannot get exclusive access to the drive, the computer must be rebooted before the conversion takes place.

```
convert [drive:] /fs:ntfs
```

Note that after you convert to NTFS, you must follow certain steps to return to a FAT or FAT32 file system: back up the current file system, delete and reformat it in either FAT or FAT32, and then restore the data from the backup.

 The exam may cover FAT, FAT32, and NTFS volumes. You should understand the different file systems and know when and how to implement them.

Files and Folders

Files and folders in Windows 2000 are used to organize, secure, and share information throughout an organization. Folders are shared so that specified users can access the folder and the files in the folder over the network. Permission restrictions can be implemented on any file or folder to make it accessible or inaccessible to everyone except specific users. Folders and their contents can also be published in Active Directory to make them more accessible to users.

Publishing Shared Folders

With Windows 2000 Server, a share can be published in Active Directory to make it more accessible to users, and easier to index and search. To share a folder, open Explorer, right-click on the folder, select Properties, and then choose the Sharing tab. This process enables administrators to allow a folder and its files to be shared on the network. Users with the correct permissions can then map a networked drive to the newly created share. After the folder is shared, follow these steps to make it available in Active Directory:

1. Open the Active Directory Users And Computers snap-in.

2. Select the domain for the location of the new share.

3. Right-click on the domain, select New, and then select Shared Folder.

4. Type the name of the shared folder that you created in Explorer, the network path, and then click OK. The new share is now available on the network and available through Active Directory to be indexed and searched by users.

Administration and Implementation of Files and Folders

Administering and implementing files and folders can be a very large task for any administrator. Files and folders have many different types of permissions to configure. We will take a brief look at the different configurations and how to administer them. To access file or folder properties, right-click on it, and select Properties.

Folder General Properties

The General properties of a folder displays the folder location, size, creation date, and attributes. The attributes dictate whether the folder is Read-Only or if it is Hidden. The Advanced tab defines archive, indexing, compression, and encryption. Figure 8.1 shows the default Advanced Attributes dialog box and the options that you can configure.

Folder Sharing Properties

The Sharing properties tab enables you to define whether a folder is to be shared on the network. If sharing is enabled, the share name can be assigned, a user limit can be set, and permissions can be configured. Figure 8.2 shows the default permissions of a shared folder. The Share Permissions dialog box is used to implement share level security to a folder.

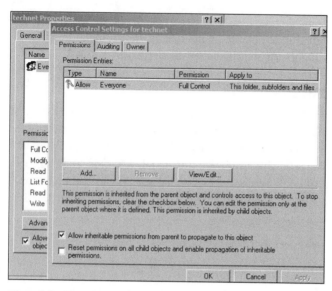

Figure 8.1   The Advanced Attributes of the General properties tab.

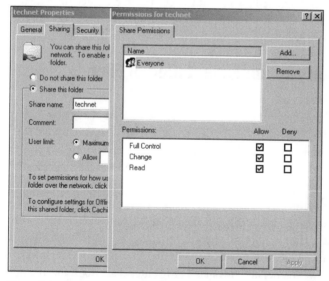

Figure 8.2   Setting up a shared folder on the Share Permissions dialog box.

Folder Security Properties

The Security tab, which provides file and folder security, is only available with NTFS volumes. Figure 8.3 displays the default Security settings for a folder. The NTFS security permissions are discussed in more detail in the following section.

The Advanced button on the Security tab provides access to advanced options such as auditing, ownership, and inheritance of permissions. Figure 8.4 displays the Access Control settings for a folder.

Offline Files

Offline files enable users to work on documents that are stored on the network, whether they are connected to the network or not. The local computer caches offline files for the user to work on when they are not connected to the network. When the computer is reconnected to the network, the changes are updated to the networked file. If you are updating a file that another person has changed, you are given the option to save your file, keep the other person's file, or save both files.

To set offline access for a shared folder, right-click on the folder, select Properties, select the Sharing tab, and click the Caching button. Figure 8.5 displays the cache settings for an offline folder and Table 8.1 displays the different settings and their function.

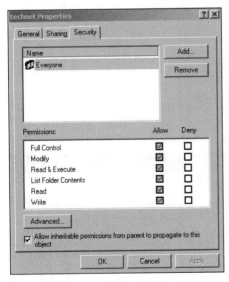

Figure 8.3   The Security settings for a folder.

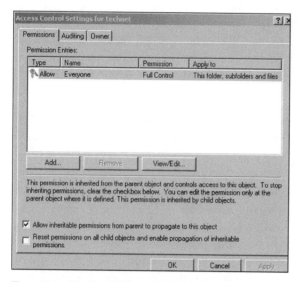

Figure 8.4   The Access Control settings for a folder.

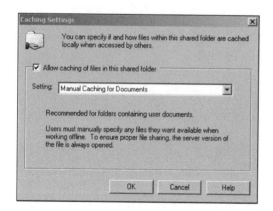

Figure 8.5   Offline folder settings.

Table 8.1	Offline folder cache settings.
Setting	**Function**
Automatic Caching For Documents	Files that are opened are automatically downloaded and made available when a user is working offline.
Automatic Caching For Programs	All the files and programs in the folder are made available for the user while working offline.
Manual Caching For Documents	A user must specify any documents that they would like to access while working offline.

Permissions

Permissions are used to control who can and cannot have access to a resource. Figures 8.2 and 8.3 display permission screens for controlling access. When you set a permission, it is configured to allow or deny access to the resources. If a user is denied access to a resource, then that permission overrides all the user's other permissions. By default, newly configured resources have the permissions set for Everyone Full Control - Allow. This means that by default, all users have full access to the resource.

 The exam may cover share permissions and security permissions. You should be familiar with permissions, how to apply different types of permissions, how to combine share and security permissions, and how permissions are inherited.

Hierarchy of Permissions

Permissions by default are inherited from folders to files and subfolders. Two types of permissions affect a hierarchy. These permissions are as follows:

➤ *Explicit permissions*—Attach directly to an object or Organizational Unit (OU), which can include file and folder permissions.

➤ *Inherited permissions*—Propagate from a parent to a child. This type of permission makes it easier for an administrator because permissions can be assigned at one level and then propagated down in the hierarchy. To disable inheritance, remove the check from the Allow Inheritable Permissions From Parent To Propagate To This Object checkbox (refer to Figure 8.3 for more detail). If inheritance is removed, you receive the warning box that appears in Figure 8.6.

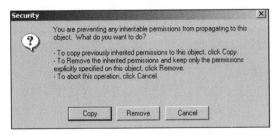

Figure 8.6 The Security warning appears when inheritance is removed.

Share Permissions

Share permissions are assigned to a folder that will be a network resource for users. The Share Permissions dialog box was shown in Figure 8.2. You use the Add and Remove buttons to add and remove users or groups from the Share Permissions properties tab. Without the correct permissions, users are not allowed to access the resource from the network. Figure 8.7 shows the Share Permissions settings for a network share that only members of the Administrators group can access. Table 8.2 defines the share permissions available and what a user can accomplish with the permission.

 Remember that share permissions have nothing to do with locally accessing resources. If a user is denied from a shared resource over the network, that user can still sit down at the local machine where the resource is located, log in, and access the resource.

Note: NTFS, FAT, and FAT32 can all have shared network folders.

Security Permissions

NTFS formatted drives provide extra file and folder security. This security, referred to as NTFS permissions or security permissions, protects files and folders at the local computer. Figure 8.8 displays the file permissions screen and Table 8.3 defines the file permissions. Figure 8.9 displays the folder permissions screen and Table 8.4 defines the folder permissions.

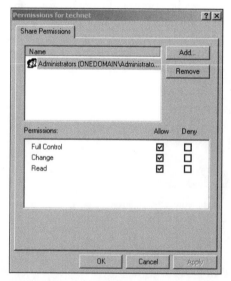

Figure 8.7 Share Permissions dialog box settings for the Administrators group.

Table 8.2 Share permissions.			
User Permission	**Full Control**	**Change**	**Read**
Viewing file and subfolder names	X	X	X
Traversing to subfolders	X	X	X
Viewing data in files and running programs	X	X	X
Adding files and subfolders to the share	X	X	
Changing data in files	X	X	
Deleting subfolders and files	X	X	

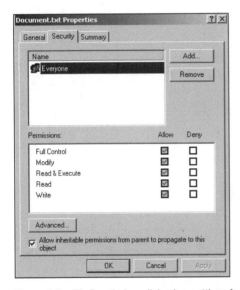

Figure 8.8 File Permissions dialog box settings for all users.

With Full Control, a user or group can delete any file in the folder regardless of the permissions assigned to the file.

Special Access Permissions

Special access can be assigned to a user or group if the default permissions are not appropriate for administrative purposes. Special access can only be assigned to a volume formatted in NTFS; otherwise this option is not available. To assign special permissions, access the Security tab, click the Advanced button, and choose View/Edit. There are two special access permissions that need to be noted because of the resources they control: Change Permissions and Take Ownership.

Table 8.3   File permissions.

Permissions	Full Control	Modify	Read & Execute	Read	Write
Traverse folder/execute file	x	x	x		
List folder/read data	x	x	x	x	
Read attributes	x	x	x	x	
Read extended attributes	x	x	x	x	
Create files/write data	x	x			x
Create folders/append data	x	x			x
Write attributes	x	x			x
Write extended attributes	x	x			x
Delete subfolders and files	x				
Delete	x	x			
Read permissions	x	x	x	x	x
Synchronize	x	x	x	x	x
Change permissions	x				
Take ownership	x				

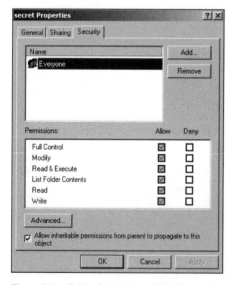

Figure 8.9   Folder Permissions dialog box settings for all users.

Table 8.4   Folder permissions.

Permissions	Full Control	Modify	Read & Execute	List Folder Content	Read	Write
Traverse folder/execute file	x	x	x	x		
List folder/read data	x	x	x	x	x	
Read attributes	x	x	x	x	x	
Read extended attributes	x	x	x	x	x	
Create files/write data	x	x				x
Create folders/append data	x	x				x
Write attributes	x	x				x
Write extended attributes	x	x				x
Delete subfolders and files	x					
Delete	x	x				
Read permissions	x	x	x	x	x	x
Synchronize	x	x	x	x	x	x
Change permissions	x					
Take ownership	x					

➤ Access to files permissions are granted or denied by using *Change Permissions*.

➤ A user can take ownership of a file or folder regardless of its current permissions using *Take Ownership permission*. The current owner of the file or an administrator can grant a user permission to Take Ownership in Windows 2000.

Note: In Windows 2000, you cannot assign file ownership to a specific user.

Copying and Moving Permissions

Security permissions may change when they are copied or moved. Table 8.5 explains how permissions are affected when they are copied or moved, in an easy-to-remember diagram that can be recreated when taking an exam to remember how permissions are copied and moved. If a file or folder is copied to the same NTFS volume, it inherits the permissions of its new location. If a file or folder is moved to the same NTFS volume, its permissions do not change. If a file or folder is copied or moved to a different NTFS volume, it inherits the permissions of its new location.

Table 8.5 Copying and moving permissions.		
	Same NTFS Volume	**Different NTFS Volume**
Copy	Inherits the NTFS permissions from the folder it is copied into.	Inherits the NTFS permissions from the folder it is copied into.
Move	Retains the NTFS permissions from the folder it was moved from.	Inherits the NTFS permissions from the folder it is moved into.

Combined Permissions

After multiple permissions are applied, it becomes confusing to determine a user's combination of permissions. If a folder has share permissions and security permissions, how does that affect the users who access those resources? Remember these points about combining permissions:

➤ If a user is a member of multiple share permissions, permissions are combined and the highest level of access is assigned.

➤ If a user is a member of multiple security permissions, permissions are combined and the highest level of access is assigned.

➤ If a user is a member of share and security permissions for a resource, the permissions are combined and the most restrictive permission is assigned.

The only exception to these three points is the Deny Access attribute. If a user is denied access, that user cannot access the resources regardless of the user's other permissions.

The exam is likely to cover combined permissions. You may be asked to combine permissions for a user with multiple groups and determine their access privileges. Do not forget that Deny Access overrules all other permissions.

Data Compression

You *compress* data to save and conserve space on a hard drive. Only drives that are formatted in NTFS can be compressed. Compressed drives cannot be encrypted. You can compress drives, files, and folders.

Remember that floppy disks cannot be compressed because compression requires the disk to be formatted in NTFS.

You should understand compression and how to calculate compression inheritance.

Drive Compression

To compress a drive:

1. In Explorer, right-click on the drive you want to compress.

2. Select Properties.

3. Check the Compress Drive To Save Disk Space checkbox.

4. Choose to compress the drive only or the drive, subfolders, and files. The newly compressed drive should appear in blue. Figure 8.10 shows a compressed drive's properties.

File and Folder Compression

To compress a file or folder:

1. In Explorer, right-click on the file or folder you want to compress.

2. Select Properties.

3. Select the Advanced button, and check the Compress Contents To Save Disk Space checkbox.

Figure 8.11 shows a compressed file's attributes.

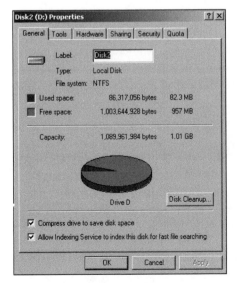

Figure 8.10   A compressed drive.

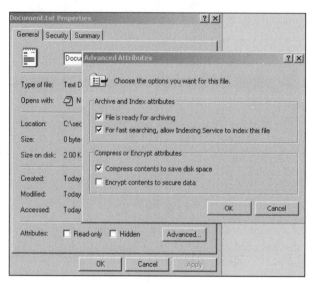

Figure 8.11 A compressed file's attributes.

Inheritance of Compression

It is important to remember how inheritance is implemented when you move and copy compressed files. If you copy a file to a compressed folder on the same drive, the file is compressed automatically. If you copy a file to a compressed folder on a different drive, the file also is compressed automatically. If you move a file to a compressed folder on the same drive, the file retains its original state. If you move a file to a compressed folder on a different drive, the file is compressed automatically. Table 8.6 defines how compression is inherited.

The **compact** Command

You use the **compact** command to change and display compressed files and directories. Table 8.7 displays the compact switches and their properties. Use the following command to compress or uncompress files and folders at the command prompt:

```
compact [/c | /u] [/s:dir] [/a /i /f]
```

Table 8.6 Inheritance of compression.		
	Same NTFS Drive	**Different NTFS Drive**
Copy	Inherits the compressed status or uncompressed status from the folder it is copied into.	Inherits the compressed status or uncompressed status from the folder it is copied into.
Move	Retains the compressed status or uncompressed status from the folder it came from.	Inherits the compressed status or uncompressed status from the folder it is moved into.

Table 8.7	Compact switches and properties.
Switch	**Property of the Switch**
none	Displays the current compression status of the directory.
/c	Compresses the file or folder.
/u	Uncompresses the file or folder.
/s	Compresses or decompresses all the subdirectories.
/a	Displays the hidden system files.
/i	Ignores any errors that are received.
/f	Forces the compression or decompression of a file or folder.

Disk Quotas

Disk quotas are a new technology implemented on Windows 2000 Server that uses NTFS as their file system. Administrators use disk quotas to set space restrictions on users. Using disk quotas, administrators can control growth and file storage on their servers. To implement and maintain quotas, you must have administrator privileges on the volume. When you implement disk quotas, remember these points:

➤ Disk quotas can only be applied to drives formatted with NTFS.

➤ Disk quotas are tracked independently for each NTFS volume.

➤ Disk quota values are calculated by the uncompressed byte value of the files or folders.

➤ Disk quota values are based on file or folder ownership. The owner of the file or folder is charged for the usage that is calculated by the disk quota entries.

 Disk quota requirements and the way in which you calculate disk quotas may appear on the exam.

Configuring Disk Quotas

As the administrator, you have different options you can employ when you implement disk quotas. Figure 8.12 displays the disk quota properties box and Table 8.8 defines the different quota options and their meaning. To enable disk quotas, follow these steps:

1. In Explorer, right-click on the drive on which you want to have quotas.

2. Select Properties.

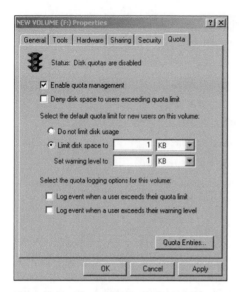

Figure 8.12   The Quota tab of the New Volume Properties dialog box.

Table 8.8 Disk Quota options and their definitions.	
Quota Option	**Definition of the Option**
Enable Quota Management	Allows quotas to be tracked and enforced on a volume. Quotas are not implemented unless this option is checked.
Deny Disk Space To Users Exceeding Quota Limit	If users exceed their limit, then this option denies additional space.
Do Not Limit Disk Usage	Enforces no space limitations on a user if this box is checked, but an administrator can still view disk space usage.
Limit Disk Space To	Restricts a user's disk space.
Set Warning Level To	Notifies the user when a preset value is reached.
Log Events	Logs exceeded quota limits and warnings to Event Viewer.
Quota Entries	Enables an administrator to view, edit, and create quota entries.

3. Select the Quota tab.

4. Put a check in the Enable Quota Management checkbox.

Figure 8.13 displays the Quota Entries management screen.

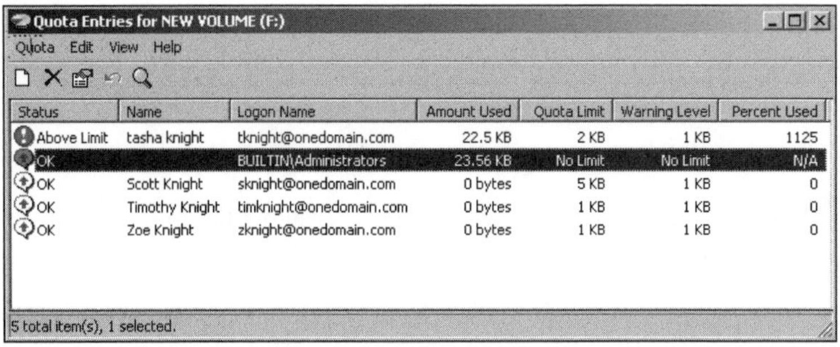

Figure 8.13   Quota Entries management screen.

Troubleshooting Disk Quota Problems

You have the option of using three main tools to troubleshoot disk quota problems: the Disk Quota tab, the Quota Entries screen, and the Event Viewer:

➤ *Disk Quota tab*—used to enable quota management, to set default quota limits, and to log events to Event Viewer when errors occur. If problems are occurring with disk quotas, first enable the log events on the Disk Quota tab. Refer to Figure 8.8 for more detail.

➤ *Quota Entries screen*—assists an administrator in determining the space a user has used, and the user's disk limitations. The Status column quickly displays the status of each user. A green status indicates the user is within the allowable limits, a red status indicates that the limit has been exceeded by the user, and a yellow status indicates the system is updating the current information for the volume. Quota limits are also administered at this screen.

➤ *Event Viewer*—displays the type, time, date, and source of the error. Double-clicking on an error provides more detailed information.

The following statements describe common disk quota errors and troubleshooting advice.

The recently applied quotas do not restrict the users:

➤ A common error in implementing quotas is to forget to check the Enable Quota Management checkbox on the Quota tab. An administrator can go to the Quota Entries button on the Quota tab, create and configure disk quotas for users, and then forget to enable quota management. The Enable Quota Management box must be checked or quotas do not restrict or control disk space for that volume.

➤ Another common error is that administrators forget to enforce quota limits. To enforce quota limits, you must check the Deny Disk Space To Users Exceeding Quota Limit checkbox. If quotas are not enforced, users can still use as much disk space as they want.

➤ Quotas are not always updated immediately, check the Quota Entries screen to verify that the users information has been updated or applied. There may be a time delay before the quota restrictions are applied to the users.

There is no Quota tab on the Volume Properties menu.

➤ The volume must be formatted in NTFS for the Quota tab to display. If the tab is not displayed, quotas cannot be implemented.

➤ You can only access quota information from the Properties screen for a volume. If you are in the Folder Properties screen, the Quota tab does not appear because quotas are set at the volume level and cannot be set on directories inside a volume.

A user receives an "insufficient disk space" error when trying to store files on the volume:

➤ This error means that the user has exceeded disk quota and that the Deny Disk Space option has been employed. The administrator can change the users quota limit, assign the user a higher disk space limit, or have the user clean up their disk space.

Practice Questions

Question 1

> Tim is a member of the Sales group and the Custom group. What are his security permissions?
>
> | Group | Permissions | Allow | Deny |
> |---|---|---|---|
> | Sales | Read | X | |
> | Marketing | Full Control | | X |
> | Custom | Write | X | |
> | Administrators | Full Control | X | |
>
> ○ a. Full Control
>
> ○ b. Write
>
> ○ c. Read
>
> ○ d. Read and Write
>
> ○ e. No Access

Answers d is correct. Answer a is incorrect because Tim is a member of the Sales group that has read access and the Custom group that has write access, which gives him a combined permission of Read and Write. Answer b is incorrect because Tim has read access from the Sales group. Answer c is incorrect because Tim has write access from the Custom group. Answer e is incorrect because Tim is not denied access on any permission.

Question 2

> The Sales folder is on the C: drive that is NTFS. The Sales folder is copied to the D: drive that is in FAT. What permissions does the Sales folder have after it is copied?
>
> ○ a. Sales keeps its original NTFS permissions.
>
> ○ b. Sales keeps its original FAT permissions.
>
> ○ c. Sales inherits the D: drive's NTFS permissions.
>
> ○ d. Sales inherits the D: drive's FAT permissions.
>
> ○ e. Sales does not have permissions in the D: drive.

Answer e is correct. FAT does not allow for NTFS or security permissions. The Sales folder is copied to the new location and no longer has security permissions.

Question 3

> A manager calls to complain that the quotas that you have set up are not restricting his employees from saving files to the Taxes folder. He has requested that you verify that quotas are functioning correctly. You open up the Quota Entries screen for the disk with the Taxes folder. You note that all of his employees have a status of green and their quota limit is set to 1K. After talking again with the manager, you find that one of his employees has just stored 10 new pictures of his baby in the Taxes folder. Why aren't disk quotas working?
>
> ○ a. The Enable Quota Management checkbox is not enabled.
>
> ○ b. The Log Event boxes do not have checks in them to allow logging to Event Viewer.
>
> ○ c. There is no Quota tab.
>
> ○ d. A green status indicates that the entries are being updated.

Answer a is correct. An administrator can still view and check the Quota Entries screen without having quotas enabled. Answer b is incorrect because logging events to Event Viewer does not affect the status of disk quotas. Answer c is incorrect because you entered into the Quota Entries screen for the disk that has the Taxes folder. Answer d is incorrect because a green status indicates that a user has not exceeded disk quotas; a yellow status indicates the entries are being updated.

Question 4

Tim is a member of the Sales group and the Marketing group. What are his security permissions?

Group	Permissions	Allow	Deny
Sales	Read		X
Marketing	Full Control	X	
Custom	Write	X	
Administrators	Full Control	X	

○ a. Full Control

○ b. Write

○ c. Read

○ d. Read and Write

○ e. No Access

Answer e is correct. Answer a is incorrect because Tim is denied access through his Sales group membership, which overrides his Full Control permissions with the Marketing group. Answer b is incorrect because Tim is not a member of the Custom group. Answers c and d are incorrect because Tim is explicitly denied access through his Sales group membership.

Question 5

The Marketing folder is available with the following share permissions. Marketing also has security permissions in place. What access does Tim have to the Marketing folder if he is a member of the Sales and Marketing groups?

Group	Share Permissions	Allow	Deny
Sales	Read	X	
Custom	Write	X	
Marketing	Read	X	
Administrators	Full Control	X	

Group	Security Permissions	Allow	Deny
Sales	Modify	X	
Custom	Write	X	
Marketing	Read		X
Administrators	Full Control	X	

○ a. Read

○ b. Write

○ c. Modify

○ d. Read and Write

○ e. Write and Modify

○ f. Full Control

○ g. No Access

Answer g is correct. Tim is a member of the Sales and Marketing groups. His combined permissions are Read-Allow for his share permissions and Modify-Allow, Read-Deny for his security permissions. Share and security permissions are combined, and the most restrictive is given to the user. Therefore Tim receives the Read-Deny permission. This means that Tim is not allowed access to the Marketing folder.

Question 6

Tim is a member of the Sales group, Marketing group, and the Custom group. What are his security permissions?

Group	Permission	Allow	Deny
Sales	Read	X	
Marketing	Modify	X	
Custom	Write	X	
Administrators	Full Control	X	

○ a. Full Control

○ b. Write

○ c. Read

○ d. Modify

○ e. Read and Write

○ f. No Access

Answer d is correct because Tim is member of the Sales, Marketing, and Custom groups. His combined permissions are Read, Write, and Modify. Modify includes Read & Execute, List Folders, Read, and Write permissions. Since Read and Write are combined into Modify, Modify has the highest level of permissions.

Question 7

The Sales folder is on the C:/ drive that is formatted in NTFS. The folder is moved to the D:/ drive that is NTFS. What permissions will the Sales folder have?

○ a. Sales keeps its original NTFS permissions.

○ b. Sales keeps its original FAT permissions.

○ c. Sales inherits the D: drive's NTFS permissions.

○ d. Sales inherits the D: drive's FAT permissions.

○ e. Sales does not have permissions.

Answers c is correct. If a folder with NTFS permissions is moved to a different volume, the folder inherits the permissions of the new location. Answer a is incorrect because folders only keep their same permissions if they are moved inside of the same volume. Answer b and d are incorrect because none of the drives are formatted in FAT, and either way FAT does not permit security permissions. Answer e is incorrect because security permissions are applied with NTFS volumes.

Question 8

Tim is a member of the Sales group and the Marketing group. What are his security permissions?

Group	Permission	Allow	Deny
Sales	Read	X	
Marketing	Full Control	X	
Custom	Write		X
Administrators	Full Control	X	

- ○ a. Full Control
- ○ b. Write
- ○ c. Read
- ○ d. Read and Write
- ○ e. No Access

Answer a is correct. Tim is a member of the Sales and Marketing groups. His combined permissions are Read and Full Control. Full Control encompasses Read; therefore, his combined permissions are Full Control. Answers b, c, d, and e are all incorrect because Tim has Full Control.

Question 9

The Sales folder is on the compressed C: drive. The folder is copied to the D: drive that is not compressed. What status does the Sales folder have after it is copied? [Check all correct answers]

❑ a. Sales is compressed.

❑ b. Sales is not compressed.

❑ c. Sales keeps its NTFS permissions.

❑ d. Sales inherits its NTFS permissions from the D: drive.

Answers b and d are correct. Answers a and c are incorrect because a folder that is copied to a different volume inherits the attributes where it is being copied. Therefore, the Sales folder inherits the D: drive's uncompressed status and its NTFS permissions.

Question 10

Which switch should be used to uncompress files using the **compact** command?

○ a. **/c**

○ b. **/u**

○ c. **/s**

○ d. **/uc**

Answer b is correct. Answer a is incorrect because **/c** compresses files or folders. Answer c is incorrect because **/s** compresses or decompresses all the subdirectories. Answer d is incorrect because **/uc** is a made up switch.

Need to Know More?

 Russel, Charlie, and Sharon Crawford: *Microsoft Windows 2000 Server Administrator's Companion*. Microsoft Press, Redmond, Washington, 2000. ISBN 1-57231-819-8. This is a valuable resource in which to learn more about implementing and administering permissions.

 Tittel, Ed, Kurt Hudson, and James Michael Stewart: *MCSE NT Server 4 Exam Cram*. The Coriolis Group, Scottsdale, AZ, 1998. ISBN 1-57610-618-7. To quickly learn more about FAT, FAT32, NTFS 4.0, and permissions, refer to Chapter 3.

 Search TechNet on the Internet at **www.microsoft.com/technet/ default.asp** or the TechNet CD for information on: NTFS, NTFS 5.0, FAT, FAT32, permissions, share permissions, NTFS permissions, folder permissions, permission inheritance, combining permissions, disk quotas, compression.

 For more information on the following terminology and implementation of that terminology refer to Microsoft Windows 2000 Help. To access this resource, click on Start and then click on Help. Terms and technologies to search for include: NTFS, NTFS 5.0, FAT, FAT32, permissions, share permissions, NTFS permissions, folder permissions, permission inheritance, combining permissions, disk quotas, and compression.

Print Servers and Web Servers

Terms you'll need to understand:

✓ Printer

✓ Print device

✓ Print server

✓ Print pool

✓ Line Printer Daemon (LPD)

✓ Line Printer Remote (LPR)

✓ Line Printer Queue (LPQ)

✓ Internet Information Services (IIS)

✓ Internet Printing Protocol (IPP)

✓ File Transfer Protocol (FTP)

✓ Simple Mail Transfer Protocol (SMTP)

✓ Network News Transfer Protocol (NNTP)

Techniques you'll need to master:

✓ Installing and configuring printers

✓ Monitoring and troubleshooting printers

✓ Setting permissions and priorities on printers

✓ Installing and configuring IIS

✓ Monitoring and troubleshooting IIS

✓ Setting permissions in IIS

This chapter addresses print server and Web server resources on a Windows 2000 network. Print servers and Web servers are usually installed on Windows 2000 member servers, which frees up their resources so that they do not replicate domain security information participating in Active Directory. You should be able to install, configure, secure, monitor, and troubleshoot print servers and Web servers.

Print Servers

Printers in Windows 2000 have vastly improved since NT 4.0. They can support more print devices, are accessible over the Web, can be managed over the Web, and can be accessed through Active Directory. The new benefits to Windows 2000 printing are as follows:

➤ Windows 2000 now supports over 2,500 different types of printers.

➤ Print device drivers are automatically downloaded and installed onto Windows 2000 operating system, without client intervention.

➤ Printing pools now make it possible to share printers anywhere on the network.

➤ Windows 2000 clients can print to any print device on the network by using a Web browser.

➤ Users can access and manage print devices through a Web page using Internet Printing Protocol (IPP).

➤ Printers can be accessed through Active Directory, making them available to all users.

Microsoft did not change the printer terminology for Windows 2000. The same terminology used in NT 4.0 is still applicable:

➤ Users send their documents to a *print server* to be printed.

➤ A *printer* is the software that is installed on the print server.

➤ A *print device* is the hardware that produces the printed output. A network print device has a network interface card (NIC) and is attached to the network.

Installing and Configuring Printers

After you configure and add a networked print device on the network, follow these steps to install a printer onto a print server:

1. From the Start menu, select Settings|Printers.

2. Double-click the Add Printer icon to start the Add Printer Wizard.

3. Select Local Printer, and make sure that the Automatically Detect And Install My Plug And Play Printer checkbox is deselected. Click Next.

The next three steps may vary depending on if you install a TCP/IP printer, a LPT printer, a COM port printer, an HP JetDirect printer, or another print device. For this example we have installed a TCP/IP printer.

4. Choose Create A New Port, and select Standard TCP/IP Port from the drop-down box. Click Next to start the Add Standard TCP/IP Printer Port Wizard. Click Next.

5. Enter the printer name or IP address, and then enter a name for the port. Click Next.

6. Click Finish to complete the Add Standard TCP/IP Printer Port Wizard.

7. At the Add Printer Wizard screen, select the type of printer, and click Next.

8. At the Printer Sharing dialog box, choose Share As and assign a name to the shared printer. Click Next.

9. Type the location information for the print device and any additional comments. Click Next.

10. Click Next to print a test page.

11. Click Finish to complete the installation of the new network print device. Figure 9.1 displays the newly configured network print device.

Note: In the Printers folder, the check next to the printer signifies that it is the default printer, and the hand under the printer signifies that the print device is shared.

A printer may need to be configured after being installed on a print server. To configure a printer, right-click on it and select Properties. Figure 9.2 displays a network printer's Properties dialog box, and Table 9.1 briefly describes each property.

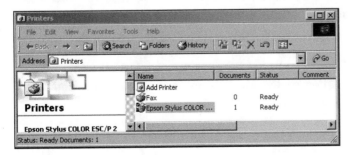

Figure 9.1   A network print device.

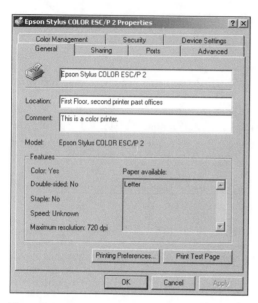

Figure 9.2 Epson Stylus color printer Properties dialog box.

The exam may cover some of the Printer Properties tabs. If you plan on taking the exam, you should be prepared to schedule a printer, enable print pooling, disable a separator page, and add security to printers. All of these topics are discussed in this chapter.

Printer Protocols

When you install a printer, you set it up on the print server with a specific port configuration. Microsoft supports six different port configurations, which can integrate with other operating systems. Table 9.2 lists the different ports and their function.

Printing Services for Unix

The exam may ask specific questions about printing services for Unix servers. The command for sending a print job to a print device in Unix is Line Printer Remote or LPR. The LPR command is issued to the Unix print server that is referred to as the Line Printer Daemon or LPD. The LPD then holds the print job in the Line Printer Queue, or LPQ, until the print device is ready to process the job. The LPR Port configuration on a Windows 2000 Server installs the LPR and the LPD services.

Remember the Unix acronyms LPR, LPD, and LPQ, because they may appear on the exam.

Table 9.1   Printer properties.

Properties Tab	Function
General	Lists the general printer information, sets printing preferences such as page rotation and paper source, and has a Print Test Page button.
Sharing	Sets printer sharing and adding print device drivers for operating systems other than Windows 2000.
Ports	Configures printer ports, including enabling print pooling.
Advanced	Schedules times the printer is available, changes print drivers, sets spooling requirements, and includes a separator page.
Color Management	Adds color profiles, if available.
Security	Configures who manages the printer and who can print to the print device.
Device Settings	Sets different form trays and letter settings.

Table 9.2   Port configuration and functions.

Port	Function
Local Port	Printing to a print device on the local computer.
TCP/IP Port	Printing to a print device that is on the network using a NIC and TCP/IP.
AppleTalk Port	Printing to an AppleTalk print device that uses the AppleTalk protocol.
HP Network Port	Printing to old Hewlett-Packard JetDirect print devices. The newer HP print devices use the TCP/IP port.
LPR Port	Printing to UNIX print devices.
Port For NetWare	Printing to NetWare print devices when NWLink and CSNW are installed.

Setting Permissions on Printers

To share a printer, right-click on the printer and select Sharing. The Sharing tab has the option to share or not share the print device. If the Share As button is selected, the box contains the name of the shared printer.

Security permissions are used to restrict users and groups from a print device. They also are used to establish who manages the printer. You can access the security permissions by right-clicking on the printer, selecting Properties, and choosing the Security tab. The default security setting for a printer is that the Everyone group has the right to print to the print device. Use the Add and Remove buttons to restrict users and groups from certain print devices. The three permissions associated with a printer are displayed in Table 9.3.

Table 9.3   Printer security permissions.

Print Permission	Print	Manage Documents	Manage Printer
Print documents	X	X	X
Pause, restart, and cancel their own document	X	X	X
Connect to a printer	X	X	X
Control job settings for all documents		X	X
Pause, restart, and delete all documents		X	X
Share a printer			X
Change printer properties			X
Delete printers			X
Change printer permissions			X

 You should understand printer permissions, printer permission combinations, how to apply permissions, and when to apply permissions to different groups.

Monitoring and Managing Network Printers

After you apply permissions to the printer, it still needs to be managed and monitored. The print server properties are used to manage settings for the print server and all of the attached printers; whereas, the printer properties are used to manage the individual printers on the print server.

The Server Properties screen is located in the Printers folder by selecting File and choosing Server Properties. With these properties, you can log information, set warnings on the spooler, add drivers, remove drivers, update drivers, change port configurations, add ports, delete ports, and set form restrictions.

The Advanced tab on the Server Properties screen enables an administrator to change the location of the print spool folder for the print server. The print spool is where print jobs are sent temporarily to wait for the print device to become available. The default spool location in Windows 2000 is systemroot\system32\spool\Printers. The location of the spool is important because disk space is consumed as print requests are sent to the spool, causing decreased system performance. To improve performance, it is recommended that the spool be moved to a hard drive other than the system root. This new location should also have adequate space to hold all the print jobs being submitted and deleted from the print spool.

In addition to the server properties, each printer has its own properties that must be maintained and can be used to set up advanced features. The following properties can be configured to improve, isolate, or segregate print jobs:

➤ A print job that is sent to a print pool prints to the next available printer in the pool. Print pooling allows multiple print devices to be associated with one printer through multiple ports on the print server. To set up print pooling, right-click on a printer, select the Ports tab, and put a check in the box marked Enable Printer Pooling. Then in the Port boxes, select all of the printer ports that will participate in the pool. Figure 9.3 displays three printer ports that are taking part in the print pool.

Because a print pool prints to the first available print device, it is recommended that the print devices be close together.

The Advanced tab for each printer contains many options that an administrator may find useful. The tab contains options to set printer priority, schedule available printer times, add a separator page, and set document spooling information. Figure 9.4 displays the Advanced Printer Properties tab.

➤ Printer Priority is used to create multiple printers with priorities. Each printer can be configured with a priority from 1 (the lowest) to 99 (the highest). For example, if your boss always needs his print jobs before everyone else, set up a printer with a 99 priority and assign that printer to your boss. Then set up a printer for everyone else with a priority of 1. These settings ensure that your boss's print jobs always print before everyone else regardless of when they enter the print queue.

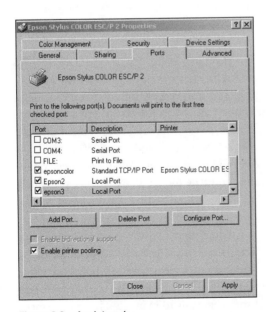

Figure 9.3 A print pool.

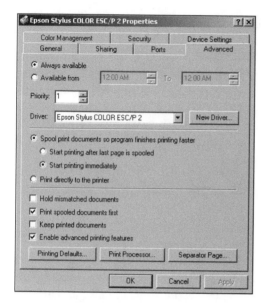

Figure 9.4   The Advanced Printer Properties tab.

> The Available From box, which is also located on the Advanced tab, can be used to set a print schedule when a printer is available. You can schedule a printer to print documents in the evening when no one is using the print device.

> Separator Page adds a sheet of paper between each document that is printed. Separator pages have a .sep file extension and can be created to have pre-configured information printed on them, including user name and date.

Adding Printers to Active Directory

Shared printers are automatically added to Active Directory when they are configured. If a printer is not shared when it is installed, an administrator can add it to Active Directory by sharing it. To share and add a printer to Active Directory right-click on the printer, select Sharing, select Share As, and confirm that the "List in the Directory" box has a checkmark in it. To add a non-Windows 2000 printer to Active Directory go to Active Directory Users And Computers, right-click an OU, select New, click Printer, and type the UNC path of the printer.

Web Printing Services

Accessing printers from a Web page is a quick and easy way to manage a network printer. In a Web browser, type "http://*servername*/printers" to obtain a list of available printers. Depending on the security, a user may have to supply a username and password because printer security is controlled through Internet Information Server 5.0. Select the printer that you want to manage. The management screen lists the documents in the queue and gives you information on the printer, depending on your permissions.

Note: Microsoft recommends using Internet Explorer 4.0 or above to manage printer documents from a Web page.

The exam may feature questions about managing and printing via a Web page. You should know what protocol is needed for Web printing, what http address is used for printing, and what http address is used for managing printers.

Accessing Windows 2000 Printers

Windows 2000 makes it easier to connect and print to a Windows 2000 network print device. A printer is installed using the Add Printer Wizard located in the Start|Settings|Printers folder. The wizard lets you select a network printer in three different ways: Find a printer in the Directory, type the name of the printer, or type the Universal Resource Locator (URL) of the printer. If you use the URL option, you can type "http://*servername*/printers/*share_name*.print".

Users can print to a print device by using the File menu and selecting Print. On the Print screen, click on Find Printer to locate a print device using Active Directory. The Print screen is displayed in Figure 9.5.

Troubleshooting Printer Problems

Many different things can go wrong with a printer. Troubleshoot printers by locating where the problem exists. Is the problem in the print device? Is the problem in the printer? Is the problem in the print server? Is there a problem with the network? Answering these questions helps locate and fix the problem.

Troubleshooting printers may be part of the Windows 2000 Server Exam. If you plan on taking the exam, you should know how to find and fix printer problems in a large networked environment.

Print Device Troubleshooting

Troubleshooting a print device usually requires being near the actual device. You or a qualified repairperson can usually easily fix these problems. If the device is not functioning, try to answer the following questions:

➤ Is the print device plugged in?

➤ Is the print device's network cable connected?

➤ Does the print device have any errors on its display panel?

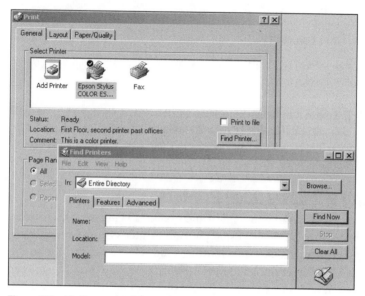

Figure 9.5 Finding a print device using Active Directory.

➤ Is the print device out of paper?

➤ Is the print device online?

Printer Troubleshooting

To troubleshoot a printer, open the Printers folder, double-click on the printer, and check the printer's status. Use the following questions to try to isolate the problem:

➤ Has the printer been paused, leading to documents piling up in the queue? The document may need to be taken off of pause, resumed, restarted, or deleted.

➤ Has the printer been set to work offline? If so, on the printer's File menu, uncheck the Use Printer Offline checkbox.

➤ Is a document stuck in the queue? If so, cancel the print job.

➤ Is it a specific user that cannot print to a printer? Does the user have permission to access the printer?

➤ Do the print jobs contain garbage or illegible symbols? Check to make sure that you are using the most current print drivers or reinstall them.

➤ Is the printer scheduled to only print during certain hours of the day? Check the Printer Properties Advanced tab to verify schedule restrictions on the printer.

Print Server Troubleshooting

If you have checked the printer and the print device, the next step is to check the print server. Check the following items:

➤ Use the Advanced tab to make sure that printer events are being logged, and then check Event Viewer for printer errors.

➤ Has a large file been sent to any of the printers? Check to ensure that the print server has sufficient hard drive space. If a hard drive uses all of its disk space before a document is spooled, the print server stops printing. If hard drive space is the problem, free up space and move the print spooler to another location.

➤ If none of the printers are printing, and nothing else seems to work, you may need to stop and restart the spooler service. To stop and restart the spooler, go to Administrative Tools, Services, and double-click Print Spooler. In the Print Spooler Properties, click Stop. After the spooler has stopped, click Start. Stopping and starting the print spooler deletes all of the queued print jobs for that print server.

Network Printer Troubleshooting

If the network seems to be the reason a printer is not functioning, check the following items:

➤ Is the network cable plugged into the printer? If not, plug it in.

➤ Can you ping the printer by IP address? If not, you should start troubleshooting the network.

➤ Can you ping the printer server? Check the print servers network cable. If it is connected, begin troubleshooting the network.

Web Services in Windows 2000

Internet Information Services (IIS) 5.0 is the Web server provided with Windows 2000. IIS 5.0 offers better security and better performance than legacy versions of IIS. Some features of IIS 5.0 include:

➤ File Transfer Protocol (FTP) enables you to have a central location for uploading and downloading files.

➤ Simple Mail Transfer Protocol (SMTP) is an easy way to send mail between servers. It does not support IMAP4 or POP3 mail.

➤ Network News Transfer Protocol (NNTP) enables you to have a centralized database of news articles that are available for users.

➤ The Internet Printing Protocol (IPP) enables you to manage printers on a Web page.

➤ Microsoft's Media Services enable high quality streaming multimedia.

➤ Active Server Pages (ASP) support server-side scripting language for creating interactive and dynamic Web applications.

➤ Distributed authoring and versioning offers remote authors and editors the ability to manage their Web pages over an HTTP connection.

Installing and Configuring IIS

Certain criteria must be achieved before installing IIS on a Windows 2000 Server. The server must have TCP/IP installed with a static IP address, and if the server will be on the Internet, it must have a registered domain name with a DNS server. After these criteria are met, you can install IIS by following these steps:

When performing an IIS 5.0 installation, Setup automatically upgrades any existing version of IIS.

1. In the Control Panel, double-click on the Add/Remove Programs icon.

2. Select the Add/Remove Windows Components option.

3. Check the Internet Information Services (IIS) checkbox and click Next.

After the installation is complete, Setup adds the Internet Services Manager menu option to the Administrative Tools and adds a snap-in option for MMC. Figure 9.6 displays the newly added Internet Services Manager.

IIS creates two new users in Active Directory:

➤ *IUSR_computername*—is a user created as a built-in anonymous access account for IIS.

➤ *IWAM_computername*—is a user created to allow IIS to start process applications such as accounting, monitoring, and scripting.

Installation has also created a directory on the hard drive called Inetpub. Inetpub is the default location for the IIS files. Figure 9.7 displays the newly created Inetpub directory. The Inetpub\wwwroot folder is the location for the default home page.

To test the installation of IIS and the default home page, open a browser, enter the name of the server in the address field, and press Enter. If this is the first time any version of IIS has been on the server, a page appears to notify you that you do not have a default document set and that users connecting will get an under construction page.

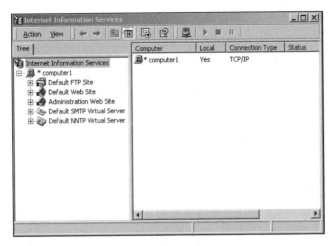

Figure 9.6   Internet Services Manager.

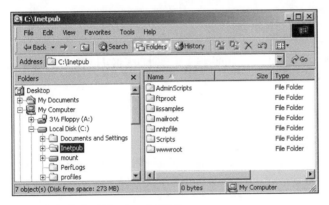

Figure 9.7   Inetpub directory for IIS files.

Configuring the IIS Server

To configure IIS and all of its services, open the Internet Services Manager, right-click on the computer name, and select Properties. Master Properties is used to edit properties for all the WWW or FTP Services. You may also assign bandwidth throttling, MIME maps, and servers.

Configuring the Default Web Site

To configure the default Web site properties, right-click the Default Web Site, and select Properties. Figure 9.8 displays the Default Web Site Properties, and Table 9.4 defines each of the property tabs.

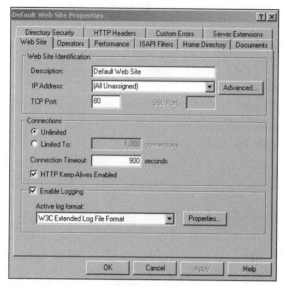

Figure 9.8 The Default Web Site Properties.

 For the exam, you should understand and know how to configure the Web Site properties.

Configuring the Default FTP Site

To configure the default FTP site properties, right-click the Default FTP Site and select Properties. Figure 9.9 displays the Default FTP Site Properties and Table 9.5 defines each of the property tabs.

 For the exam, you should understand and know how to configure the FTP Site properties.

Web Ports

The exam may cover how to allow Web access through a firewall; Table 9.6 lists the default TCP ports and what protocol should be enabled.

Permission to Web Resources

Securing a Web site and all of its resources can be a large task for an administrator. The administrator can use NTFS security permissions in conjunction with Web sharing permissions. To access the Web sharing permissions, open Explorer, select Inetpub, right-click wwwroot, select Properties, and go to the Web

Table 9.4	The Default Web Site Properties tabs.
Properties Tab	**Function**
Web Site	The Web Site Identification section is used to change the description, IP address, and TCP port number. The Connections section can be used to limit connections and implement HTTP Keep-Alives. The Enable Logging section is used for configuring a log file format.
Operators	Enables you to add or remove operators for the Web site.
Performance	Enables you to monitor performance. The Performance Tuning section has a slider to mark expected hits per day. The Enable Bandwidth section can be used to define the maximum network bandwidth used by IIS, and the Enable Process Throttling can be used to define maximum CPU usage.
ISAPI Filters	Enables Internet Server Application Programming Interface (ISAPI) filters and processing.
Home Directory	Defines where the default Web content is located, enables you to change the wwwroot path, and set permissions on the pages to be browsed. The Application Settings section is used to add and configure applications.
Documents	Defines the default document, adds the ability to have multiple documents, and has the ability to add a document footer.
Directory Security	Enables you to configure Anonymous Authentication, Basic Authentication, Digest Authentication for Windows Domain Servers, and Integrated Windows Authentication in the Anonymous Access and Authentically Control section. The IP Address and Domain Name Restrictions section is used to grant or deny access to computers, groups of computers, or domain names. Use the Secure Communications section to add a Certificate Server to IIS for secure transactions.
HTTP Headers	Enables you to expire pages, add custom HTTP headers, change content rating, and set MIME mapping.
Custom Errors	Enables you to edit and define custom error messages.
Server Extensions	The Enable Authoring section is used to set version control, performance, and client scripting. Use the Options section to set up email contacts for required mail delivery. The Don't Inherit Security Settings section is used to log actions, manage permissions, and require Secure Socket Layers (SSL).

Sharing tab. To change wwwroot permissions, click Add. Figure 9.10 displays the folder properties of the wwwroot with the additional permissions screen. Table 9.7 explains the different Web access permissions and their function.

Authentication Options

IIS 5.0 has four levels of authentication. The different levels protect the Web server in varying degrees. When implementing different authentication levels, a

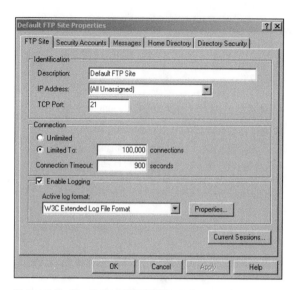

Figure 9.9 The Default FTP Site Properties.

Table 9.5	The Default FTP Site Properties tab.
Properties Tab	**Function**
FTP Site	The Identification section is used to change the description, the IP address, and the TCP port. The Connection Section can be used to limit connections to the site and set connection timeouts. The Enable Logging section can be used to define log formats. The Current Sessions button is used to view users who are connected to the site.
Security Accounts	The Allow Anonymous Connections section can be used to change the anonymous account. The FTP Site Operators section is used to grant operator privileges to users.
Messages	The FTP Site Message section can be used to enter a welcome message to users of the site. The Exit section can be used for an exit message, and the Maximum Connections can be used for displaying a message when the site has reached its maximum user limit.
Home Directory	This option defines where the default FTP files are located, used to change the ftproot path, set permissions on the site, and select a directory listing style.
Directory Security	This option grants or denies certain computers, groups of computers, or domains from accessing the FTP site.

Table 9.6   TCP ports.

Default TCP Port	Description
80	HTTP
21	FTP
20	Alternate FTP port
25	SMTP
119	NNTP
23	Telnet
389	LDAP

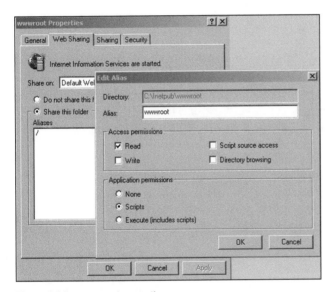

Figure 9.10   wwwroot properties.

Table 9.7   Web access permissions and functions.

Permission	Function
Access Permissions	
Read	Used to read and display the Web page.
Write	Used to read, display, and make changes to the Web page.
Script Source Access	Used to get access to the script code.
Directory Browsing	Used to view a hypertext listing of files in the directory.
Application Permissions	
None	Prevents programs and scripts from running.
Scripts	Allows scripts to be run.
Execute (includes scripts)	Enables scripts, dlls, and exe programs to run.

user must be validated by a username and password. The four levels of authentication are found on the Directory Security tab under the Anonymous Access And Authentication Control Edit button.

➤ Anonymous Authentication provides access to public areas of your Web site. It uses the IUSR_computername account.

➤ Basic Authentication transmits passwords in clear text. It is supported by most browsers but is not secure. Secure Socket Layer (SSL) must also be used to secure basic authentication.

➤ Digest Authentication uses a process called hashing to authenticate. Hashing converts the password into a numeric value that corresponds with a server's hashing table. Digest authentication has two drawbacks. Only Internet Explorer 5.0 supports it, and only Windows 2000 domain controllers can make this option available.

➤ Integrated Windows Authentication uses the logon username and password so that passwords are not sent over the network. There are three drawbacks to integrated windows authentication. First, only Internet Explorer 2.0 and above support it. Second, it does not work over HTTP Proxy connections. Finally, the user must be authenticated by a domain logon.

 You should know how to secure the IIS 5.0 Web services and FTP services. The exam may feature questions on restricting accesses, limiting usage, and basic configuration options.

IP Security

Restricting access by IP, computer, or domain is a property of IIS. To restrict access, go to the Web or FTP resource in Internet Services Manager, select Properties, go to the Directory Security tab, and click Edit under the IP Address And Domain Name Restriction tab. You can grant or deny access to computers using the IP Address And Domain Name Restriction screen.

Secure Communications

IIS can be configured for secure transactions using a Server Certificate Authority. To set up secure communications, go to the Web resource in Internet Services Manager, select Properties, go to the Directory Security tab, and click Secure Certificate under the Secure Communication section. The Web Server Certificate Wizard walks you through the steps of setting up secure transactions.

Monitoring Web Resources

You can use Site Server to monitor and map a Web site. Site Server uses a Web crawler to explore a Web site and report broken links. It displays the Web site in an easy to use format and can be queried for certain criteria.

IIS tracks events using log files for the FTP and Web services. These logs are located in the systemroot\system32\logfiles folder. They can be imported into the Usage Import program. Report Writer is then used to import the Usage Importer data. Report Writer gives statistical information for analyzing Web and FTP resources.

Troubleshooting Web Resources

You have many options in troubleshooting Web resources. The following section provides solutions to common problems.

If users cannot access the Web pages, check the following items:

➤ Check the Web sharing permissions on the folder using Explorer.

➤ Check NTFS permissions on the folder using Explorer.

➤ Check restrictions in Internet Services Manager on the Directory Security tab of the folder.

➤ In Explorer and the Internet Services Manager, verify that there is a default document.

➤ Stop the Web service by right-clicking the Web site in Internet Services Manager and selecting Stop. Then start the Web service by right-clicking the Web site and selecting Start.

➤ Check Event Viewer for Web service errors.

If users cannot access the FTP site, check the following items:

➤ Check Web sharing permissions on the folder using Explorer.

➤ Check NTFS permissions on the folder using Explorer.

➤ Check restrictions in the Directory Security tab of the folder in Internet Services Manager.

➤ Check the number of current sessions and the connection limits.

➤ Stop the FTP service by right-clicking the FTP site in Internet Services Manager and selecting Stop. Then start the FTP service by right-clicking the FTP site and selecting Start.

➤ Check Event Viewer for FTP errors.

Practice Questions

Question 1

You are the printer manager for an organization that has configured five printers for one print device. The following users have access to printers: Scott prints to Printer1, Tim prints to Printer2, Nancy prints to Printer3, Mike prints to Printer4, and Bob prints to Printer5. The printers have the following configurations.

Printer	Separator Page	Print Schedule	Priority	Logging Enabled
Printer1	N	N	50	Y
Printer2	Y	N	10	Y
Printer3	N	N	60	Y
Printer4	N	N	50	Y
Printer5	Y	N	20	Y

Whose print job will be printed first if all the users submit their jobs at the same time?

○ a. Scott

○ b. Tim

○ c. Nancy

○ d. Mike

○ e. Bob

Answer c is correct. Printing priorities are ranked from 1 being the lowest priority to 99 being the highest. This signifies that Nancy will receive her print job first if they all print at the same time.

Question 2

What is the default FTP port?

○ a. 11

○ b. 21

○ c. 31

○ d. 80

Answer b is correct. The default port for FTP is port 21.

Question 3

Match the following ports with their appropriate protocol.

Port	Protocol
21	FTP
23	HTTP
25	NNTP
80	SMTP
119	Telnet

Answer:

Port	Protocol
80	HTTP
21	FTP
25	SMTP
119	NNTP
23	Telnet

Question 4

The following screen, shown in Figure 9.11, displays the printer properties. Use checkmarks to create a print pooling for the Epson Color, the Epson2, and Epson4.

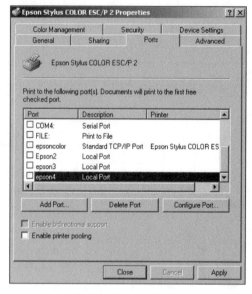

Figure 9.11 Printer Properties screen.

Answer: See Figure 9.12. There should be four checkmarks: one before the Epson Color, one before the Epson 2, one before the Epson 3, and one before Enable Print Pooling.

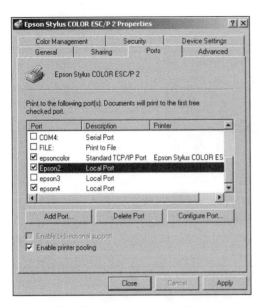

Figure 9.12 Printer Properties screen for print pooling.

Question 5

How do you configure the IP Address Access Restrictions screen (shown in Figure 9.13) so that only the following computers will be able to connect to the Web site?

　　　　122.1.14.2

　　　　111.2.15.11

　　　　180.130.5.3

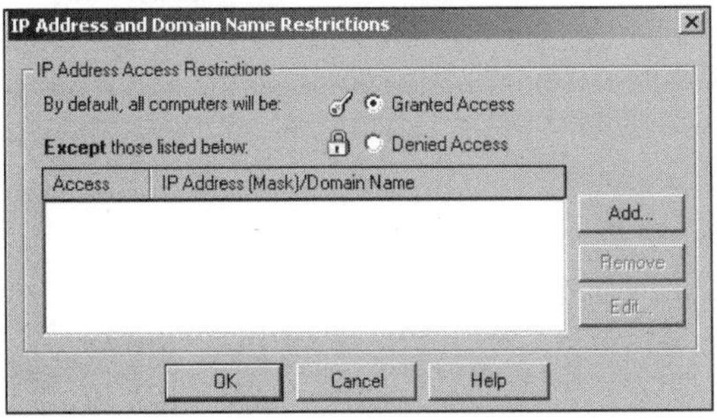

Figure 9.13　IP Address Access Restrictions screen.

Answer: See Figure 9.14.

Figure 9.14   IP Address Access Restrictions screen configured.

Question 6

What are the drawbacks for using Integrated Windows Authentication? [Check all correct answers]

❑ a. The password is not sent over the network.

❑ b. It only supports Internet Explorer 2.0 and above.

❑ c. It only supports Internet Explorer 5.0.

❑ d. It does not work over HTTP Proxy.

❑ e. It allows users who have not authenticated with a domain controller to logon.

❑ f. It requires the user to be authenticated by a domain controller.

Answers b, d, and f are correct because Integrated Windows Authentication uses the logon username and password so that passwords are not sent over the network. The three drawbacks include: only Internet Explorer 2.0 and above support it, it does not work over HTTP Proxy connections, and only users who authenticate with a domain controller can use it.

Question 7

> You have been asked to install IIS 5.0. What are the requirements before you install? [Check all correct answers]
>
> ❑ a. Windows NT 4.0
>
> ❑ b. Windows 2000
>
> ❑ c. A TCP/IP address
>
> ❑ d. NWLink is installed
>
> ❑ e. Registered with a DNS
>
> ❑ f. Registered with a DHCP

Answers b, c, and e are correct. Answer a is incorrect because IIS 5.0 requires Windows 2000 Server. Answer d is incorrect because IIS 5.0 only requires TCP/IP; it does not require NWLink. Answer f is incorrect because the server should have a static IP address, not an address assigned by DHCP.

Question 8

> When IIS 5.0 is installed, what are the two built-in accounts that it creates? [Check all correct answers]
>
> ❑ a. ISUR_computername
>
> ❑ b. ISUR_domainname
>
> ❑ c. IUSR_computername
>
> ❑ d. IUSR_domainname
>
> ❑ e. IMAW_computername
>
> ❑ f. IMAW_domainname
>
> ❑ g. IWAM_domainname
>
> ❑ h. IWAM_computername

Answers c and h are correct. The two built-in names that IIS 5.0 creates are IUSR_computername and IWAM_computername. The rest of the answers are made up.

Question 9

> What protocol does IIS 5.0 implement to allow managing printers through a browser?
>
> ○ a. II
>
> ○ b IP
>
> ○ c. IIP
>
> ○ d. IPP
>
> ○ e. IPT

Answer d is correct. IIS 5.0 implements the Internet Printing Protocol (IPP) to allow printers to be managed through a Web page.

Question 10

> You have set up IIS 5.0 on your Windows 2000 Server. Now you want to manage printers using the Web. Which Web address do you type in a Web browser?
>
> ○ a. **http://*servername*/printers**
>
> ○ b. **http://*domainname*/printers**
>
> ○ c. **http://*servername*/print**
>
> ○ d. **http://*servertree*/print**

Answer a is correct. When IIS 5.0 is installed, the printers can be managed by accessing **http://*servername*/printers** from a Web browser.

Need to Know More?

 Russel, Charlie, and Sharon Crawford: *Microsoft Windows 2000 Server Administrator's Companion*. Microsoft Press, Redmond, Washington, 2000. ISBN 1-57231-819-8. This book is a valuable resource from which to learn more about installing and administering print servers and IIS 5.0.

 Search TechNet on the Internet at **www.microsoft.com/technet/ default.asp** or the TechNet CD for information on: print server, printer, print device, IIS 5.0, authentication, IPP, LPR, LPQ, LPD, and Unix integration.

 For more information on the following terminology and implementation of that terminology refer to Microsoft Windows 2000 Help. To access this resource, click on Start and then click on Help. Terms and technologies to search for include: auditing printer activity, setting up a printer, Internet Information Services, Internet Information Services features, managing printers, printer overview, publishing a printer in Active Directory, Transmission Control Protocol (TCP), Windows 2000 Command Reference Main Page.

Network Resources

Terms you'll need to understand:

✓ Windows Installer

✓ Software Installation And Maintenance

✓ Assigned

✓ Published

✓ Remote Installation Services (RIS)

✓ Standalone Distributed file system (Dfs)

✓ Domain Dfs

✓ Terminal Services

✓ Terminal Services server

✓ Terminal Services client

✓ Application server mode

✓ Remote administration mode

✓ Routing And Remote Access

✓ Remote Access Services (RRAS)

✓ Virtual Private Network (VPN)

Techniques you'll need to master:

✓ Installing software using Windows Installer and Software Installation And Maintenance

✓ Installing and maintaining standalone Dfs

✓ Installing and maintaining domain Dfs

✓ Creating a Dfs root

✓ Installing and securing a Terminal Services server

✓ Configuring clients to access the Terminal Services server

✓ Logging onto a Terminal Services server from a Terminal Services client

✓ Understanding the difference between Application Server mode and Remote Administration mode

✓ Installing, monitoring, and configuring Routing And Remote Access

✓ Configuring a VPN

This chapter addresses the network resources that are available in Windows 2000. It covers software management and how to use Group Policy Objects (GPOs) to remotely install software without having to access the computer. It also explains the creation of Distributed file systems (Dfs) to make it easy for users to access networked resources. Terminal Services will be discussed along with Routing and Remote Access to Windows 2000 servers. The exam may cover all of these topics. It is important for anyone taking the exam to be familiar with all of the network resources available in Windows 2000.

Software Management

Windows 2000 has the capability to deploy and manage software throughout an organization using the Windows Installer and Software Installation And Maintenance tools. These products use GPOs to install and maintain software for computers and users.

Windows Installer

You use Windows Installer to manage the installation of software on remote computers. The installer determines how packages are installed and uninstalled on computers or for users. The package that is created uses a file with an .msi extension, which replaces the setup.exe program that is normally used for installing software. You can use Windows Installer to manage installed software components. It can add, delete, or repair software installations and components. It also can silently detect and repair critical files that have been deleted. Windows Installer also cleanly removes any program that it has installed without leaving orphaned files on the system or deleting critical files that are needed by other programs.

Windows Installer manages software programs by using an already existing package or by using a repackaged application so that the Software Installation And Maintenance program can use it. After Windows Installer packages an application, it should be placed in a shared network folder.

 Remember that the Windows Installer application files have an .msi extension for the installation.

Software Installation And Maintenance

The Software Installation And Maintenance program uses the Windows Installer files to deploy and manage the software throughout an organization by Group Policy Objects (GPOs). Many administrators use the Software Installation And Maintenance program because it does not require an administrator to go to every machine and install software. An administrator can install a software package, upgrade different versions of software, and remove software, all by adding information to the software section of a GPO.

Note: The Software Installation And Maintenance program only operates with Windows 2000 clients.

A software application that is assigned to a GPO can be applied to a user or a computer. If an application is assigned to a user through the GPO, the applications icon appears on the user's desktop. The application is available to the user regardless of which computer the user is logged on to. The application is not installed until the user double-clicks on the application. Only applications that are used are deployed, which limits the hard drive space and the server load. If an application is published to a user through a GPO, the application only appears in the Add/Remove Programs icon in the Control Panel. The user must know to open Add/Remove Programs to install the software application. If a GPO software package is assigned to a computer, the application is available on that computer regardless of who logs on. The application package is automatically loaded when a computer boots; it does not wait for a user to access the software.

After you configure a software package for a GPO, you have three different ways to deploy the package. Table 10.1 defines the different deployment options, and Figure 10.1 displays the GPO with the deployment options.

The exam may cover Windows Installer, the Software Installation And Maintenance program, and the way in which applications are assigned and published.

Table 10.1	GPO deployment options.
Option	**Function**
Assigned	Makes an application available from the Start menu and displays an icon on the desktop. The application is not loaded onto the computer until the user initiates the application.
Published	Makes an application available through the Add/Remove Programs icon in Control Panel. The user must access Add/Remove Programs to install the application. The computer cannot be set up to have an application published.
Advanced published or assigned	Upgrades, modifies, or uninstalls software packages that have already been either published or assigned.

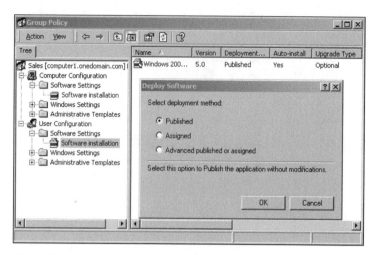

Figure 10.1   Deploying a software package for a user.

The Software Installation And Maintenance program can be used to apply service packs, fix applications, upgrade applications, and delete applications. This powerful administrative tool does not require a person to install an application manually on every machine. After an application is configured and packaged with Windows Installer, then the Software Installation And Maintenance program installs it as part of a GPO.

Remote Installation Services (RIS)

Remote Installation Services (RIS) is used to remotely install Windows 2000 Professional. If the remote computer supports a network card that is Preboot Execution Environment (PXE), the installation can take place without someone needing to visit each computer on which it needs to be installed. If the remote computer does not support remote boot, it must be started by a remote-boot floppy. RIS makes it easy to install multiple versions of Windows 2000 Professional with software preinstalled, without personnel overhead.

RIS requires Active Directory, a Windows 2000 Professional CD-ROM, a DHCP server, and a DNS service be available. To install RIS on a Windows 2000 Server, follow these instructions:

1. In the Control Panel, select Add/Remove Programs. Then select Add/Remove Windows Components, and choose the Remote Installation Services option. The computer must be rebooted.

2. In the Add/Remove Programs dialog box, select Configure Remote Installation Services.

3. The Wizard asks you to type a remote installation folder path. Click Next.

4. Select whether you want RIS to respond to client computer requests. Click Next.

5. Enter the path to the Windows 2000 Professional CD-ROM. Click Next.

6. Type a folder name for the Professional image information. Click Next.

7. Type a user-friendly description for the help text and any additional help text information. Click Next.

8. Click Finish to complete the Remote Installation Services Wizard. Figure 10.2 displays the actions that the Wizard takes to install RIS.

To administer RIS, go to Active Directory Users And Computers, right-click the server that RIS is installed on, select Properties, and click on the Remote Install tab. Figure 10.3 displays the Remote Install tab for Computer1. You can use the Remote Install tab to show clients, add clients to be imaged, change the Windows 2000 Professional image, and add additional Remote Install tools.

Distributed File System (Dfs)

A Distributed file system (Dfs) is used to create a logical hierarchical file system for users. This logical hierarchy is made up of shared folders from different locations, but they are seen by the users as one common logical file system. One common file system makes it easier for users to locate and use shared network resources. The physical location of the files is independent of what the user sees in the Dfs. Figure 10.4 depicts the physical location of the shared folders compared to the logical directory that the users access. The first shared network resource in a Dfs is the Dfs root. All additional shared network resources that are added to the Dfs root are called Dfs links.

Figure 10.2   Remote Installation Services Setup Wizard task screen.

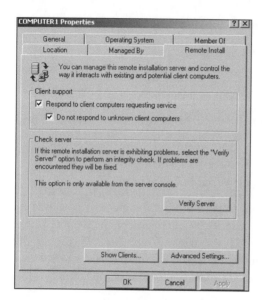

Figure 10.3 Remote Installation Configuration tab.

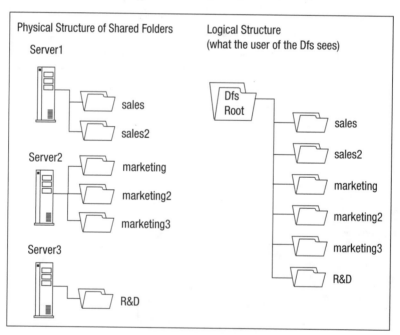

Figure 10.4 The physical and virtual layout of a Distributed file system.

Distributed file systems make it easy for users to access shared resources because they access a central location for their shared network resources without mapping different network drives. It also makes it easy for an administrator to change the physical location of a shared folder without affecting how the users access the resources.

Dfs was available in Windows NT 4.0, but it has been enhanced in Windows 2000. There are two types of distributed files systems: standalone Dfs and domain Dfs. A standalone Dfs displays the file system from one single computer; it is not a part of Active Directory. The drawback of a standalone Dfs is that there is no fault tolerance built in. A domain Dfs displays the file systems from many computers and is stored in Active Directory. The advantage to a domain Dfs is that it provides fault tolerance.

Standalone and domain Distributed file systems may be covered on the exam. You should be familiar with both these technologies and know how to deploy them.

Standalone Dfs

A stand-alone Dfs is installed on the same server that houses the shared network resources. Although it can use either a FAT or NTFS file system, remember that NTFS is the file system to use if security is important.

Setup and Configuration of a Standalone Dfs

To install a standalone Dfs, follow these steps:

1. Open the Distributed File System console on the Administrative Tools menu.

2. Right-click on Distributed File System and select New Dfs Root.

3. Click Next on the New Dfs Root Wizard.

4. Select Create A Standalone Dfs Root as seen in Figure 10.5.

5. Enter the name of the server that will house the Dfs root. Click Next.

6. Select an existing shared folder to be your new Dfs root, or create a new share. Click Next.

7. Enter a comment on the new Dfs root and click Next.

8. Click Finish to complete the new standalone Dfs root.

To create Dfs links to the Dfs root, follow these steps:

1. Right-click on the Dfs root to which you want to add a link.

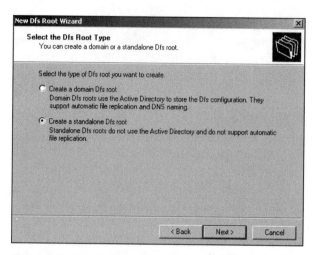

Figure 10.5 Selecting a new Dfs root.

2. Select New Dfs Link.

3. Enter the new link name, the shared folder that is being linked, and any additional comments. Then click OK. Figure 10.6 displays the new Dfs root with a link to the shared folders.

Domain Dfs

You can configure a domain Dfs on a Windows 2000 member server or domain controller. A domain Dfs also supports FAT or NTFS files systems. The domain Dfs offers the advantage of being published to Active Directory and this provides fault tolerance. Because it uses Active Directory, a domain Dfs can replicate information to other domain controllers. If the shared resources become unavailable from one location, the user can be redirected to the replica. A damaged

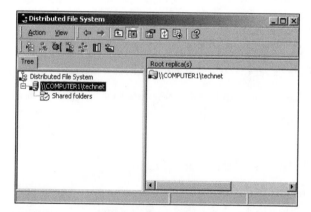

Figure 10.6 A new Distributed file system with a link to shared folders.

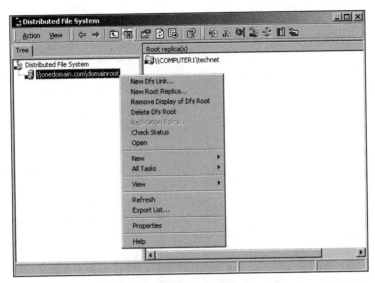

Figure 10.7   A new domain Distributed file system and configuration options.

network resource can also be used to help repair a replica. Figure 10.7 displays some of the options for a domain Dfs root, including the creation of a replica.

A domain Dfs root and a standalone Dfs root are installed and configured the same way. A new domain Dfs root is established by starting the New Dfs Wizard and selecting Create A Domain Dfs Root, as seen in Figure 10.5. After the root Dfs is established, an administrator can add new Dfs links by right-clicking on the root Dfs and selecting New Dfs Link, as seen in Figure 10.7.

Client Access to Dfs

Dfs client software 4.x or 5.0 must be loaded before the client can access a Dfs. Windows 98, Windows NT 4.0, and Windows 2000 include Dfs client software. Client software for Windows 95 must be downloaded and installed. Dfs access is not supported for DOS, Windows 3.x, or other non-Windows operating systems.

Terminal Services

Terminal Services is loaded on a server so that clients and administrators can run applications on the server's desktop without using client resources. A terminal emulator enables a very low-end client machine to display a Windows 2000 desktop and enables the client to control the desktop by using a keyboard and a mouse. Terminal Services give low-end client machines, high-end client machines, and other operating systems the capability to run applications or administer Windows 2000 from a different location.

Terminal Services consist of three different parts: the Terminal Services server, a client, and a Remote Desktop Protocol (RDP). The Terminal Services server houses the software and the environment for the terminal emulation. A client connects to the Terminal Services server to gain access to applications and resources. RDP is the communication protocol that uses TCP/IP to interface between the server and the client. You can configure the Terminal Services server in Application Server mode or Remote Administrative mode.

Application Server Mode

If Terminal Services are installed using the Application Server mode, the clients access the server to use the Windows 2000 desktop and Windows applications. Application Server mode can be implemented on low-end clients and non-Windows computers so they can have access to the Windows 2000 desktop and applications.

 Configuring Terminal Services and application sharing may appear on the exam. You should be familiar with both of these topics.

Remote Administrator Mode

Administrators can remotely manage Windows 2000 Servers from anywhere on the network when Terminal Services are installed in Remote Administrator mode. Administrator mode is a secure method of administering a network on minimal hardware.

 Configuring administrative access to Terminal Services may appear on the exam. You should be familiar with how to remotely administer Terminal Services.

Installation of Terminal Services

Because of the system overhead of running Terminal Services, it is recommended that it be installed on a member server. For security, it also should be installed on an NTFS volume. To install Terminal Services, follow these steps:

1. Open Add/Remove Programs in Control Panel.

2. Select the Add/Remove Windows Components option.

3. In the Windows Component box, select Terminal Services And Terminal Services Licensing. Click Next.

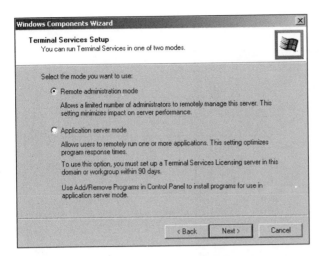

Figure 10.8   The Terminal Services server modes.

4. Choose either Remote Administration mode or Application Server mode. Figure 10.8 displays the Terminal Services server modes.

5. Complete the Wizard's instructions to install either Remote Administration mode or Application Server mode.

 You should be familiar with installing and configuring Terminal Services because these topics could be on the exam.

Configuring Terminal Services

You can configure, manage, and secure Terminal services in many different ways. The best way to secure Terminal Services, is to use NTFS volumes. You should also monitor how the users are configured and how the server is configured.

Users' Configurations for Terminal Services

By default, all users are granted permission to log on to a Terminal Server. In the Active Directory Users And Computers option, each user has four property tabs that control the Terminal services:

➤ The Environment tab, as seen in Figure 10.9, is used to designate programs to run when a user logs on onto a Terminal Server. It is also used to determine printer and network drive connections.

➤ The Sessions tab, as seen in Figure 10.10, is used to set timeouts and set rules for reconnecting to the server.

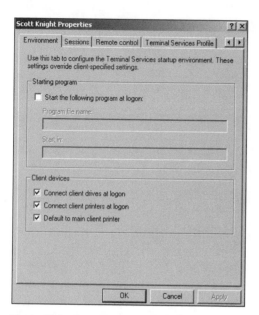

Figure 10.9 A user's Environment tab.

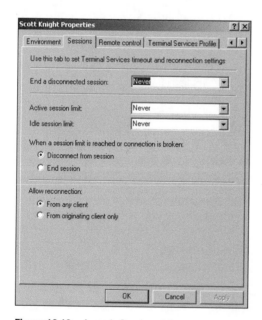

Figure 10.10 A user's Sessions tab.

➤ The Remote Control tab, as seen in Figure 10.11, enables you to set control levels on monitoring a user's desktop that is using the server. The settings dictate whether the administrator must inform a user when monitoring the user and the level of control an administrator has over the user's desktop.

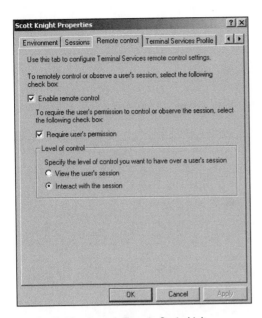

Figure 10.11   A user's Remote Control tab.

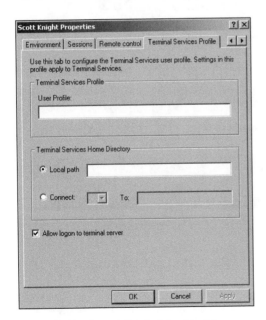

Figure 10.12   A user's Terminal Services tab.

➤ The Terminal Services Profile tab, as seen in Figure 10.12, is used to allow users to log on to the Terminal server, set user profiles, and map network drives.

Server Configuration of Terminal Services

Besides the users configuration, two administrative tools are used to manage Terminal Services. These tools include:

➤ Terminal Services Configuration, as seen in Figure 10.13, is used to add different network connections and to change server settings.

➤ Terminal Services Manager, as seen in Figure 10.14, is used to monitor the server, monitor users, connect users, disconnect users, remotely control users, and send messages to users.

Licensing Terminal Services

Each client connecting to a Terminal Services server in Application mode needs to have a client access license. When you install Terminal Services in Application Server mode, you should also install the Terminal Services Licensing on a domain controller. Terminal Services Licensing helps manage Client Access Licenses (CAL).

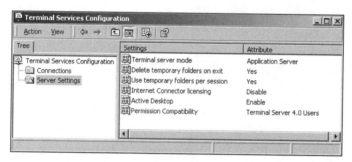

Figure 10.13   The Terminal Services Configuration screen.

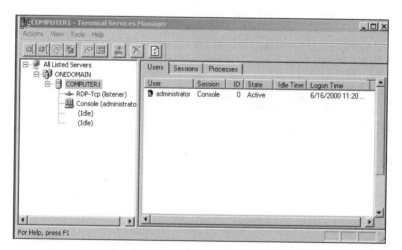

Figure 10.14   The Terminal Services Manager screen.

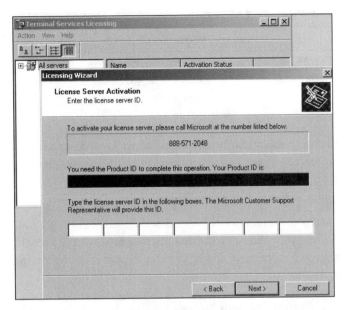

Figure 10.15   The Licensing Wizard ID screen.

To configure Terminal Services Licensing, go to Administrative Tools, Terminal Services Licensing, right-click on the server, and select Activate Server. The Licensing Wizard walks you through the steps of setting up client access licenses. Figure 10.15 displays the server activation license screen needed to complete the installation. The following licensing information applies to each Terminal Services client connecting to the Terminal:

> Terminal Services Client Access Licenses must be purchased for anyone that is not a Windows 2000 client that plans on connecting to the Terminal Services.

> Built-in Licenses are automatically available for Windows 2000 clients connecting to the Terminal Services.

> Terminal Services Internet Connector Licenses must be purchased for users who connect anonymously to the Terminal Services over the Internet.

Client Access to Terminal Services

After the licenses are purchased, each client that connects to a Terminal Services server must have client software installed. Terminal Services is emulating the server's desktop; there is little load on the client because the server handles most of the processing. Table 10.2 displays the minimal client requirements.

A Terminal Services client computer also must have TCP/IP and the Terminal Services client software installed. The client software can be installed using installation disks or from a shared network folder:

Table 10.2   The minimal Terminal Services client requirements.

Operating System	Minimal Requirements
Windows 3.11 and Windows 95	16MB of RAM, 386 processor
Windows 98 and Windows NT 4.0	16MB of RAM, 486 processor
Windows 2000	32MB of RAM, Pentium processor

➤ Installation disks are created from the Administrative Tools Terminal Services Client Creator. The Wizard displays options to create Terminal Services client software for 16-bit or 32-bit Windows. Follow the setup Wizard on the client computer to complete the installation.

➤ To install the client over the network, the systemroot\system32\clients\tsclient folder must be a shared folder.. After a client is connected to the network share, run the setup.exe program, and follow the Wizard to complete the client software installation.

Connecting to a Terminal Services Server

After a user has the correct permissions to log on and the client software is loaded, a user can start the Terminal Services client. The user then connects to the server by selecting it, choosing the area of the terminal emulation screen, selecting the line speed that is being used, and then pressing Connect. After the user has authenticated, the terminal emulation session begins.

Ending a Terminal Services Server Connection

There are two ways to end a Terminal Services server connection. These methods include the following:

➤ Disconnecting from a session ends the session for the client but leaves applications running on the server open. This option is used for log processes that need to finish executing before the session is logged off.

➤ Logging off from a session ends the session for the client and closes all open applications on the server, which frees up the resources.

Routing And Remote Access

Users can authenticate on the server and access local area network (LAN) resources using Routing And Remote Access Services (RRAS). Windows 2000 uses Routing And Remote Access to make authenticating and accessing resources easier for administrators and clients. Remote Access Services are still supported, but now Windows 2000 includes a routing feature as well. Table 10.3 displays the different ways to configure Routing And Remote Access. Windows 2000 supports different remote access protocols, which are discussed in the next section.

Table 10.3 Routing And Remote Access options.	
Option	Function
Internet Connection Server	Grants computers access to the Internet.
Remote Access Server	Provides dial-in access to the network.
Virtual Private Network (VPN) Server	Provides a connection to the network over a secure Internet connection.
Network Router	Facilitates communication between different networks.
Manually Configured Server	Configures the server with default settings.

Remote Access Protocols

Windows NT 4.0 supports different authentication protocols. Windows 2000 now supports these older technologies and many new protocols. The following section includes new and the old protocols.

The older authentication protocols and their main properties include:

➤ Password Authentication Protocol (PAP) sends passwords in clear text.

➤ Challenge Handshake Authentication Protocol (CHAP) securely sends passwords.

➤ Microsoft CHAP (MS-CHAP) is the Microsoft version of CHAP that sends passwords securely over the network.

➤ Point-to-Point Tunneling Protocol (PPTP) securely encapsulates information inside of network protocols such as IP or IPX.

New Windows 2000 Authentication Protocols include:

➤ Extensible Authentication Protocol (EAP) is an extension of Point-to-Point (PPP) protocol that works with token cards, Kerberos, smart cards, certificates, and other security devices. The secure transmission helps guard against known ways to crack passwords.

➤ Remote Authentication Dial-In User Services (RADIUS) is an accounting and authorizing tool, mainly used by ISPs, to provide reliable and secure dial-in access. For communication to take place, a RADIUS client can use the Internet to connect to a RADIUS server.

➤ Layer 2 Tunneling Protocol (L2TP) is a secure tunneling protocol that can be used over different types of media. It uses PPP, can be encrypted, and supports tunnel authentication for untrusted networks. It requires IPSec for encryption, which is discussed in the Chapter 11.

➤ Bandwidth Allocation Protocol (BAP) is used to dynamically control multilink for better use of network bandwidth.

Configuration of a Remote Access Server

Follow these steps to configure Routing And Remote Access for a server:

1. Open the Routing And Remote Access menu item under the Administrative Tools. This screen is used to add, enable, and configure remote access and routing. If the current computer has a red arrow in front of it, the server is not configured.

2. Right-click on the server and select Configure And Enable Routing And Remote Access to start the Wizard. Click Next. Figure 10.16 displays the routing and remote access configurations that are available.

3. Select Remote Access Server (RAS). Click Next.

4. Choose whether to automatically assign clients IP addresses using DHCP or to specify a specified range of IP addresses. Click Next.

5. Choose Yes or No to install a RADIUS server. Click Next.

6. Click Finish to complete the setup of the RAS. Figure 10.17 displays the Routing And Remote Access screen for the newly created RAS.

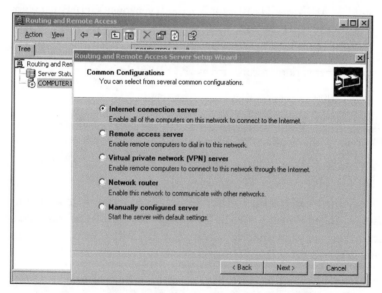

Figure 10.16 The Routing And Remote Access Server configuration options.

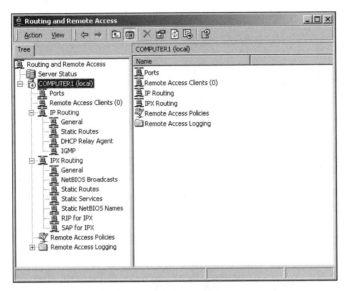

Figure 10.17   Routing And Remote Access screen.

Configuring Remote Access Permissions and Policies

You can configure and manage remote access through the Routing And Remote Access server properties and a user's properties. Routing And Remote Access properties give an administrator control of the server, remote policies, and different network connection interfaces. A user's properties are specific to an individual using a dial-in or VPN connection.

User Remote Access Properties

A user's properties can be accessed by double-clicking the user in Active Directory Users And Computers. Use the Dial-In tab to control an individual's access to the Remote Access server. Figure 10.18 displays a user's dial-in properties. The Dial-In tab enables you to control logon access, set callback options, assign a static IP address, and apply static routes.

Routing And Remote Access Manager

Administrators can control Remote Access Services by using the Routing And Remote Access properties screen, as seen in Figure 10.17. Use the following options to configure Remote Access Services:

➤ Remote Access Clients determines which users are logged onto the server and how long they have been connected.

➤ Ports determines which remote access ports are active. You also can get statistical information about the port by double-clicking on it.

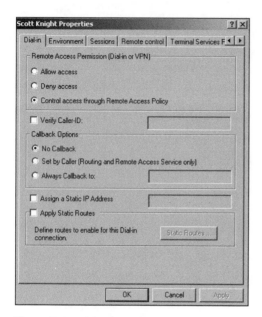

Figure 10.18   A user's dial-in properties.

➤ Remote Access Policies lets the administrator assign guidelines to the remote access server. The only default policy is to allow access to the server if dial-in access is granted. To add additional policies, right-click on the Remote Access Policies icon and select New Remote Access Policy.

➤ Remote Access Logging designates the location of the remote access logging files.

Managing Routing

The following items are used to manage and monitor routing on a Windows 2000 Server with Routing And Remote Access enabled:

➤ Routing Interface monitors dial-in interfaces. It can also be used to add new IP tunnels and demand-dial interfaces.

➤ IP Routing monitors and manages IP traffic for your Routing And Remote Access Server.

   ➤ General is used to add new remote access interfaces or routing protocols. It also lets you view TCP/IP statistics, address translation, IP addresses, IP routing tables, TCP connections, and UPD Listener port information.

   ➤ Static Routes is used to add a new static route and display the IP routing table.

➤ DHCP Relay Agents is used add and monitor DHCP relay agents.

➤ IGMP or Internet Group Membership Protocol reports group member-ship of multicast routers that are near this router.

➤ IPX Routing (if enabled) monitors and manages IPX traffic for your Routing And Remote Access Server.

   ➤ General is used add new remote access interfaces or routing protocols. It also lets you view IPX statistics, IPX routing table, and IPX service table information.

   ➤ NetBIOS Broadcasts is used to view NetBIOS broadcast information. You also can access the interface's properties to reject and control broad-cast traffic.

   ➤ Static Routes is used to add static routes and view the IPX routing table.

   ➤ Static Services is used to add a new static service and view the IPX service table.

   ➤ Static NetBIOS Names is used to add and view static NetBIOS name information.

   ➤ RIP for IPX or Routing Information Protocol for IPX is used to view IPX routing information. You also can access the network devices inter-face properties to control RIP traffic, set RIP filters, and advertised rout-ing information.

   ➤ SAP for IPX or Service Advertising Protocol for IPX is used to display advertised services on the network. You also can access the network de-vices interface properties to disable SAP, advertise SAP information, and set SAP filters.

Virtual Private Network (VPN)

A *Virtual Private Network* (VPN) is a secure encrypted transmission used to con-nect to a remote access server. A user can connect to the server by using the Internet, a phone line, or an Internet Service Provider (ISP). VPN can use different network protocols, including TCP/IP, IPX/SPX, and NetBEUI. VPNs can use PPTP, MS-CHAP, EAP, and L2TP to securely transmit packets. To further secure the server, remote access policies can be implemented with different access restrictions.

Configuring a VPN

Follow these instructions to install the VPN remote access service:

1. Open the Routing And Remote Access menu item under the Administra-tive Tools.

2. Right-click on the server and select Configure And Enable Routing And Remote Access to start the Wizard. Click Next. Figure 10.16 displays the routing and remote access configurations that are available.

3. Select Virtual Private Network (VPN) Server and click Next.

4. Select or add protocols for the remote client. Click Next.

5. Select the Internet connection for the VPN Server to use. Click Next.

6. Choose whether to automatically assign clients IP addresses using DHCP or to specify a specified range of IP addresses. Click Next.

7. Choose Yes or No to install a RADIUS server. Click Next.

8. Click Finish to complete the setup of the VPN Server. Figure 10.19 displays the newly created VPN.

Monitoring and Securing a VPN

You can monitor and configure VPNs through the Routing And Remote Access snap-in. The Ports option displays the status of open connections. The Remote Access Clients displays the users who are logged in and how long their connection has been active. If you need more information on the network interface that is supporting the VPN, use the IP Routing and IPX Routing options to display statistical information. Figure 10.19 displays the monitoring options that are available using the Routing And Remote Access snap-in.

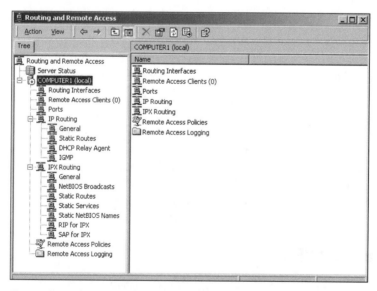

Figure 10.19   Routing And Remote Access screen for a VPN.

User properties and remote access policies are two ways to secure a VPN. A user's properties screen is seen in Figure 10.18. Adding remote access policies gives an administrator the flexibility to customize the VPN's structure. To add a new policy, right-click on the Remote Access Policies option and select New Remote Access Policy. Create policies for your VPN using the Wizard. Figure 10.20 displays the policy options for a VPN.

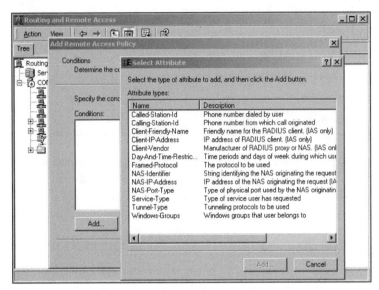

Figure 10.20   Adding Remote Access policies for a VPN.

Practice Questions

Question 1

> Which software packages do you use to remotely install Word on all com-
> puters in your organization? [Check all correct answers]
>
> ❑ a. Remote Installer
>
> ❑ b. Remote Installation Services
>
> ❑ c. Software Installation And Maintenance
>
> ❑ d. Windows Installer
>
> ❑ e. Word Installer

Answers c and d are correct. Answer a is incorrect because it does not exist. Answer b is incorrect because Remote Installation Services is used to remotely install Windows 2000 Professional. Answer e is incorrect because Word Installer is
not a real program.

Question 2

> Which two administrative programs are used to remotely install software
> packages for a server onto a client computer? [Check all correct answers]
>
> ❑ a. Add/Remove Programs
>
> ❑ b. Remote Installation Services
>
> ❑ c. Setup Manager
>
> ❑ d. Software Installation And Maintenance
>
> ❑ e. Windows Installer

Answers d and e are correct. Answer a is incorrect because the Add/Remove
Programs icon is used by the client to install software locally. Answer b is incorrect because Remote Installation Services are used to remotely install Windows
2000 Professional. Answer c is incorrect because Setup Manager is used to automatically install Windows 2000.

Question 3

After using Windows Installer to package a file, what file extension is used?

- ○ a. .exe
- ○ b. .xex
- ○ c. .mis
- ○ d. .msi
- ○ e. .paz

Answer d is correct. Windows Installer packages use the .msi file to replace the setup.exe file.

Question 4

The table below displays the criteria for Workstation1 and User2. How do you deploy the software remotely? [Check all correct answers]

User or Computer	Software and Criteria
Workstation1	Excel must always be loaded and available.
User2	Word must be loaded if the user accesses it.
User2	PowerPoint must be available for the user to load if necessary.

- ❑ a. Assign Excel to Workstation1
- ❑ b. Publish Excel to Workstation1
- ❑ c. Assign Word to User2
- ❑ d. Publish Word to User2
- ❑ e. Assign PowerPoint to User2
- ❑ f. Publish PowerPoint to User2

Answers a, c, and f are correct. Answer b is incorrect because a computer cannot have software published to it. Answer d is incorrect because publishing software requires that the user go to the Add/Remove Programs to install Word. Answer e is incorrect because assigning software makes PowerPoint available for use on the desktop and the Start menu.

Question 5

> You have been instructed to install a Dfs root to make accessing shared
> folders easier for users. Which kind of Dfs do you install if fault tolerance is
> of the utmost importance?
>
> ○ a. Domain Dfs
>
> ○ b. Domain multiple Dfs
>
> ○ c. Standalone Dfs
>
> ○ d. Standing Dfs
>
> ○ e. Fault tolerant Dfs
>
> ○ f. Robust Dfs

Answer a is correct. A domain Dfs provides fault tolerance through the use of
replicas. Answers b, d, e, and f are not real Dfs root types. Answer c is incorrect
because a standalone Dfs does not provide any fault tolerance.

Question 6

> How do you add a Dfs link to a domain Dfs root?
>
> ○ a. Right-click the domain Dfs root in the Active Directory File System
> snap-in, select New Dfs Link, and complete the Wizard.
>
> ○ b. Right-click the domain Dfs root in the Distributed File System
> snap-in, select New Dfs Link, and complete the Wizard.
>
> ○ c. Right-click the domain Dfs root in the Active Directory File System
> snap-in, select Add Domain Link, and complete the Wizard.
>
> ○ d. Right-click the domain Dfs root in the Distributed File System
> snap-in, select Add Domain Link, and complete the Wizard.

Answer b is correct. Answers a and c are incorrect because there is not an Active
Directory File System snap-in. Answer d is incorrect because the option to add a
link to a Dfs root is New Dfs Link, not Add Domain Link.

Question 7

Which two modes can you configure Terminal Services in? [Check all correct answers]

☐ a. Application server mode

☐ b. Administrative mode

☐ c. Advanced server mode

☐ d. Organizational server mode

☐ e. Organizational mode

Answers a and b are correct. Answer c, d, and e are made up terms. Terminal Services supports two modes: Server mode, which can be implemented on low-end clients and non-Windows computers so they can have access to the Windows 2000 desktop and applications; and Administrative mode, which can be a secure method of administering a network on minimal hardware.

Question 8

Using the Routing And Remote Access Manager, where do you access the IP routing tables? On Figure 10.21, highlight the correct option under the IP Routing options.

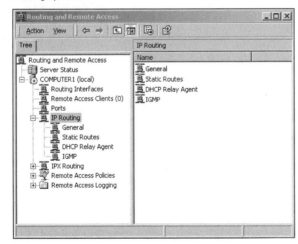

Figure 10.21   Routing And Remote Access Manager.

Answer: The General option under the IP Routing option should be highlighted, as shown in Figure 10.22. Under the General icon select an interface, right-click, and select IP Routing Table.

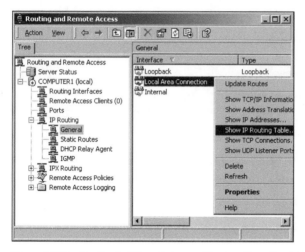

Figure 10.22 Routing And Remote Access Manager IP routing tables.

Question 9

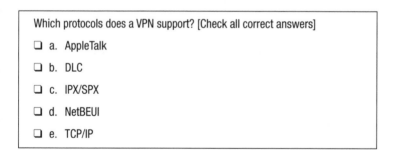

Which protocols does a VPN support? [Check all correct answers]

❑ a. AppleTalk

❑ b. DLC

❑ c. IPX/SPX

❑ d. NetBEUI

❑ e. TCP/IP

Answers c, d, and e are correct. Answers a and b are incorrect because a VPN connection does not support AppleTalk or DLC.

Question 10

> Which three methods can be used to secure a VPN? [Check all correct answers]
>
> ❏ a. NTFS
>
> ❏ b. FAT
>
> ❏ c   User accounts in Active Directory Users And Computer
>
> ❏ d. Computer accounts in Active Directory Users And Computer
>
> ❏ e. Access Policies
>
> ❏ f. Remote Access Policies

Answers a, c, and f are correct. Answer b is incorrect because FAT does not support file level security. Answer d is incorrect because only user accounts have the Dial-In tab to configure user access, callback options, and static IP addresses. Answer e is incorrect because Access Policies do not exist.

Need to Know More?

Russel, Charlie, and Sharon Crawford: *Microsoft Windows 2000 Server Administrator's Companion*. Microsoft Press, Redmond, Washington, 2000. ISBN 1-57231-819-8. This is a valuable reference from which to learn more about implementing and administering networking services.

Search TechNet on the Internet at **www.microsoft.com/technet/ default.asp** or the TechNet CD for information on: Windows Installer, Software Installation And Maintenance, Remote Installation Services, Windows 2000 Professional, Terminal Services, Routing And Remote Access, RAS, Remote Access, Virtual Private Network, VPN.

For more information on the following terminology and implementation of that terminology, refer to Microsoft Windows 2000 Help. To access this resource, choose Help from the Start menu. Terms and technologies to search for include: Windows Installer, Software Installation And Maintenance, published software, assigned software, software installation overview, Remote Installation Preparation Wizard, RIS, Remote Installation Services, Remote Installation overview, Terminal Services, Terminal Services administering, Terminal Services logging, Terminal Services modes, Routing And Remote Access, Routing And Remote Access overview, Routing And Remote Access authentication, Routing And Remote Access enabling, RAS, RAS overview, VPN, VPN overview.

Windows 2000 Security

Terms you'll need to understand:

- ✓ Security policies
- ✓ Group Policy Objects (GPOs)
- ✓ Local security policy
- ✓ Account policy
- ✓ Domain security policy
- ✓ Security Configuration And Analysis tool
- ✓ Security template
- ✓ Security permissions
- ✓ Auditing
- ✓ Local audit policy
- ✓ Encrypting File System (EFS)
- ✓ Recovery Agent
- ✓ IPSec
- ✓ Delegation of Control Wizard

Techniques you'll need to master:

- ✓ Configuring local and domain security policies
- ✓ Using the Security Configuration And Analysis snap-in to secure and analyze a server
- ✓ Creating a security template
- ✓ Implementing security permissions
- ✓ Configuring and accessing audited events
- ✓ Using the Encrypting File System to secure a server
- ✓ Troubleshooting an EFS using the Recovery Agent and **cipher**

The Windows 2000 security features discussed in this chapter include permissions, policies, auditing, the Encrypting File System, and the security configuration tool. Windows 2000 has many security features, and most likely, Microsoft will test your knowledge of security on the exam. Studying this chapter will help prepare you for the security portion of the exam.

Manually Configuring Security Policies

Policies are rules that are applied to users and computers either locally or globally throughout an organization. The types of policies that you can manually configure to secure Windows 2000 are group policies, local security policies, and domain security policies.

Group Policies

Group Policy Objects (GPOs) are implemented to control users' local desktops, computer settings, and user rights. GPOs help administrators control and secure computers on the domain. For more information about GPOs, refer to Chapter 6. Local GPOs are stored and applied to the local computer, whereas domain GPOs are stored on a domain controller and are implemented by Active Directory. If there is a local and a domain GPO that conflict, the local GPO is overridden. Administrators can use both types of policies to secure their organization.

 GPOs and policies may appear on the exam. You should be familiar with how they work, how they are implemented, and how they are inherited.

Local Security Policy

A *local security policy* is used to protect and secure the local computer. The three categories in a local policy include audit polices, user rights assignment, and security options. To configure the local security policies, select the Local Security Policy option from the Administrative Tools menu. Table 11.1 defines the different categories of the local policy and their functions. Figure 11.1 displays the

Table 11.1 Local policy categories.	
Local Policy	**Function**
Audit Policy	Used to determine which security events are logged
User Rights Assignment	Used to determine the tasks a user can perform on the local system
Security Options	Used to determine how to protect the local machine from intrusion

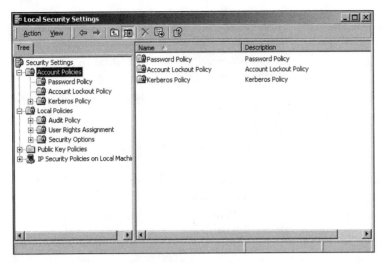

Figure 11.1   Local Policy snap-in.

Local Policy snap-in and Table 11.2 defines some of the over 70 local policies that can be configured.

You can open and edit a policy by double-clicking it. The following steps demonstrate how to edit the policy that deletes the name of the last user who logged onto the system out of the logon box:

1. Select Local Security Policy from the Administrative Tools menu.

2. Choose Local Policies.

3. Choose Security Options.

4. Double-click the Do Not Display Last User Name in logon screen policy.

5. Select the Define This Policy Setting checkbox.

6. Select Enable, and click OK to finish editing the policy.

Account Policy

Account policy is an important category of the Local Policy because it is the policy that restricts password settings, account lockouts, and Kerberos settings. To configure the account policy, select Local Security Policy from the Administrative Tools menu. Table 11.3 defines the three different types of account policies. Figure 11.2 displays the account policies and Table 11.4 defines the different policies and their default configurations.

Table 11.2 Local policies and default settings.		
Type of Local Policy	**Policy**	**Default Setting**
Security policy	Additional restrictions for anonymous connections	Not defined
Security policy	Allow server operators to schedule tasks (domain controllers only)	Not defined
Security policy	Allow system to be shut down without having to log on	Not defined
Security policy	Automatically log off users when logon time expires (local)	Not defined
Security policy	Disable Ctrl+Alt+Del requirement for logon	Not defined
Security policy	Do not display last user name in logon screen	Not defined
Security policy	Message text for users attempting to log on	Not defined
Security policy	Message title for users attempting to log on	Not defined
Security policy	Prevent system maintenance of computer account password	Not defined
Security policy	Restrict floppy access to locally logged-on user only	Not defined
User rights assignment	Access this computer from the network	Not defined
User rights assignment	Act as part of the operating system	Not defined
User rights assignment	Add workstations to domain	Not defined
User rights assignment	Change the system time	Not defined
User rights assignment	Force shutdown from a remote system	Not defined
User rights assignment	Increase quotas	Not defined
User rights assignment	Load and unload device drivers	Not defined
User rights assignment	Log on as a batch job	Not defined
User rights assignment	Log on as a service	Not defined
User rights assignment	Log on locally	Not defined
User rights assignment	Shut down the system	Not defined

Table 11.3 Account policies and their functions.	
Account Policy	**Function**
Password policy	Used to determine the minimum and maximum password length, defines when users must change their passwords, and defines if they must always use unique passwords.
Account lockout policy	Used to determine when a user is restricted from logging into the domain because of unsuccessful login attempts. It also defines how long they will not be able to access the domain and when their unsuccessful login attempts are set back to zero.
Kerberos policy	Used with Kerberos V5 authentication protocol to determine how long the Kerberos data is valid and when the data can be renewed.

Table 11.4 Account policies and their default configurations.		
Type of Account Policy	**Policy**	**Default Configuration**
Password policy	Enforce password history	1; remembers one password
Password policy	Maximum password age	42 days
Password policy	Minimum password age	0 days
Password policy	Minimum password length	0 characters
Password policy	Password must meet complexity requirements	disabled
Password policy	Store password using reversible encryption for all users in the domain	disabled
Account lockout policy	Account lockout duration	not defined
Account lockout policy	Account lockout threshold	0 invalid logon attempts
Account lockout policy	Reset account lockout counter after a defined set of time	not defined
Kerberos policy	Enforce user logon restrictions	enabled
Kerberos policy	Maximum lifetime for service ticket	600 minutes
Kerberos policy	Maximum lifetime for user ticket	10 hours
Kerberos policy	Maximum lifetime for user ticket renewal	7 days
Kerberos policy	Maximum tolerance for computer clock synchronization	5 minutes

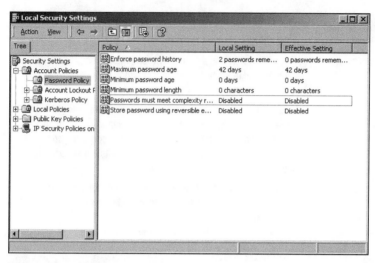

Figure 11.2 Account policies.

Domain Security Policy

A domain security policy is applied to the domain using GPOs, whereas the local security policy is configured for a local computer. The domain security policy has the same configuration and category settings as the local security policy. It includes additional settings for the Event Log, groups, services, Registry, and file system. Figure 11.3 displays the Domain Security Policy snap-in, and Table 11.5 defines the default configuration categories.

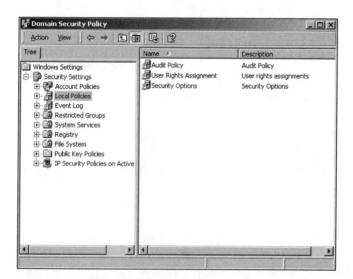

Figure 11.3 Domain Security Policy snap-in.

Table 11.5   Security Configuration And Analysis tool options.

Security Option	Function
Account policies	Configures password policies, user lockout policies, and Kerberos security settings.
Local policies	Configures the computer's auditing policy, the policies of users on the local computer, and policies for computer security.
Event log	Configures how long logs are maintained, the maximum size of the logs, and other settings for the logs.
Restricted groups	Configures membership of restricted groups.
System services	Configures the services that are running on the computer.
Registry	Enables security to be set on registry keys.
File system	Configures security on the local file system.

If you implement a local security policy and a domain security policy on a computer, the domain policy overrides the local security settings. To track the combined or effective permissions of the two policies, open the Local Security Policy snap-in, select a policy, and note the local settings and the effective settings.

Note: Windows 2000 allows only one account policy per domain, and it becomes the default policy for members of the domain through the Domain Security Policy.

Security Configuration And Analysis Tool

You use the Security Configuration And Analysis tool to configure your server against security holes and attacks. It uses different security templates to analyze and secure the computer. There are 13 different security templates to configure and analyze your computer. The tool generates a text file report and graphically displays consistencies and inconsistencies.

Configuring and Analyzing a Computer

After you add the Security Configuration And Analysis snap-in, you create a new database with a security template. The database is used to analyze the security settings on the computer, and the security template compares its security information with the computer's security information. Consistencies and inconsistencies between the security template and the computer system can be analyzed. The following methods are used to create a new database, install a security template, configure the computer, and analyze the computer.

To create a new database with the Security Configuration And Analysis tool, follow these steps:

1. Right-click the Security Configuration And Analysis snap-in.

2. Select Open Database.

3. In the Open Database box, type the name of the new database and click Open.

4. Select the basicsv.inf security template and click Open. The following section discusses how to configure your own security template.

Note: basicsv.inf is a preconfigured security template that defines a set of default security for a Windows 2000 Server.

To configure a computer with the new database and security template information, follow these steps:

1. Right-click the Security Configuration And Analysis snap-in.

2. Select Configure Computer Now.

3. Click OK to save the error log at the designated path.

To compare the computer's current security settings to the security template, follow these steps:

1. Right-click the Security Configuration And Analysis snap-in.

2. Select Analyze Computer Now.

3. Click OK to save the error log at the designated path.

4. To check the log file, right-click the Security Configuration And Analysis snap-in and select View Log File.

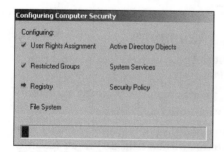

Figure 11.4   The Configuring Computer Security dialog box displays the configuration progress.

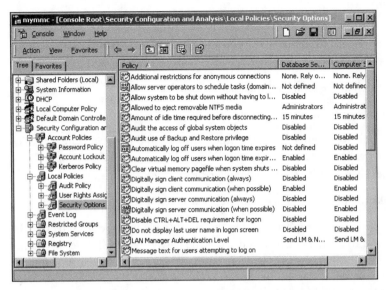

Figure 11.5 The Security Configuration And Analysis snap-in after configuration and analysis.

5. To view analyzed information, browse through the Security Configuration And Analysis snap-in. Figure 11.5 displays the different responses to the original configuration using the basicsv.inf file.

The Security Configuration And Analysis snap-in can provide the following analysis:

➤ A red X signifies that there is a difference in the original configuration.

➤ A green check signifies that the original configuration has remained the same.

➤ If an icon does not appear, it indicates that the configuration option was not included in the security template.

Security Templates

The Security Configuration And Analysis tool for Windows 2000 Server comes with 13 security templates. These templates are created so that one or two can be used throughout an organization as a consistent policy. If the templates that are provided do not meet your needs, you can configure your own security templates. You can create security templates by using the Security Template snap-in and exporting a local security policy.

Security Template Snap-In

The Security Template snap-in helps administrators create security templates. After you create a security template, you can import it onto other computers.

Follow these steps to modify an existing security template:

1. In the Security Templates snap-in, select a template to modify. This example uses the basicsv.inf template.

2. Right-click the template, and choose Save As.

3. Name the new template and choose Save.

4. The Security Templates snap-in now displays the new template. Double-click the new template to open it. Figure 11.6 displays the Security Templates snap-in with the new template highlighted.

5. Make the necessary changes to the security template.

6. The new template is then used in the Security Configuration And Analysis snap-in to open a database and select the newly created INF security template. By default, the templates are saved in the C:\winnt\security\templates folder.

Note: You can use the command line utility secedit.exe to configure and refresh security templates.

Exporting a Local Security Policy

An administrator easily can adjust the domain security policy so that it can be used rather than local policies by exporting a local security policy. After the template is created, it can be imported to other computer systems by using a GPO. To configure a local policy to be implemented at the domain level, follow these steps:

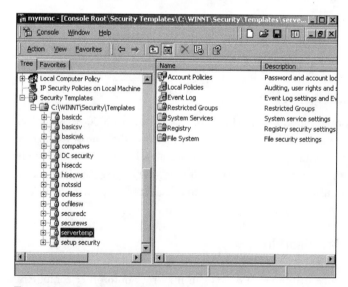

Figure 11.6   Security Templates snap-in.

1. Under the Administrative Tools menu, open the Domain Security Policy.

2. Select Security Settings, right-click, and go to Import Policy.

3. Select the domain policy and click Open.

4. Reboot the computer.

5. In the Administrative Tools, open the Local Security Policy.

6. Open the Security Settings.

7. Configure the policies for your new security template.

 Remember to compare the Local Settings and the Effective Settings to understand which options will be implemented. Adjust the Domain Security Policy so that it does not interfere with the Local Policy settings. Figure 11.2 displayed the Local and Effective Settings.

8. After the Effective Settings are correct, click the Local Policy|Security Settings, select Export Policy, and then select Effective Policy.

9. Name the new template and save it. This policy can now be used as the domain security policy and local security policies do not have to be implemented.

Security Permissions

Security permissions are accessible on an NTFS volume. It is the only file system that supports security and auditing of local files, folders, and printers. NTFS should be used to secure local and remote access to a server. Remember that NTFS permissions restrict the local file system so that a user who logs onto the server is restricted by his or her permissions. When security permissions and share permissions are combined, they make a good security defense.

Another security measure is to only assign security permissions to the necessary users and groups. Figure 11.7 displays the security permissions that are used to secure a shared folder. In addition to security permissions on this share, an administrator should control the share level access, as seen in Figure 11.8. Refer to Chapter 8 for more details on users, groups, share permissions, and security permissions.

Auditing

Auditing a server is one way to monitor and improve the security procedures that you have implemented. With Windows 2000 the administrator can audit users,

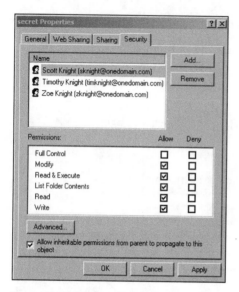

Figure 11.7   Security permissions.

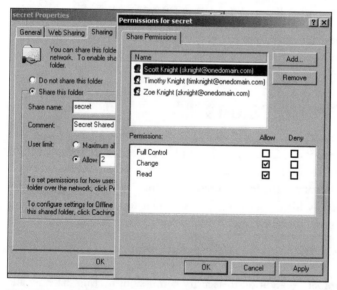

Figure 11.8   Share permissions.

file and folder access, system events, system changes, and Active Directory. An administrator can also configure auditing of files and folders and implement auditing through domain security policy and local security policy.

Auditing Files and Folders

Files and folders that are on an NTFS volume can be audited. Auditing files and folders enables you to monitor successful and failed attempts to access the resources. To enable local auditing for files and folders, follow these steps:

1. Right-click on an NTFS file or folder.

2. Select Properties.

3. Choose the Security tab.

4. Select the Advanced button.

5. Choose the Auditing tab.

6. Select Add and choose the groups or users you want to audit.

7. Check the boxes for auditing successful or failed events, as shown in Figure 11.9.

 For a further understanding of auditing files and folders, review the access permissions that are being tracked for success or failure. These access permissions are listed in Figure 11.9.

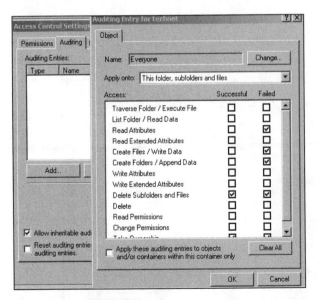

Figure 11.9 Auditing Entry interface.

Auditing Printers

An administrator can keep track of who is printing or cannot print and how the printer is being managed by auditing printers. Follow these steps listed to audit a printer:

1. Right-click on the printer you want to audit.

2. Select Properties.

3. Choose the Security tab.

4. Select the Advanced button.

5. Choose the Auditing tab.

6. Select Add, and choose the groups or users you want to audit.

7. Check the boxes for auditing successful or failed events, as seen in Figure 11.10.

 For a further understanding of auditing printer success or failure, review the access permissions that are listed in Figure 11.10.

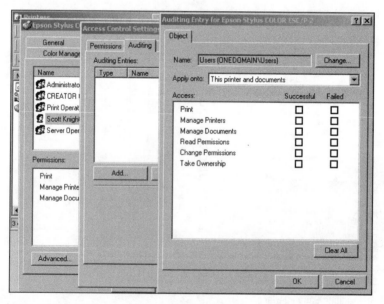

Figue 11.10 Auditing Entry interface for a printer.

Local Audit Policy

Audit policies make it possible to track logon events, object access, system events, and account management. They can be defined through a Local Security Policy and a Domain Security Policy. Figure 11.11 displays the events that can be audited.

Note: The auditing policies have been changed in Figure 11.11; by default all of the policies are set as Not Defined until an administrator changes them.

To configure a local audit policy, follow these steps:

1. Under the Administrative Tools menu, open the Local Security Policy.

2. Select Local Policies.

3. Select Audit Policies.

4. Double-click on the policy you want to edit. Then select Define These Policy Settings, check the Success or Failure boxes, and click OK.

Configuring auditing is implemented the same way in domain security policy.

Accessing Audited Events

Event Viewer displays the audited events after auditing has been configured. You can access Event Viewer by selecting Administrative Tools|Event Viewer.

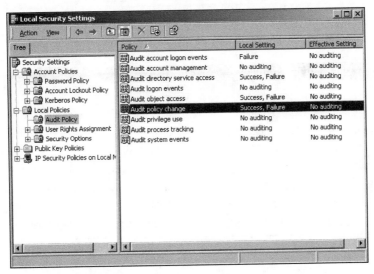

Figure 11.11   Local Audit Policy.

Figure 11.12 displays the Event Viewer and Table 11.6 defines the different categories of event logs.

Note: Certain programs implemented on a Windows 2000 Server add additional Event Viewer logs.

Table 11.7 explains the different types of events that are logged in Event Viewer.

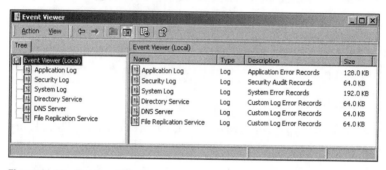

Figure 11.12   The Event Viewer.

Table 11.6 Event Viewer log descriptions.	
Type of Log	**Description**
Application Log	Events relating to the program are logged here. These events include program errors and missing data information.
Security Log	Events relating to computer security are logged here. These events include audited events such as logon attempts and folder access.
System Log	Events relating to the system components are logged here. These events include startup information, shutdown information, and driver information.

Table 11.7 Log event descriptions.		
Symbol	**Log Type**	**Description**
Red circle with an "X"	Error	A serious problem has occurred
Circle with a blue "i"	Information	An event has successfully completed
Yellow triangle with an "!"	Warning	A non-serious problem has occurred
Closed lock	Success Audit	An audited event has a successful status
Open lock	Failure Audit	An audited event has a failed status

Encrypting File System (EFS)

An Encrypting File System (EFS) uses public key encryption to secure files and folders on an NTFS volume. After a file or folder is encrypted, only the user who encrypted it can access it. When a user tries to access an encrypted file, the user's private access certificate is checked against the file. The user is granted or denied access to the file depending on the certificate. If granted access, the file appears in normal text and decryption is transparent to the user. If the user is denied access, a No Access message appears in place of the document. Only the owner of the file and a recovery agent can access an encrypted file. In addition, encrypted files cannot be shared or have their permissions changed to give access to other users.

Encrypting Using EFS

You can configure encryption the same way that you configure compression. Follow these steps to configure encryption for a file or folder:

1. Right-click the file or folder you want to encrypt.

2. Select Properties.

3. Click the Advanced button.

4. Select the Encrypt Contents to Secure Data checkbox, as seen in Figure 11.13. Click OK. Click OK to confirm attribute changes.

5. Choose Apply Changes To This Folder Only or Apply Changes To This Folder, Subfolders And Files radio button, as seen in Figure 11.14. Click OK.

Files and folders can either be encrypted or compressed; they cannot be encrypted and compressed simultaneously.

Figure 11.13   The Advanced Attributes dialog box is used to enable encryption.

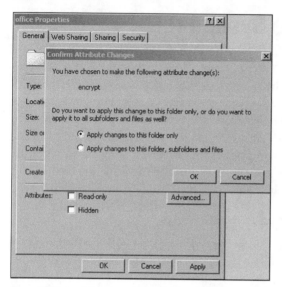

Figure 11.14 The Confirm Attribute Changes dialog box for encyption.

 EFS questions may appear on the exam. You should be prepared to configure encryption, decrypt files, and recover files using the GUI interface or the Cipher command-line utility.

Decrypting Using EFS

Decrypting a file is transparent to the user who encrypted the file. When the user opens or closes a file, it is decrypted and encrypted for them. To permanently decrypt a file or folder, you use the same process used to encrypt a file or folder. If a file no longer needs to be encrypted, deselect the Encrypt Contents To Secure Data checkbox. If a file needs to be decrypted but the user is unavailable to decrypt, a recovery agent is needed.

Troubleshooting EFS

The exam may cover troubleshooting EFS problems. Problems could range from losing an encryption key to advanced encryption or decryption features. If a key is lost or a user is unavailable to decrypt a file or folder, an EFS Recovery Agent is used. If the GUI interface to encrypt files does not give you enough control, the cipher.exe command-line utility can be used. The following sections address these troubleshooting topics.

EFS Recovery Agent

If necessary, an EFS Recovery Agent is used to decrypt a file. If the original owner of the file is unavailable or the user's key has been lost, the recovery agent is the only way to access the encrypted files and folders. The domain administrator, by default, is the recovery agent for the domain, and local administrators are recovery agents for standalone computers. To create additional recovery agents, you must create and assign certificates, and must specify them in a group policy. A recovery agent implements these steps to decrypt an EFS file:

1. Copy the file to the recovery agent's computer.

Note: Files that are copied or moved to other locations remain encrypted with the original users private key. They are moved to the recovery agent's computer so that the agent's private key is not copied to other computers on the network.

2. Right-click the file and select Properties.

3. Click the Advanced button on the General tab.

4. Deselect the Encrypt Contents To Secure Data checkbox.

5. Move the decrypted file back to the user's computer.

cipher Command

Cipher is a command-line utility that is used by an administrator to mange encryption. This utility gives an administrator greater control over the encryption and decryption of files and folders. Table 11.8 displays the **cipher** command switches and their functions.

IP Security (IPSec)

IP Security, or IPSec, can provide encryption and secure communication between computers and uses Kerberos authentication. It supports public and private key encryption, IP filtering, and Encapsulated Security Payload (ESP) to encrypt the IP packets. These features make IPSec a great tool against attackers. IPSec is controlled through the IP Security Policy Management snap-in. When you add the snap-in, you are asked which computer to manage, as seen in Figure 11.15.

Table 11.8 Cipher.exe command switches.	
Switch	**Function**
/a	Includes files and folders
/d	Decrypts the folder
/e	Encrypts the folder
/f	Forces encryption
/h	Includes hidden files
/i	Continues operations if errors occur
/k	Creates a new encryption key

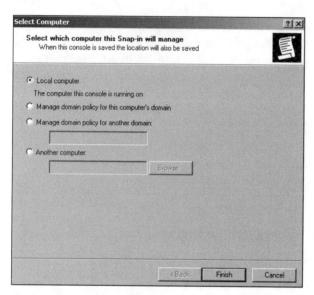

Figure 11.15 The IP Security Policy Management computer option.

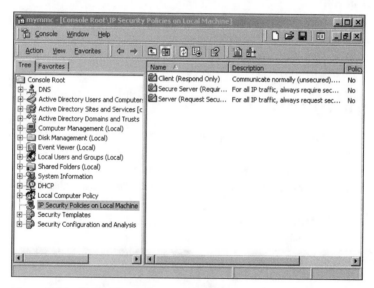

Figure 11.16 The IP Security Policy Management snap-in.

The IP Security Policy Management enables you to set policies for IP security. These policies include setting filters for client computers, configuring Kerberos settings, securing client transactions, and securing server communications. Figure 11.16 displays the IP Security Policy Management snap-in.

Delegation of Control Wizard

The Delegation of Control Wizard is used in Active Directory to assign permissions to users and groups to manage OUs. The Wizard helps administrators spread the administrative overhead to different people, without giving them administrator rights to the whole domain. This feature assists in distributing the administrator's load, while keeping the security of Active Directory in place.

To delegate control to another user or group, follow these steps:

1. Right-click on the OU that you want to delegate.

2. Select Delegate Control to start the Delegation of Control Wizard.

3. Click Add, and select the users and groups that will gain control.

4. Select which tasks the users or groups can control. Refer to Figure 11.17.

5. Click Finish to complete the Delegation of Control Wizard.

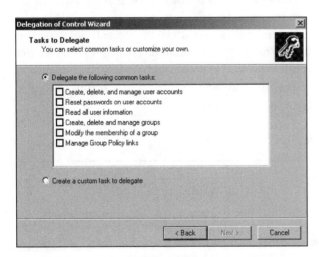

Figure 11.17   Delegation of Control Wizard.

Practice Questions

Question 1

> An accounting manager has abruptly left the company. His account files were in an encrypted folder. What tool must be used to access these files?
>
> ○ a. Decrypt File System
>
> ○ b. IPSec
>
> ○ c. Recover Agent
>
> ○ d. secedit.exe
>
> ○ e. Security Configuration And Analysis tool

Answer c is correct. The user who encrypts the files and folders can access them, and if necessary, the Recovery Agent. Answer a is incorrect because there is not a tool named Decrypt File System. Answer b is incorrect because IPSec is used for IP security and cannot be used to decrypt the accounting manager's files. Answer d is incorrect because secedit.exe is used to update and create security templates. Answer e is incorrect because the Security Configuration And Analysis tool is used to implement and check computer security.

Question 2

> Which **cipher** switches are used to encrypt and decrypt a file? [Check all correct answers]
>
> ❑ a. **/a**
>
> ❑ b. **/d**
>
> ❑ c. **/e**
>
> ❑ d. **/i**
>
> ❑ e. **/k**

Answers b and c are correct. The **/d** switch decrypts a file or folder, and **/e** encrypts a file or folder. Answer a is incorrect because **/a** includes files and folders in the **cipher** command. Answer d is incorrect because **/i** is used to continue operations if an errors occur. Answer e is incorrect because **/k** is used to create a new encryption key.

Question 3

You are given the task of auditing a printer. In the screen shown in Figure 11.18, check those boxes which will allow you to audit the following requests.

You want to know if someone unsuccessfully tried to access a printer.

You want to know if someone successfully took ownership of the printer.

You want to know if someone could not print to the printer.

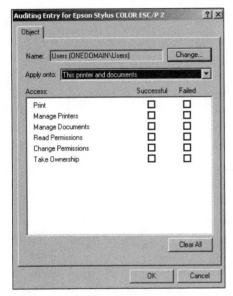

Figure 11.18 Auditing a printer.

Answer: One check should be on Read Permissions Failed, one check should be on Take Ownership Successful, and one check should be on Print Failed, as shown in Figure 11.19.

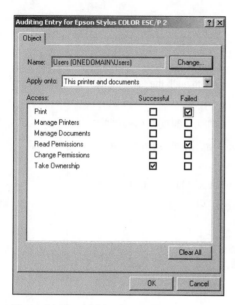

Figure 11.19 Auditing Printer answer.

Question 4

Match the following symbols in Event Viewer with their meaning.

Symbol:	Meaning:
Red circle with an "X"	An event has successfully completed
Circle with a blue "i"	A non-serious problem has occurred
Yellow Triangle with an "!"	A serious problem has occurred

Answer:

A red circle with an "X" is an error, meaning that a serious problem has occurred.

A circle with a blue "i" is an informational message, which notifies when an event has successfully completed.

A yellow triangle with an "!" is a warning, which notifies that a non-serious problem has occurred.

Question 5

As an administrator of 100 Windows 2000 Professional computers, what do you use to track the same security features on all the computers?

O a. EFS

O b. IPSec

O c. Local Policy

O d. Security Configuration And Control tool

O e. Security templates

Answer e is correct. Answer a is incorrect because EFS is used to encrypt files and folders. Answer b is incorrect because IPSec is used to secure IP packets between computers. Answer c is incorrect because a local policy is used to secure the computer, not to track security features. Answer d is incorrect because there is not a Security Configuration And Control tool. There is a Security Configuration And Analysis tool that is used in conjunction with the Security templates.

Question 6

Who can access and read an encrypted file? [Check all correct answers]

❑ a. Administrators

❑ b. All users

❑ c. The user who encrypted the file

❑ d. The Recovery Agent

❑ e. Administrators who log on to the computer on which the files are located

❑ f. Users who log on to the computer on which the files are located

Answers c and d are correct. The only people that can access an encrypted file are the person who encrypted the file and the Recovery Agent. Answer a is incorrect because administrators do not have rights to other users encrypted files. Answer b is incorrect because all users cannot access other users' encrypted files. Answers e and f are incorrect because it does not matter who logs onto the computer on which the files are located. The file is still encrypted.

Question 7

Which tool do you use to give someone else control of an OU?

○ a. Delegation of Control Wizard

○ b. OU Control Wizard

○ c. Share permissions

○ d. Security permissions

○ e. Security templates

Answer a is correct. Answer b is incorrect because there is not an OU Control Wizard. Answer c and d are incorrect because share and security permissions do not dictate who controls an OU in Active Directory. Answer e is incorrect because security templates do not set policies on who controls OUs.

Question 8

By default, who is the Recovery Agent in a domain?

○ a. Administrators

○ b. Backup Operators

○ c. Domain Administrators

○ d. EFS Administrators

○ e. Enterprise Administrators

Answer c is correct. Answers a, b, and e are incorrect because these groups do not have the Recovery Agent capability. Answer d is incorrect because there is not an EFS Administrators group.

Question 9

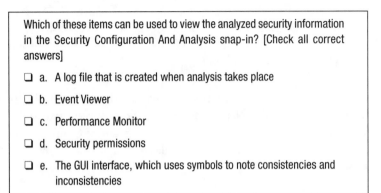

Which of these items can be used to view the analyzed security information in the Security Configuration And Analysis snap-in? [Check all correct answers]

- ❑ a. A log file that is created when analysis takes place
- ❑ b. Event Viewer
- ❑ c. Performance Monitor
- ❑ d. Security permissions
- ❑ e. The GUI interface, which uses symbols to note consistencies and inconsistencies

Answers a and e are correct. Answer b is incorrect because Event Viewer is used to access audited events and system events, and it cannot be accessed in the Security Configuration And Analysis snap-in. Answer c is incorrect because Performance Monitor is used to analyze a computer system, not security events. Answer d is incorrect because security permissions do not involve analyzing Security Configuration And Analysis data.

Need to Know More?

 Russel, Charlie, and Sharon Crawford: *Microsoft Windows 2000 Server Administrator's Companion*. Microsoft Press, Redmond, Washington, 2000. ISBN 1-57231-819-8. To learn more about implementing and administering security, refer to Chapters 17 and 19.

 Search TechNet on the Internet at **www.microsoft.com/technet/ default.asp** or the TechNet CD for information on: security permissions, GPO, local policies, domain policies, Security Configuration And Analysis tool, security templates, delegation of Control Wizard, IPSec.

 For more information on the following terminology and implementation, refer to Microsoft Windows 2000 Help. To access this resource, choose Help from the Start menu. Terms and technologies to search for include: Active Directory security, account policy best practices, common asks for managing security, Windows 2000 Concepts, IPSec Authentication, local policies, security areas, Security Configuration And Analysis overview, Security Configuration And Analysis tool, security templates overview, delegation of Control Wizard, GPO, and security permissions.

Backup and Recovery

Terms you'll need to understand:

✓ Backup

✓ Restore

✓ Schedule

✓ System State data

✓ Authoritative restore of Active Directory

✓ Non-authoritative restore of Active Directory

✓ Advanced Startup Options

✓ F8 startup option

✓ Safe Mode

✓ Safe Mode With Networking

✓ Enable VGA Mode

✓ Last Known Good Configuration

✓ Recovery Console

✓ winnt32 /cmdcons

✓ Emergency repair disk (ERD)

✓ Advanced RISC computing (ARC) naming path

Techniques you'll need to master:

✓ Using the Advanced Startup options to troubleshoot a Windows 2000 Server

✓ Backing up and restoring a Windows 2000 Server

✓ Backing up and restoring System State data

✓ Installing and using the Recovery Console

✓ Creating and implementing an emergency repair disk (ERD)

✓ Editing a boot.ini ARC path to boot to the good disk of a failed mirror

This chapter addresses backing up and restoring Windows 2000 Server. The tools that come with Windows 2000 Server include a backup program, a restore program, a scheduler program, an advanced set of startup options, a Recovery Console, and a program to make an emergency repair disk (ERD). We will look at these tools and how to implement them in Windows 2000 Server. The exam may cover the backup and restore options that are included with Windows 2000; therefore, you should be familiar with the topics covered in this chapter.

Windows 2000 Backup

The Windows 2000 Backup program protects against data loss, disk failures, data loss due to viruses, power failure damage, and, if stored off site, natural disasters. Backups should be scheduled on a regular basis. After data is backed up, a log should be kept of the backups, some backups should be kept off site, the backups should be verified, and data restoration should be tested frequently. Access the backup interface by opening the Start menu and selecting Programs|Accessories|System Tools|Backup. Figure 12.1 displays the Backup program's welcome screen, which includes three backup Wizards.

Windows 2000 Backup combines programs to back up, restore, make an ERD, and schedule backup jobs. You can perform these tasks manually or by following a Wizard. You must be an administrator or backup operator to back up or restore a Windows 2000 Server. Users can back up files that they own and files with Read, Read and Execute, Modify, or Full Control permissions.

Note: The Backup program supports hard drives, floppies, tape drives, CD-ROM, and removable disks.

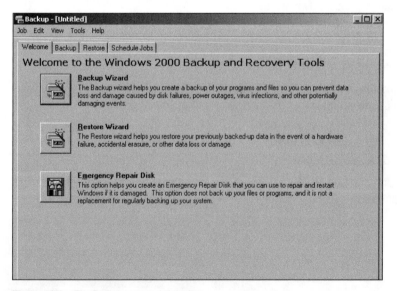

Figure 12.1 The Backup program interface.

Backing Up Files and Folders

You should back up the operating system, including files and folders, on a regular basis to protect against data loss. The next sections address the different types of backup strategies and how to manually backup a Windows 2000 Server.

Types of Backup Strategies

The types of backup strategies for Windows 2000 define which files are backed up and whether the files are marked as backed up. Some strategies back up only the files that have changed since the last backup; other strategies back up all the files on the systems. The backup strategy that you use will dictate how many tapes you need to restore if data is lost. Table 12.1 displays the types of backup strategies and which files they back up.

 You should be familiar with the types of backups, how and when to use each kind of backup, and how to plan a restoration depending on the type of backups used.

Configuring a Backup

To manually configure a backup for Windows 2000, use the Backup program as specified in the following steps:

1. In the Backup program, select the Backup tab as seen in Figure 12.2.

2. Check the files and folders that you want to back up. Select the backup destination. Select the backup file name.

3. Click the Start Backup button.

4. In the Backup Job Information dialog box, enter a backup description, check whether to append or replace data on the media, and specify a name to identify the new media.

Table 12.1 Backup types.		
Types of Backups	What Is Backed Up	Marked as Backed Up
Copy	Specified files	No
Daisy	Files that have changed that day	No
Differential	Files that have changed since the last normal or incremental backup	No
Incremental	Files that have changed since the last normal or incremental backup	Yes
Normal	Specified files	Yes

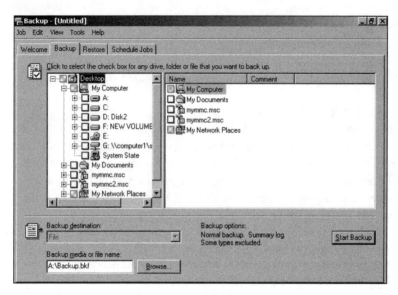

Figure 12.2   The Backup tab.

5. Set up a schedule using the Schedule button. Save your backup job information and log on as an administrator. Enter the job name and set properties as seen in Figure 12.3.

6. The Advanced button gives you the option to choose the type of backup to perform, whether you want the data verified after the backup, and whether

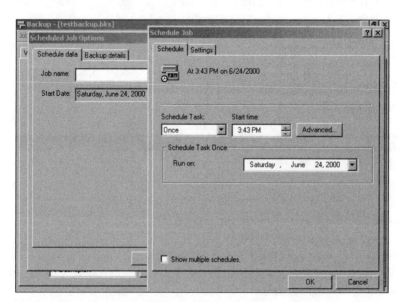

Figure 12.3   Scheduled Job options.

you are backing up data to remote storage. The Advanced button options appear in Figure 12.4.

7. After you complete all of the configuration options, click the Start Backup button. Figure 12.5 displays the Backup Progress screen.

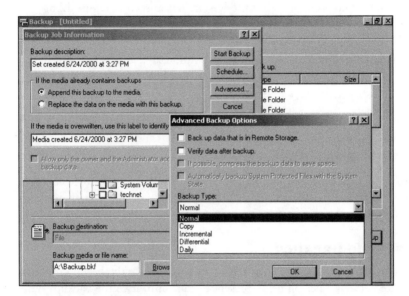

Figure 12.4 The Backup Job Information and Advanced Backup options dialog boxes.

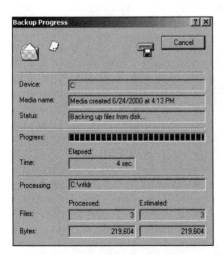

Figure 12.5 The Backup Progress screen.

Restoring Files and Folders

After you back up data, use the Backup program to restore the data as necessary. Log on as a backup operator or an administrator, open up the Backup program, and follow these steps:

1. In the Backup program, select the Restore tab, as seen in Figure 12.6.

2. Select which files to restore.

3. Choose to restore files to their original location, an alternate location, or to a single folder. If you choose to restore into a folder or an alternate location, you must specify where to restore the files.

4. After you configure the Restore options, click the Start Restore button. Figure 12.7 displays the Confirm Restore dialog box and the Advanced Restore Options that are available.

5. After you start the restoration, you are asked where the restored media is located. The restoration begins and the progress screen tracks the restoration, as seen in Figure 12.8.

Scheduling Backups

Scheduling backups enables an administrator to configure the backup program to execute without a person being present to start or oversee the backup. Windows 2000 scheduling software is located on the Schedule Jobs tab. You also have the option of using the Scheduled Tasks program, which you access by choosing

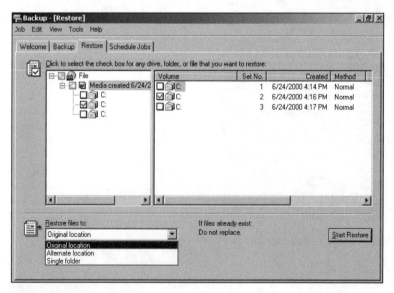

Figure 12.6   The Restore tab.

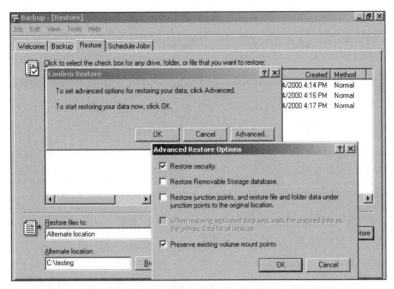

Figure 12.7 The Confirm Restore and Advanced Restore options dialog boxes.

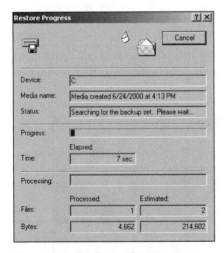

Figure 12.8 The Restore Progress screen.

Accessories|System Tools. To schedule a backup task using the Backup program, follow these steps:

1. In the Backup program, select the Schedule Jobs tab. Use the arrows to go backward or forward through the calendar, and the Today button highlights today's date.

2. Click the Add Job button to start the Backup Wizard.

3. Select from the following options: Back Up Everything On My Computer, Back Up Selected Files, Drives, Or Network Data, or Only Back Up The System State Data. Click Next.

4. Select where to back up the files and enter the backup file name. Click Next.

5. Select the type of backup and whether you are going to back up to remote storage. Click Next.

6. Select whether the data should be verified after the backup and whether to use compression, if it is available. Click Next.

7. Select to append or replace the current data on the tape. Click Next.

8. Type a label for the backup and the media. Click Next.

9. In the Set Account Information field, type the administrator password and then confirm it. Click OK.

10. Select whether to start the backup now or later, enter the name of the scheduled job you are creating, and click the Set Schedule button.

11. Specify the time, data, and frequency of the new job. Click OK and click Finish to complete the Wizard. Figure 12.9 displays a newly created job on the Schedule Jobs tab that is set to run two times a week. At any time you can double-click on the Backup program icon on the calendar to change its configuration.

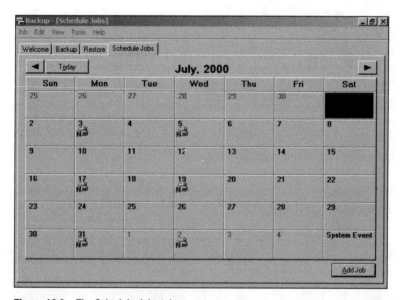

Figure 12.9   The Schedule Jobs tab.

System State Data

System State data is a combination of important Windows 2000 Server system components packaged together for easy backup and restoration. The System State data should be backed up regularly because it contains important components. The following system components combine to make System State data:

➤ The Registry is a hierarchical database that is made up of hives, keys, subkeys, and values. It contains the computer's configuration for hardware, software, user information, and installed software.

➤ System Startup files are the system and boot files to start the server.

➤ The Component Services Class Registration database contains the standards for writing software.

➤ The Certificate Services database contains the X.509 certificates, if it is installed on the server.

➤ The Active Directory database. (If the server is a domain controller.)

➤ The Sysvol directory is a shared directory that contains files that are replicated to domain controllers, if the server is a domain controller.

When backing up a Windows 2000 Server, you have the option to back up the System State data. Refer to the checkbox in Figure 12.10. System State data is backed up and restored as a package; you cannot back up or restore single parts of the System State data.

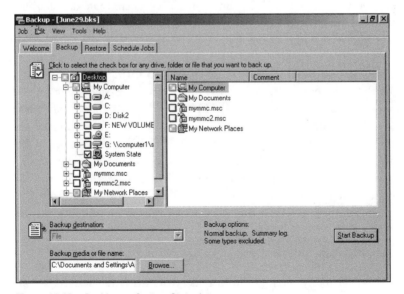

Figure 12.10   Backing up System State data.

System State data can only be backed up on the local computer. It cannot be backed up from a remote computer.

Restoring System State Data

All of the components of the System State data are restored together because of their dependencies on each other. Use the following steps to restore System State data onto a computer that is not a domain controller:

1. In the Backup program, select the Restore tab.

2. Select the media that has the System State information.

3. Select the restore location and click Start Restore.

4. After the information is restored, reboot the server to complete the operation.

Restoring System State Data on a Domain Controller

If you backed up the System State data for a domain controller, the restore process becomes a little more difficult. The domain controller participates in Active Directory, which keeps track of changes in a domain using Update Sequence Numbers (USN). If a domain controller has Organizational Units (OUs) or objects that were deleted and the System State data needs to be restored on the domain controller, the last backup has USNs associated with the deleted data. You have two ways to restore a domain controller's System State data for and Active Directory restore: authoritative restore of Active Directory or a non-authoritative restore of Active Directory.

Performing an Authoritative Restore of Active Directory

An authoritative restore assigns new USNs to the restored System State data so that the old USNs are not used. If the old USNs were used, the rest of Active Directory would know not to replicate the changes because of the outdated sequence number. An authoritative restore changes the USN so that the rest of the domain controllers know that the restored replicated information is valid and should be replicated throughout the domain. If OUs or objects are accidentally deleted out of Active Directory, an authoritative restore must be performed to restore them back on the domain controller. To perform an authoritative restore, follow these steps:

1. Reboot the server, and press F8 to access the Advanced Options.

2. Select the Directory Service Restore mode. After the system restarts in Safe Mode, log on as administrator.

3. Open the Backup program, select the Restore tab, and click the System State data checkbox, as seen in Figure 12.11.

4. After the data is restored, type "ntdsutil.exe" at the command prompt.

5. At the prompt, type "authoritative restore".

6. At the Authoritative Restore prompt, type "restore" and the name of the object to restore. An example is "restore subtree OU=secret,DC=computer1, DC=com". Refer to Figure 12.12 for more details.

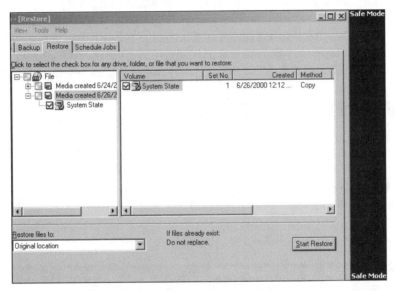

Figure 12.11   Restoring System State data.

Figure 12.12   An example of an Authoritative Restore syntax.

7. Exit ntdsutil and reboot. The authoritative restore ensures that the OU=secret is restored to its original backed up condition, and it is replicated throughout Active Directory.

 You should know how to use ntdsutil to restore Active Directory OUs and objects because it may be on the exam.

Performing a Non-Authoritative Restore of Active Directory

To perform a non-authoritative restore, follow the preceding steps except reboot the server after the data is stored rather than running ntdsutil. A non-authoritative restore restores the System State data to its original USN, but the restored information is not replicated throughout the domain because the USN is outdated.

Advanced Startup Options

You can access a menu for advanced troubleshooting and startup options before the Windows 2000 Server operating system starts. During the boot process, press the F8 function key. An administrator can troubleshoot a Windows 2000 server in different modes using the Advanced Startup options. Table 12.2 displays the Advanced Startup options and their functions. These options are used to troubleshoot an operating system that has driver problems, video problems, services that are not loading, or a server that is just not responding to a normal startup procedure.

Table 12.2 The Advanced Startup options.		
Startup Option	**Function**	**Log File**
Safe Mode	Loads only the basic operating system to start Windows 2000 Server.	Yes
Safe Mode With Networking	Loads only the basic operating system, plus networking, to start Windows 2000 Server.	Yes
Safe Mode With Command Prompt	Starts Windows 2000 Server with a command prompt, not a GUI.	Yes
Enable Boot Logging	Creates a file called systemroot\ntbtlog.txt that lists all of the drivers and services and their status on startup.	Yes
Enable VGA Mode	Starts Windows 2000 Server using minimal VGA support. Used for video problems.	No
Last Known Good Configuration	Uses the Registry to load the last system configuration that was saved the last time a user successfully logged on.	No

(continued)

Table 12.2   The Advanced Startup options *(continued)*.

Startup Option	Function	Log File
Directory Services Restore Mode (Windows 2000 domain controllers only)	Enables the restoration of Active Directory.	Yes
Debugging Mode	Uses a cable to send debugging information to a remote computer.	Yes
Boot Normal	Continues to start Windows 2000 Server without Advanced Startup Option changes.	No

The Recovery Console

If all attempts at repairing the operating system using the Advanced Startup options fail, you can use the Recovery Console. The Recovery Console is a command prompt utility that enables an administrator to start and stop services, access the server's drives, copy files, delete files, log on to the server, and format a server's hard drives. You must install the Recovery Console or run it from the CD-ROM setup. Table 12.3 displays some of the commands you can use at the Recovery Console.

Note: To run the Recovery Console, you must be an administrator.

Table 12.3   Recovery Console commands.

Command	Function
chdsk	Lists the status of the disks.
copy	Copies a file.
delete	Deletes a file.
disable	Disables a service or driver.
enable	Enables a service or driver.
exit	Closes the console and reboots the server.
fixboot	Creates a new boot sector.
fixmbr	Creates a new master boot record.
format	Formats a hard drive.
help	Displays a list of the Recovery Console commands.
listsrv	Displays the drivers and services.
logon	Lets you log on to the system.
type	Displays a text file.

You should be familiar with the Recovery Console and the commands that are associated with it. These topics may be on the exam.

Installing Recovery Console

To install the Recovery Console so that it is available from the Startup menu, follow these steps:

1. At the command prompt, access the Windows 2000 Server CD-ROM and type "\i386\winnt32.exe\cmdcons". Figure 12.13 displays the Recovery Console Setup dialog box.

2. Click Yes. The setup begins and completes without intervention.

3. Reboot the server. Windows 2000 Server Recovery Console is now an option on the Start menu.

To access the Recovery Console when the system reboots, follow these steps:

1. Select the Windows 2000 Server Recovery Console Startup option.

2. Enter the number on the screen that correlates with the operating system you want to recover and press Enter.

3. Type the administrator password and press Enter. After logon, you can execute the Recovery Console commands from the Recovery Console prompt.

Executing Recovery Console from the Setup CD-ROM

If the system fails before you have a chance to install the Recovery Console, follow these steps:

1. Boot the system using the Windows 2000 Server CD-ROM or the four setup floppies.

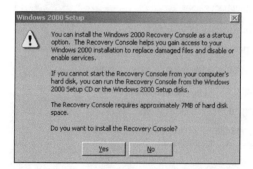

Figure 12.13   The Recovery Console Setup dialog box.

2. During the setup, choose to repair the operating system. Then select Recovery Console as your repair method.

3. Follow the instructions to log on to the Recovery Console.

Emergency Repair Disk (ERD)

An *emergency repair disk* (ERD) contains information about the Windows 2000 Server system settings that helps repair damaged boot sector and system files. Use the ERD only after the Advanced Startup Options and Recovery Console have failed to fix the server's problem. An ERD must be created in advance of a system failure. You should create an ERD when installing the system or when major system changes occur.

Note: An ERD does not hold a copy of the Registry; therefore, you cannot repair the Registry from the floppy.

Creating an ERD

Use the following steps to create an ERD:

1. In the Backup program, select the Tools menu.

2. Select Create An Emergency Repair Disk.

3. Insert a blank floppy into Drive A, select the box to back up the Registry in the repair directory, and then click OK.

4. Click OK when the disk has been created and label it ERD.

The disk now contains these files: an autoexec.nt, a config.nt, and a setup.log. If you checked the box to back up the Registry, the systemroot\repair folder contains additional backup and repair information.

Repairing a Server Using an ERD

Use the following steps to repair a Windows 2000 Server using an ERD:

1. Boot the server with either the Windows 2000 Server CD-ROM or the four setup floppies.

2. During the setup, select R to repair the current Windows 2000 Server. The server requests the Windows 2000 Server CD-ROM, and the repair process begins.

3. When prompted, choose F for Fast Repair or M for Manual Repair.

Note: Only experienced administrators should use the Manual Repair option. It requires indepth knowledge of the operating system.

4. Insert the ERD when the setup program requests it.

5. When the system reboots, the repair process is complete.

6. Remove the ERD from the drive, and store it in a safe location for future use.

 You should know when and how to implement the following items: a restoration of data, the Advanced Startup Options, a Recovery Console, and an ERD.

A Windows 2000 Boot Disk

You can use a boot disk to start a Windows 2000 Server computer that has a corrupt master boot record (MBR), a corrupt boot sector, a missing ntldr file, a missing ntdetect.com, or a failed mirror. To create a boot disk, follow these steps:

1. Format a floppy disk under the Windows 2000 Server operating system.

2. Copy the ntldr, boot.ini, and ntdetect.com files from the boot partition to the floppy.

3. Restart the server using the boot floppy to ensure that it functions properly.

ARC Path Naming Conventions

The *advanced RISC computing* (ARC) naming path is specified in the BOOT.INI file. The path informs the server where the system and boot files are for the Windows 2000 server operating system. Remember the following facts about ARC paths:

➤ multi is used for SCSI, IDE, and EIDE controllers.

➤ scsi is used for SCSI controllers without the SCSI BIOS enabled.

➤ scsi( ) and disk( ) function together, and rdisk( ) is not used.

➤ multi( ) and rdisk( ) function together, and disk( ) is not used.

➤ multi( ), scsi( ), disk( ), and rdisk( ) always start with the number 0 and then 1, 2, 3. The 0 signifies the first controller or disk in the series, 1 the second controller or disk in the series, and so on.

➤ partition( ) always start with the number 1 and then 2, 3, 4. Partition 1 being the first partition, partition 2 being the second, and so on.

Understanding and being able to edit an ARC path should be fully understood by anyone taking the exam. Two common ARC paths are as follows:

multi(0)disk(0)rdisk(0)partition(1) or scsi(0)disk(0)rdisk(0)partition(1)

The first path signifies the first partition on the first disk on the first controller. The second path signifies the first partition on the first disk on the first controller that does not have the SCSI BIOS enabled. Remember the following information about ARC paths:

➤ multi(0) signifies the first controller, multi(1) signifies the second controller, and so on.

➤ scsi(0) signifies the first controller without the SCSI BIOS enabled, scsi(1) signifies the second controller without the SCSI BIOS enabled, and so on.

➤ rdisk(0) signifies the first disk on the controller, rdisk(1) signifies the second disk on the controller, and so on.

➤ disk(0) signifies the first disk on the controller without the SCSI BIOS enabled, disk(1) signifies the second disk on the controller, and so on.

➤ partition(1) signifies the first partition on the disk or rdisk, partition(2) signifies the second partition on the disk or rdisk, and so on.

You should understand the ARC naming conventions. If given an ARC path, you should be able to select the disk to which the path is referring. You should also be able to edit the ARC path for a boot disk to start Windows 2000 Server on the working disk in a failed mirror.

Practice Questions

Question 1

Which users are allowed to back up a Windows 2000 Server operating system? [Check all correct answers]

❑ a. Administrators
❑ b. Account operators
❑ c. Server operators
❑ d. Backup operators
❑ e. Users

Answers a and d are correct. Answer b is incorrect because account operators administer users and groups; they do not back up the operating system. Answer c is incorrect because server operators maintain servers for a domain. Answer e is incorrect because the users do not have authority to back up a Windows 2000 Server, although they can back up files and folders that they own.

Question 2

Which key is used to access the Windows 2000 Server Advanced Startup Options menu on startup?

○ a. F2
○ b. F5
○ c. F8
○ d. The ESC key
○ e. The Windows key

Answer c is correct. Answers a, b, d, and e are all incorrect because the only way to access the Advanced Options menu on startup is the F8 function key.

Question 3

> Which program do you use to make an ERD?
>
> ○ a. The Advanced Startup Options menu
> ○ b. The Backup program
> ○ c. Typing "ERD" at the command prompt
> ○ d. Typing "EDR" at the command prompt
> ○ e. The **makeboot** command

Answer b is correct. Answer a is incorrect because the Advanced Startup Options menu is used for troubleshooting and repairing a Windows 2000 Server. Answers c and d are incorrect because there are no programs accessible from the command prompt called ERD or EDR. Answer e is incorrect because the **makeboot** command is used to make the four setup floppies used for installation.

Question 4

> Which installation is executed to start the Recovery Console command?
>
> ○ a. **winnt /cmdcons**
> ○ b. **winnt32 /cmdcons**
> ○ c. **winnt /conscmd**
> ○ d. **winnt32 /conscmd**
> ○ e. **rconsole**
> ○ f. **recoverc**

Answer b is correct. Answer a is incorrect because the **winnt** command is used on 16-bit operating systems. Answers c and d are incorrect because /**conscmd** is not a valid switch. Answers e and f are incorrect because these commands do not exist.

Question 5

> Who can execute and run commands in the Recovery Console? [Check all correct answers]
>
> ❏ a. Administrators
> ❏ b. Anyone with full control over the systemroot
> ❏ c. Backup operators
> ❏ d. Everyone
> ❏ e. Server operators
> ❏ f. Users

Answer a is correct. Answers b, c, d, e, and f are incorrect because only the administrators can execute and run commands in the Recovery Console.

Question 6

> You have implemented the following backup schedule. How many tapes are used to restore the operating system if it needs to be restored on Friday?
>
> | Day of Backup | Type of Backup |
> | --- | --- |
> | Saturday | Normal |
> | Monday | Incremental |
> | Tuesday | Incremental |
> | Wednesday | Incremental |
> | Thursday | Differential |
> | Friday | Differential |
>
> ○ a. 2
> ○ b. 3
> ○ c. 4
> ○ d. 5
> ○ e. 6

Answer d is correct: normal backup (1), incremental Monday (2), incremental Tuesday (3), incremental Wednesday (4), and differential Friday (5). Incremental backups back up the files that have changed since the last normal or incremental backup, and they mark the files as being backed up. Differential backups back up the files that have changed since the last normal or incremental backup, and they do not mark the files as being backed up (that is why you do not need to restore differential Thursday).

Question 7

Where is the Backup program for Windows 2000 Server located?

○ a. In Control Panel|Backup

○ b. In Control Panel|System|Backup

○ c. Under Accessories|Backup

○ d. Under Accessories|System Tools|Backup

○ e. Under Administrative Tools|Backup

Answer d is correct. The Backup program is located under the Accessories|System Tools option. Answers a, b, c, and e are incorrect default locations of the backup program.

Question 8

You have implemented the following backup schedule. How many tapes are used to restore the operating system if it crashes on Friday?

Day of Backup	Type of Backup
Saturday	Normal
Monday	Differential
Tuesday	Differential
Wednesday	Differential
Thursday	Differential
Friday	Differential

○ a. 2

○ b. 3

○ c. 4

○ d. 5

○ e. 6

Answer a is correct: Saturday normal (1) and the Friday differential (2). The differential backs up the files that were not backed up since the last normal or incremental backup, and they do not mark the files as being backed up. Therefore, you would need the normal backup and the last differential that you have.

Question 9

> Which types of media does Windows 2000 Server Backup support? [Check all correct answers]
>
> ❑ a. CD-ROMs
> ❑ b. Floppies
> ❑ c. Hard drives
> ❑ d. Removable disks
> ❑ e. Tape drives

Answers a, b, c, d, and e are correct. Windows 2000 Server Backup supports CD-ROMs, floppies, hard drives, removable disks, and tape drives.

Question 10

> Which of the following components make up the System State data for a Windows 2000 Server? [Check all correct answers]
>
> ❑ a. Catastrophic database file
> ❑ b. Component Services Class Registration database
> ❑ c. Registry
> ❑ d. System log files
> ❑ e. System Startup files

Answers b, c, and e are correct. Answer a in incorrect because a catastrophic database file does not exist. Answer d is incorrect because the System State data does not include system log files.

Question 11

Match the type of backup with its definition.

Type of Backup:

> Copy
>
> Daily
>
> Differential
>
> Incremental
>
> Normal

Definition:

> Backs up files that have been changed that day, and does not mark them as backed up.
>
> Backs up files that have changed since the last normal or incremental backup, and marks them as backed up.
>
> Backs up files that have changed since the last normal or incremental backup, and does not mark them as backed up.
>
> Backs up specified files, and does not mark them as backed up.
>
> Backs up specified files, and marks them as backed up.

Answer:

> Copy—Backs up specified files, and does not mark them as backed up.
>
> Daily—Backs up files that have been changed that day, and does not mark them as backed up.
>
> Differential—Backs up files that have changed since the last normal or incremental backup, and does not mark them as backed up.
>
> Incremental—Backs up files that have changed since the last normal or incremental backup, and marks them as backed up.
>
> Normal—Backs up specified files, and marks them as backed up.

Need to Know More?

Russel, Charlie, and Sharon Crawford: *Microsoft Windows 2000 Server Administrator's Companion*. Microsoft Press, Redmond, Washington, 2000. ISBN 1-57231-819-8. To learn more about implementing a backup plan, backing up a Windows 2000 Server, and repairing Windows 2000, refer to Chapters 33, 34, and 37.

Search TechNet on the Internet at **www.microsoft.com/technet/default.asp** or TechNet CD for information on: backup, restore, ERD, Recovery Console, class registration, backup and domain controllers, authoritative restore, advanced startup options.

For more information on the following terminology and implementation of that terminology, refer to Microsoft Windows 2000 Help. To access this resource, select Start and then choose Help. Terms and technologies to search for include: emergency repair disks, emergency repair disks creating, emergency repair disks for system repair, backup domain controllers, backup media, backup operators, Recovery Console overview, Recovery Console commands, Safe Mode, Startup services, Startup menu.

For more information on Microsoft white papers on backup and recovery access, go to **www.microsoft.com/ISN/whitepapers.asp**.

Troubleshooting
Windows 2000

· ·

Terms you'll need to understand:

✓ System Monitor

✓ Network Monitor

✓ Event Viewer

✓ Task Manager

✓ Regedit and Regedt32

✓ Disk Defragmenter

✓ Disk Cleanup

✓ Resource Kit

✓ TechNet

✓ Hardware Compatibility List (HCL)

✓ **winnt** and **winnt32** command switches

✓ Advanced Startup Options

✓ Recovery Console

✓ Emergency repair disk (ERD)

Techniques you'll need to master:

✓ Troubleshooting and repairing a Windows 2000 installation

✓ Troubleshooting and repairing a Windows 2000 Server that does not boot

✓ Troubleshooting and repairing network devices, drivers, and network services

✓ Using Windows 2000 tools to troubleshoot a Windows 2000 Server

✓ Reallocating resources to avoid operating system congestion and slowness

This chapter addresses troubleshooting Windows 2000 Server. Part of the exam may assume that you can successfully troubleshoot, repair, and optimize a Windows 2000 Server in a large multiple domain environment. This chapter reviews the tools that are available to an administrator to detect and repair problems. Mastering the topics in this chapter can help you be successful on the troubleshooting portion of the exam.

Installation Troubleshooting

The first problem you may encounter with Windows 2000 Server is trouble installing the operating system. The four ways to install Windows 2000 Server are addressed in Chapter 3; refer to it for more in-depth repair solutions. If problems do occur during installation of Windows 2000, check the following list of items to help you troubleshoot:

➤ Check the Hardware Compatibility List (HCL) to verify that your computer hardware is compliant.

➤ Use the **winnt** and its switches to upgrade 16-bit operating systems.

➤ Use the **winnt32** and its switches to upgrade 32-bit operating systems.

➤ Use the Windows 2000 CD-ROM or the four setup floppies to install a new copy of Windows 2000.

➤ Use the F6 key to install a manufacture's hardware abstraction layer (HAL).

➤ Verify that there is enough drive space to install Windows 2000 Server.

➤ Use a distribution server if the CD-ROM drive is not accessible.

Boot Process Troubleshooting

Use the following tools to help troubleshoot and repair a Windows 2000 Server that fails to boot:

➤ Use the Windows 2000 CD-ROM to boot into the Windows 2000 Setup program, and then use Setup to start a repair process.

➤ Use the four setup floppies to boot into the Windows 2000 Server Setup program for a computer that does not support a bootable CD-ROM. You can use Setup to start a repair process.

➤ Use the Advanced Startup Options to boot the server into Safe Mode, Safe Mode With Networking, Last Known Good Configuration, Directory Service Restore, Enabled VGA Mode, or Enabled Boot Logging.

➤ Use the Recovery Console, which is a command-line utility that can copy files, start and stop services, repair a master boot record (MBR), and format hard drives.

➤ Use the emergency repair disk (ERD) in conjunction with the Setup program to repair damaged system settings.

➤ Use a Windows 2000 boot disk to boot a Windows 2000 Server that has a corrupt MBR, a corrupt boot sector, a missing ntldr, a missing ntdetect.com, or a failed mirror.

Hardware Troubleshooting

Troubleshooting hardware can be a difficult task because multiple problems can occur, and you have many ways to repair the problems. A person taking the exam should be familiar with troubleshooting and repairing Windows 2000 Server hardware problems.

When troubleshooting any hardware problem, check the HCL for compatibility and Device Manager for interrupt request (IRQ) or memory conflicts. Use the Add/Remove Hardware Wizard whenever possible to add new hardware, or use the manufacturer's setup program as a secondary method. Chapter 4 addresses most of these hardware issues in depth, including IRQ default settings and updating driver information. The following sections briefly cover different kinds of hardware problems and repairs.

HAL Troubleshooting

Installing a new hardware abstraction layer (HAL) can be completed at setup by selecting F6 to install third party HAL drivers. If you update a HAL after installation, and a conflict exists, try the following methods to fix it:

➤ Use the Windows 2000 CD-ROM to boot, select R to Repair, choose to perform a Manual repair, and select F to run all repair options. On startup, choose F8 and select the Last Known Good Configuration.

➤ Use the Windows 2000 CD-ROM to boot, select R to Repair, choose C for the Recovery Console, and then copy and rename HAL files to the winnt\system32 directory.

NIC Troubleshooting

If you are troubleshooting a network interface card (NIC), do not forget to check the following items:

➤ Make sure that there is not a duplicate IP address, MAC address, or computer name.

➤ Make sure that the correct drivers were added or updated.

➤ Diagnostics and resource conflicts have been checked in Device Manager.

➤ Make sure that a DHCP server available if using DHCP.

➤ If you are using TCP/IP, verify TCP/IP settings and communication using **ipconfig** and **ping**.

➤ If you are using NWLink, verify that the correct frame type, network number, and internal network number are being used by the NWLink protocol·

Modem Troubleshooting

If you are troubleshooting a modem, do not forget to check the following items:

➤ Use the Device Manager to run the diagnostics and verify that no resource conflicts exists.

➤ Make sure that the correct drivers are loaded and updated.

➤ Activate the Query Modem button in the Modem Properties dialog box by selecting Control Panel|Phone And Modem Options to check the modem hardware.

➤ Verify that the phone line, Routing And Remote Access Service (RRAS), or Internet Service Provider (ISP) settings are correct and responding to the modem commands.

Updating Drivers Troubleshooting

If driver problems occur or an older driver needs to be updated, use the Update Driver button in Device Manager to update the driver. If an incorrect driver is loaded and Device Manager cannot be accessed, try to access the Last Known Good Configuration. The next recovery step is to boot the server using the Windows 2000 CD-ROM and select the Repair option.

Network Services Troubleshooting

Troubleshooting network services can be a tedious task for any administrator because complex problems can arise in large networking environments. The following section briefly addresses some network services troubleshooting. A person taking the exam should be familiar with these services and be able to troubleshoot them in a large environment.

CSNW and GSNW Troubleshooting

Client Services For NetWare (CSNW) and Gateway Services For NetWare (GSNW) troubleshooting require Windows 2000 and NetWare experience. If CSNW or GSNW are not functioning properly, check the following items:

➤ Verify that the correct password and account information is being supplied.

➤ Verify that the correct frame type, network number, and internal network number are being used by the NWLink protocol.

➤ Check the default tree and context settings. They should be the same as the available NetWare servers.

➤ Use the command **net view /network:nw** to view the available NetWare servers.

DHCP Troubleshooting

To troubleshoot Dynamic Host Configuration Protocol (DHCP) check the following items:

➤ Verify that the DHCP servers have IP addresses available in their scopes and that Automatic Private IP Addressing (APIPA) has not been initiated on the client.

➤ Ensure that the scope is activated and that the DHCP Server Service is started.

➤ If the DHCP traffic is crossing a router, verify that the router supports DHCP/BOOTP. If DHCP/BOOTP is not supported, you must configure a DHCP Relay Agent.

DNS Troubleshooting

Two or more servers usually provide Domain Name System (DNS) services in a large environment. Communication between the servers is important for transferring computer and IP information. Refer to Chapter 5 for more details on DNS. Check the following items when troubleshooting a DNS service environment:

➤ When using DNS, other than Windows 2000 DNS, verify that Service Resource Records (SRVs) are supported.

➤ Verify that full and incremental zone transfers are replicating information to designated DNS servers.

➤ Check the configuration of the Primary Zone, Secondary Zones, and Active Directory Zones.

➤ Ensure that the DNS service is always available by using Active Directory Integrated Zones.

Network service troubleshooting may appear on the exam. You should be familiar with the network services and how they function in a large Windows 2000 environment.

Troubleshooting Tools

An administrator can use a variety of tools to monitor and troubleshoot Windows 2000 Server. The following sections briefly define these tools and their capabilities to help you repair problems. A person taking the exam should be familiar with all of these tools.

System Monitor

System Monitor monitors local or remote system resources. Figure 13.1 displays the System Monitor tool, and Chapter 4 takes a more in-depth look its capabilities.

 System Monitor counters and process monitoring may appear on the exam. You should be familiar with the available counters and how to use them to monitor Windows 2000 Server. You should be able to monitor processors, disks, disk resources, memory, and individual processes.

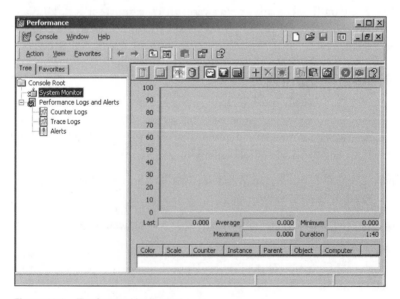

Figure 13.1 The System Monitor tool.

Network Monitor

Network Monitor is used to view network statistics and packet information. It enables you to isolate and troubleshoot network traffic problems. Use the Add/Remove Programs icon in the Control Panel to install Network Monitor. Figure 13.2 displays the Network Monitor interface.

Event Viewer

Event Viewer enables you to access log files that are being compiled by the server. The three default logs are application, system, and security. Event Viewer lists the severity and a brief description of the logged event. You can use other tools in conjunction with Event Viewer to track and fix problems with Windows 2000 Server. Chapter 4 presents a more in-depth view of Event Viewer.

Managing Processes

Process management can be controlled using Task Manager or command-line utilities. It is important to manage processes because if you are working on a Windows 2000 Server that is being used by clients, your actions can slow the client's processes. Use the following tools to run processes at different priorities to manage resources on the server.

Task Manager

You can access Task Manager by right-clicking on the taskbar and selecting Task Manager. It can be used to start and stop applications, check the memory usage, check the CPU usage, and to manage processes. Changing a process's priority can help clients who are trying to access other server resources. Figure 13.3 displays the

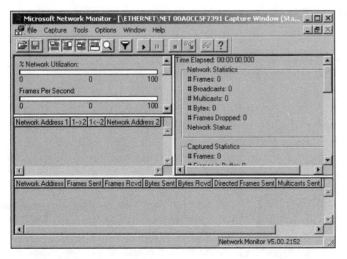

Figure 13.2   The Network Monitor.

Figure 13.3   Task Manager screen.

Task Manager Processes screen with the priority options, and Chapter 4 discusses Task Manager in more depth. You also can use Task Manager to assign different processes to different CPUs.

 You should know the different process priorities and how to configure them because this topic may be on the exam. Refer to Figure 13.3 for a list of Task Manager priorities. Process priorities can also be configured from command-line utilities.

Command-Line Utilities
You can use command-line utilities to monitor and control a Windows 2000 Server. To access a command prompt, select Start|Run, and type "cmd.exe". Table 13.1 lists some helpful command-line utilities.

Backup
Use the Backup utility to back up and restore Windows 2000 Server. You also can use this utility to make an ERD. Refer to Chapter 12 for more information on Windows 2000 Backup and Recovery.

Regedit and Regedt32
Use Regedit and Regedt32 to edit the Windows 2000 Registry. Only experienced administrator should edit the Registry because incorrectly editing the Registry can cause system wide problems including system failure. Type "regedit.exe"

Table 13.1   Command-line utilities.

Command	Function
arp	Monitors and changes the address translation tables
at	Schedules programs to run at a specified time
cipher	Encrypts and decrypts files
compact	Compresses and decompresses files and folders
convert	Changes a FAT or FAT32 volume to NTFS volume
diskperf	Starts disk counters for System Monitor
ipconfig	Enables viewing of system TCP/IP information
nbtstat	Enables viewing of NetBIOS over TCP/IP statistics
net start	Starts Windows 2000 services
net use	Maps or unmaps network drives
print	Prints files from the command prompt
start	Runs a specified program. It can be used with **/low** and **/high** to set process priority
tracert	Used to view packet routes
xcopy	Copies files, directories, and subdirectories

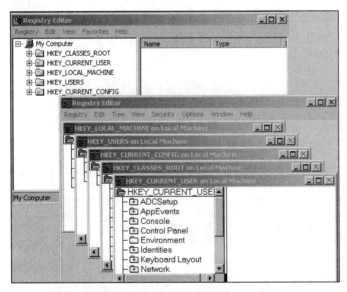

Figure 13.4   The Regedit and Regedt32 interfaces.

(the 16-bit version) or "regedt32.exe" (the 32-bit version) to run a Registry editor. Remember that Microsoft does not support editing the Registry. Figure 13.4 displays the two Registry editors.

Disk Utilities

The two main tools used to troubleshoot and prevent problems with hard drives are the Disk Defragmenter and the Disk Cleanup utility.

Disk Defragmenter

The Disk Defragmenter is located under the System Tools menu. Use this tool to arrange files, programs, and free space on a hard drive. It enables you to organize the hard drive to increase program and file access speed. If programs are slow or users are noticing an increased access time for files, it is a good idea to run the Disk Defragmenter. Figure 13.5 displays the Disk Defragmenter program.

Disk Cleanup Utilty

The Disk Cleanup utility is located under the System Tools menu. This utility scans a selected hard drive, reports how much disk space it can free up, and then prompts for input on files to delete. Figure 13.6 displays the Disk Cleanup utility after it has scanned a hard drive.

Resource Kit

Microsoft's *Windows 2000 Server Resource Kit* is a highly recommended product for any administrator. The kit is an add-on product that must be purchased. This kit provides additional Windows 2000 tools to improve troubleshooting your server. It also supplies documentation and software to help you support your Windows 2000 Server.

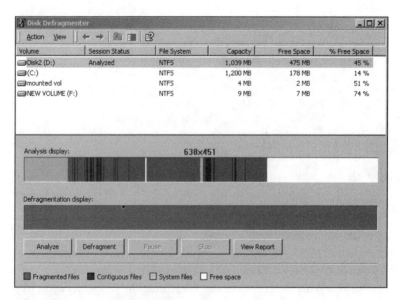

Figure 13.5   The Disk Defragmenter.

Figure 13.6   Disk Cleanup utility.

TechNet

Microsoft's TechNet provides up to date information about all Microsoft products. You can subscribe to TechNet or access it on Microsoft's Web site. If you subscribe, your paid yearly subscription includes a monthly set of CD-ROMs with Knowledge Base, Technical Information, Service Packs, software, beta software, and other useful Microsoft tools. If you access the free Microsoft's Web site at **www.microsoft.com/technet/default.asp**, you receive the Knowledge Base, Technical Information, Service Packs, and other useful information.

Practice Questions

Question 1

> You are installing Windows 2000 Server on a new computer. A new 12GB hard drive has been added that has a manufacturer's HAL. How should you install the new HAL?
>
> ○ a. Press F6 during setup to access the HAL configuration screen
>
> ○ b. Press F8 during setup to access the HAL configuration screen
>
> ○ c. After the setup has completed, run the Add/Remove Software program
>
> ○ d. After the setup has completed, run the Add/Remove HAL program

Answer a is correct. Use the F6 key to install a manufacturer's HAL during the setup process. Answer b is incorrect because F8 is used to access the Advanced Startup Options screen during normal startup; it is not used during the setup and installation of Windows 2000. Answer c is incorrect because the Add/Remove Software program is for adding new programs and applications to the Windows 2000 Server. Answer d is incorrect because there is no program called Add/Remove HAL.

Question 2

> The advanced RISC computing (ARC) path for a mirror that has failed is multi(0)disk(0)rdisk(1)partition(1). Which hard drive needs to be replaced?
>
> ○ a. The first hard drive on the first controller
>
> ○ b. The first hard drive on the second controller
>
> ○ c. The second hard drive on the first controller
>
> ○ d. The second hard drive on the second controller

Answer c is correct. Answers b, c, and d are incorrect because multi(0) signifies the first controller, disk(0) is reserved for scsi(0), rdisk(1) signifies the second disk. Therefore, the failed mirror was on the second disk of the first controller.

Question 3

> Which command do you use to start Word on a server so it does not inter-
> fere with users accessing to the server?
>
> ○ a. **start word.exe /low**
>
> ○ b. **start word.exe /high**
>
> ○ c. **start word.exe /normal**
>
> ○ d. **start csrss.exe /low**
>
> ○ e. **start csrss.exe /high**
>
> ○ f. **start csrss.exe /normal**

Answer a is correct. Answers b is incorrect because starting a process at a high
setting gives it a higher priority to the processor. Answer c is incorrect because
starting a process at Normal has the potential to interfere with users, whereas
starting a process at a low setting does not. Answers d, e, and f are incorrect
because the csrss.exe process is a client server runtime subsystem that is continually running on Windows 2000 Server.

Question 4

> Which product is the best to purchase to provide your Windows 2000 Server
> with additional programs and documentation?
>
> ○ a. Event Viewer
>
> ○ b. The Regedt32
>
> ○ c. The Resource Kit
>
> ○ d. TechWin

Answer c is correct. Answer a is incorrect because Event Viewer is a program that
is installed with Windows 2000. Answer b is incorrect because the Registry editor is also a program that comes installed with Windows 2000. Answer d is
incorrect because TechWin is not a real product.

Question 5

> Which program do you use to free up disk space on a Windows 2000 Server?
>
> ○ a. Disk Cleanup
>
> ○ b. Disk Defragmenter
>
> ○ c. Disk Destroyer
>
> ○ d. Disk Doctor

Answer a is correct. Answer b is incorrect because Disk Defragmenter is used to arrange files, programs, and free space on a hard drive. Answers c and d are incorrect because these programs do not exist.

Question 6

> A new server has been configured and added to the network. It is mainly used as an application server. After a few months, users complain that the server does not seem to be as fast as it was. What can you do?
>
> ○ a. Run the Disk Cleanup utility
>
> ○ b. Run the Disk Defragmenter utility
>
> ○ c. Reboot the server once a day
>
> ○ d. Nothing; this tends to happen with servers

Answer b is correct. Answer a is incorrect because the Disk Cleanup utility helps an administrator delete files from the hard drive to free up space. Answer c is incorrect because Windows 2000 should not have to be rebooted every day. Answer d is incorrect because more than likely your hard drive is becoming defragmented.

Question 7

A new server had been configured as a file and print server. After a few months you are using the server to graph a spreadsheet on printer statistics. Users complain that printing time has become unacceptably slow. What should you do?

○ a. Add a new server

○ b. Add an additional spreadsheet

○ c. Set the excel.exe process to Normal

○ d. Set the excel.exe process to Low

○ e. Reboot the server, and take it offline

Answer d is correct. Answer a is incorrect because you are using the server and taking up processing time; therefore, adding a new server will not fix the problem. Answer b is incorrect because running an additional spreadsheet does not fix the problem of slow printing. Answer c is incorrect because when you start Excel, it automatically runs at normal. Answer e is incorrect because rebooting the server and taking it offline prevents users from printing.

Question 8

Which is the best program to use to troubleshoot TCP/IP traffic?

○ a. Network Monitor

○ b. System Monitor

○ c. TCP/IP Monitor

○ d. tracert

Answer a is correct. Answer b is incorrect because System Monitor can be used to track TCP/IP traffic; it does not have the functions that Network Monitor provides. Answer c is incorrect because there no program called TCP/IP Monitor. Answer d is incorrect because tracert is used to trace packets, but it does not provide individual packet information like Network Monitor.

Need to Know More?

 Russel, Charlie, and Sharon Crawford: *Microsoft Windows 2000 Server Administrator's Companion*. Microsoft Press, Redmond, Washington, 2000. ISBN 1-57231-819-8. This book covers troubleshooting skills in most of the chapters.

  Search TechNet on the Internet at **www.microsoft.com/technet/default.asp** or TechNet CD for information on: troubleshooting boot processes, troubleshooting installation, troubleshooting DNS, troubleshooting DHCP, troubleshooting protocols, troubleshooting hardware, Task Manager, Event Viewer, TechNet, and Windows 2000 Server Resource Kit.

 For more information on the following terminology and implementation of that terminology refer to Microsoft Windows 2000 Help. To access this resource, select Start|Help. Terms and technologies to search for include: TechNet, Windows 2000 Server Resource Kit, Hardware Compatibility List, boot process troubleshooting, installation troubleshooting, troubleshooting DNS servers, command-line utilities, troubleshooting process, troubleshooting DHCP, troubleshooting TCP/IP, and troubleshooting modems.

For Microsoft white papers on backup and recovery access, go to **www.microsoft.com/ISN/whitepapers.asp**.

Sample Test

Question 1

A Windows 2000 Server has a mirrored set on Disk0 and Disk1. Disk1 fails, and a disk from another server's volume is added to repair the mirror. What should the administrator do to fix the mirrored set? [Check all correct answers]

- ☐ a. Format the other server's hard drive and revert to a basic disk
- ☐ b. Format the other server's hard drive and revert to a dynamic disk
- ☐ c. Format the other server's hard drive
- ☐ d. Repair Volume and Resynchronize Mirror
- ☐ e. Repair Set and Resynchronize Mirror

Question 2

The current network configuration includes 1,000 Windows Professional computers, 50 Windows NT Workstation computers, and 40 Windows 2000 servers in native mode. There are 10 DHCP servers, 2 IIS servers, 4 Terminal servers, 4 DNS servers on the network, and 2 RRAS servers. You are assigned to make sure that all the clients can access DNS resources at all times. What should you do?

- ○ a. Enable DHCP/BOOTP
- ○ b. Enable Active Directory Integrated Zones for DNS
- ○ c. Enable Incremental Zones for DNS
- ○ d. Enable RIP

Question 3

You are working on a server that has a striped volume with parity on dynamic disks. One of the four disks in the volume fails. What recovery options can you employ? [Check all correct answers]

❑ a. Reactivate the disk and repair

❑ b. Repair the volume

❑ c. Recover from a backup

❑ d. Replace the failed disk and Disk Management will recreate the volume

Question 4

Place a check in Figure 14.1 over the area that would enable clients to view Web files as a list for the Default Web Site.

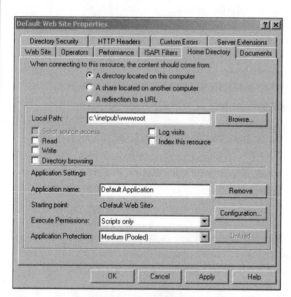

Figure 14.1   Default Web site properties.

Question 5

You have just purchased 10 new computers, with only DOS, that require Windows 2000 Servers. Which options can be used to install Windows 2000 Server? [Check all correct answers]

❏ a. Add the individual computer information to the UDF

❏ b. Add the individual computer information to the unattended.txt file

❏ c. Make a boot disk

Link to a distribution server

Run **winnt32 /u /udf**

❏ d. Make a boot disk

Link to a distribution server

Run **winnt /u /udf**

Question 6

On a Windows 2000 Server you have just installed an updated HAL for your hard drive. When you reboot the server you get a startup error and are unable to boot the server. Which options can you use to repair the server? [Check the two best answers]

❏ a. Boot to the Windows 2000 CD-ROM

Go into the Recovery Console, and copy the old HAL files to the drivers folder

Reboot the machine

❏ b. Boot to the Windows 2000 CD-ROM

Go into the Recovery Console, and select Safe Mode

Reboot the machine

❏ c. Boot the machine and press F8 to access the Last Known Good Configuration

❏ d. Boot the machine and press F9 to access the Last Known Good Configuration

Question 7

In Figure 14.2 put a check in the box that enables authentication to occur without passwords being sent over the network.

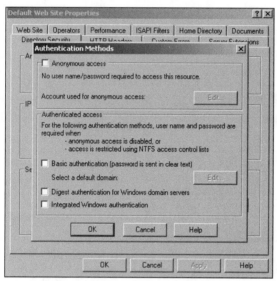

Figure 14.2 Authentication methods.

Question 8

After the new company takes over your department, you are required to copy all of the annual reports to a new location. You are assigned to copy all of the annual report information from the E:\projects folder, that has Full Control security permissions for everyone, to the Q:\projectsnew, that has Read security permissions for the Administrators group. What permissions will the annual reports have?

- ○ a. Full Control - Everyone
- ○ b. Full Control - Administrators
- ○ c. Read - Everyone
- ○ d. Read - Administrators

Question 9

A network contains 100 Windows Professional computers, 40 Windows 95 computers, 5 computers in native mode, and 3 Windows 2000 Servers. In Active Directory, an administrator deleted an OU from the onedomain computer that contained all of the users for the Management group. Which option do you use to recover the OU?

○ a. Reboot the computer into Safe Mode

Restore from a backup

Reboot the computer

○ b Reboot the computer into Safe Mode With Networking

Restore from a backup

Reboot the computer

○ c. Reboot the computer into Directory Service Restore Mode

Restore from a backup

Reboot the computer

○ d. Reboot the computer into Directory Service Restore Mode

Restore from a backup

Run **ntdsutil** and reboot the computer

Question 10

A server has been upgraded from NT 4.0 to Windows 2000. The striped set that is on the server fails. What should you do to recover the striped set?

○ a. Revert to basic disks and choose to regenerate

○ b. Revert to dynamic disks and choose to regenerate

○ c. Upgrade to basic disks and recover from a backup

○ d. Upgrade to dynamic disks and recover from a backup

Question 11

Clients access a SQL database on an application server over the network, and you use Word on the local machine in the mornings. After six months the clients start to complain that the server is unacceptably slow between 10 A.M. and 11 A.M. What can you do on the local machine to alleviate the problem?

○ a. Start SQL with a priority of Normal

○ b. Start SQL with a priority of Low

○ c. Start Word with a priority of Normal

○ d. Start Word with a priority of Low

Question 12

You are assigned to install Windows 2000 on 10 servers using the **winnt.exe** command. An answer file and a definition file need to be assigned. Which switches should you use?

○ a. **winnt /u /definition**

○ b. **winnt /u /udf**

○ c. **winnt /unattend /definition**

○ d. **winnt /unattend /udf**

Question 13

You maintain a Windows 2000 Server that has the boot partition mirrored. The second disk on your server fails, and the server will no longer boot. How do you edit the ARC path on the boot floppy if the good half of the mirror is on the first partition of the fourth disk?

○ a. multi(0)disk(0)rdisk(2)partition(0)

○ b. multi(0)disk(0)rdisk(2)partition(1)

○ c. multi(0)disk(0)rdisk(3)partition(0)

○ d. multi(0)disk(0)rdisk(3)partition(1)

○ e. multi(0)disk(0)rdisk(4)partition(0)

○ f. multi(0)disk(0)rdisk(4)partition(1)

Question 14

You successfully configured a Windows 2000 Server with the following items: a keyboard, a mouse, a COM1 printer, a sound card, a NIC, a primary SCSI controller, and a secondary SCSI controller. After a few months your boss suggests that another NIC needs to be added to handle all of the network traffic. You try to install the NIC, but are unsuccessful. The first NIC is working on IRQ 13. What IRQ should you be trying to use for the second NIC?

○ a. IRQ 8

○ b. IRQ 9

○ c. IRQ 10

○ d. IRQ 11

Question 15

Your boss assigns you to manually install a new Windows 2000 Server for the network. Before the server arrives for configuration, your boss purchases a mass storage device that she wants to add to the new system. The new device has a custom HAL that must be installed for the device to work. What is the fastest way to set up and configure the new server? [Check the two best answers]

❑ a. Run the Setup Wizard

❑ b. Run the Setup Manager

❑ c. Install the HAL during setup

❑ d. Install the HAL using the Add/Remove Hardware Wizard

Question 16

The D: drive on the new server has been reserved for storing company documents. There are two groups configured with quota entries: Designers and Managers. The company currently has over 80 Designers that should be limited to 45MB of storage; whereas, the 5 Managers should be able to store at least 100MB each. What should you do to set up this configuration? [Check all correct answers]

❑ a. Enable Quota Management

❑ b. Enable Disk Management

❑ c. Set the default Limit Disk Space to 45MB

❑ d. Set the default Limit Disk Space to 100MB

❑ e. Change the Managers quota to 45MB

❑ f. Change the Managers quota to 100MB

Question 17

Every year the administrators try to clean up the servers by moving and copying files to their correct location. You have moved the account folder and copied the sales folder and the marketing folder to different locations on the same hard drive to fulfill your cleanup responsibility. Only the account folder and all of its files are compressed. What can you assume happened during the cleanup? [Check all correct answers]

❑ a. The account folder was compressed in its original location.

❑ b. The account folder was not compressed in its original location.

❑ c. The drive is compressed.

❑ d. The drive is not compressed.

Question 18

You are working on a Windows 2000 Server that has a failed mirrored volume. What are the two most likely ways to recover from this failure? [Check the two best answers]

❑ a. Recover the mirror from a backup

❑ b. Remove the mirror, replace the disk, and reestablish the mirror

❑ c. Try to reactivate the mirror

❑ d. Try to reinitiate the mirror

Question 19

A user is having problems accessing the System icon in Control Panel. After investigating, you find that the user has a local policy, an NT policy, a domain policy, and a site policy. Which policy is the last to be implemented?

○ a. The domain policy

○ b. The local policy

○ c. The NT policy

○ d. The site policy

Question 20

You are rebooting a Windows 2000 Server, and you receive the following message.

```
Missing NTLDR. Insert disk and press Enter.
```

Which is the best option to employ next?

○ a. Press Enter to boot the server

○ b. Select NTLDR option and boot the server

○ c. Put the NTLDR on a disk and boot the server

○ d. Boot the server with a boot disk

Question 21

You have set up IIS 5.0 on your Windows 2000 Server. Now you want to manage printers using the Web. Which Web address do you type in a Web browser?

○ a. **http://servername/printers**

○ b. **http://domainname/printers**

○ c. **http://servername/printers.print**

○ d. **http://domainname/printers.print**

Question 22

Zoe is a member of the Marketing and Sales groups. What are her security permissions?

Group	Security Permissions	Allow	Deny
Marketing	Read	X	
Custom	Full Control		X
Sales	Write	X	
Customers	Read		X

○ a. Read

○ b. Write

○ c. Read and Write

○ d. Full Control

○ e. No Access

Question 23

What does Software Installation And Maintenance use to globally distribute Windows Installer packages? [Check all correct answers]

❑ a. An .ism package

❑ b. An .msi package

❑ c. An .smi package

❑ d. A Global Catalog Server

❑ e. A GPO

❑ f. A RIS

Question 24

You are assigned to automate processes on a Windows 2000 Server. You are writing programs that will start processes at different priorities during the day. Which line do you insert to make the Access program that does calculations, usually taking all day, to finish faster while still going about regular server maintenance?

○ a. start access.exe /low

○ b. start access.exe /normal

○ c. start access.exe /high

○ d. start access.exe /realtime

Question 25

You just installed a new video driver and rebooted the server. When the logon screen appears, you cannot read the screen. What should you do?

○ a. Log on by memory and access the Display icon

○ b. Log on by memory and access the Registry

○ c. Restart the server and go into Last Known Good Configuration

○ d. Restart the server and go into Safe Mode

Question 26

Which program should be used to remotely install Windows 2000 Professional on 200 computers with Word, Excel, and PowerPoint preconfigured?

○ a. Remote Installation Services

○ b. Setup Manager

○ c. Setup Wizard

○ d. Software Installation And Maintenance

Question 27

You are instructing a user on how to access the printers on the server "webo" for the domain **weboramaprint.com**. The share name for the printers is "webos" and the users need to access the printers using a URL. Which address should they access?

- ○ a. **http://webo/printers/webos.print**
- ○ b. **http://webo/printers/webos/print**
- ○ c. **http://weboramaprint.com/printers/webos.print**
- ○ d. **http://weboramaprint.com/printers/webos/print**

Question 28

Jennifer needs to access the Sales2 folder. Which group can she be a member of and only get access to the Sales2 folder?

Folder	Group Membership
Sales	Sales1, Sales3, Sales4
Sales2	Sales, Sales3, Sales4
Accounting	Account1, Account2
Accounts	Account2, Account3

- ○ a. Sales
- ○ b. Sales1
- ○ c. Sales2
- ○ d. Sales3
- ○ e. Sales4

Question 29

You are working on a server that has a striped volume on dynamic disks. One of the four disks in the volume fails. What recovery options can you employ?

- ○ a. Reactivate the disk and repair the volume
- ○ b. Reactivate the volume
- ○ c. Recover from a backup
- ○ d. Replace the failed disk and Disk Management recreates the volume

Question 30

The LaserMaster printer has been restricted so that only three groups are allowed to print to it: Adhocs, Designers, and CAD. The CAD group has permission to manage documents, and the Designers group has permission to manage the printer. You want Scott to be able to control the job settings for all documents, but you do not want him to be able to change permissions of the printer. To which group should Scott be a member?

○ a. The Adhocs group

○ b. The CAD group

○ c. The Designers group

○ d. Scott can print and control job settings by default; therefore, he should not be added to a group

Question 31

Nancy is a new user who needs to be able to access all of the Accounting folders. The following groups need to be configured on the network. What is the proper way to configure these groups in a large forest environment so that the Accounting folder is accessible?

Group Type	Group Name	Accessible Folders
Domain local	Account	Sales, Marketing
Domain local	Account2	Marketing, Accounting
Global	Account3	Marketing, Accounting
Global	Account4	Sales, Marketing

○ a. Add Nancy to the Account2 group, and then add that group to the Account3 group

○ b. Add Nancy to the Account group, and then add that group to the Account4 group

○ c. Add Nancy to the Account3 group, and then add that group to the Account2 group

○ d. Add Nancy to the Account4 group, and then add that group to the Account group

Question 32

Zoe is a member of the Sales and the Planning groups. What permission does she have to the yearend.doc file that is part of the Yearend folder?

Group	Share Permission	Allow	Deny
Customer	Read		X
Planning	Read	X	
Sales	Read	X	
Administration	Full Control	X	
Group	Security Permission	Allow	Deny
Customer	Modify	X	
Planning	Modify	X	
Sales	Read		X
Administration	Full Control	X	

○ a. Read

○ b. Modify

○ c. Full Control

○ d. No Access

Question 33

Jennifer is a member of the Accounting group, the Account1 group, and Accounts group. What access permissions does she have to the Accounting Folder on the local machine where only the following permissions apply?

Accounting Folder Group	Share Permission	Allow	Deny
Accounting	Write	X	
Account1	Read	X	
Accounts	Read		X
Accounting2	Full Control	X	

○ a. Read

○ b. Write

○ c. Read and Write

○ d. Full Control

○ e. No Access

Question 34

You are preparing your servers for easy restore from system failures. You decide that the Recovery Console should be accessible on bootup. Which program should be executed to make the console available?

○ a. It cannot be accessed from bootup

○ b. **recoveryc /cons**

○ c. **recoveryc /nosidgen**

○ d. **winnt /cmdcons**

○ e. **winnt32 /cmdcons**

Question 35

The administrator for two different subnets is implementing DHCP on both networks. There is one DHCP server on each subnet. The router does not support RFC 2132 or RFC 1542, and it is not able to handle DHCP traffic. How can the administrator easily configure the network so that DHCP address can be accessed if one of the servers crashes?

○ a. Install a BOOTP Relay Agent

○ b. Install another DHCP server on each subnet

○ c. Install DNS

○ d. There is nothing that can be done

Question 36

The organization that you work for currently has 15 servers configured with GSNW. After configuring another server with GSNW, you realize that this server cannot access any of the 25 Novell servers. What is most likely the problem?

○ a. The wrong internal network number has been assigned.

○ b. The wrong frame type has been configured.

○ c. The wrong network frame has been configured.

○ d. NWLink also needs to be installed.

Question 37

Zoe is a member of the Sales and the Planning group. What permission does she have to the yearend.doc file that is part of the Yearend folder?

Group	Share Permission	Allow	Deny
Customer	Read		X
Planning	Read	X	
Sales	Read	X	
Administration	Full Control	X	
Group	**Security Permission**	**Allow**	**Deny**
Customer	Modify		X
Planning	Read	X	
Sales	Read	X	
Administration	Full Control	X	

○ a. Read

○ b. Modify

○ c. Full Control

○ d. No Access

Question 38

> Due to the annual cleanup schedule, you have been assigned to move and copy files to their correct location. The c:\projects folder has Read security permissions, and the c:\archive\projects folder has Write security permissions. The following configurations need to take place.
>
> | Folder | Current Location | Proposed Location |
> |---|---|---|
> | yeartodate | c:\projects | c:\projects |
> | yearend | c:\projects | c:\archive\projects |
> | yearbegin | c:\projects | c:\archive\projects |
> | yeartotal | c:\projects | c:\archive\projects |
>
> What permissions will the yearend folder have if it is moved to the new location?
>
> ○ a. Read
>
> ○ b. Write
>
> ○ c. Read and Write
>
> ○ d. It will not be accessible in the new location

Question 39

> The organization consists of 2,000 Windows 2000 Professional computers, 200 Windows 2000 domain controllers, and 100 Windows 2000 member servers. Microsoft just released a new Service Pack. What is the easiest way to install it onto all of your Windows 2000 Servers?
>
> ○ a. Manually install the SP on every server
>
> ○ b. Set up a distribution server and configure the servers from there
>
> ○ c. Use Software Installation And Maintenance
>
> ○ d. Use Remote Services Installation

Question 40

Which GPO has the highest priority? Refer to Figure 14.3.

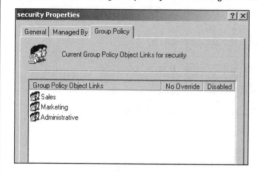

Figure 14.3 Group Policy Properties screen.

Question 41

Jennifer has compressed the annualsales.ppt file that needs to be presented at the annual sales meeting. She then copied the file into the Presentation folder on the Marketing computer that will be shipped to the convention. Nancy logs onto the Marketing computer and has security permission Full Control on the uncompressed Presentation folder. What has happened to the annualsales.ppt file? [Check all correct answers]

❏ a. The file is compressed.

❏ b. The file is uncompressed.

❏ c. Nancy has Full Control of the file.

❏ d. Nancy cannot access the file.

Question 42

Jennifer has received a promotion to the Accounting department. Which groups should the administrator add her to so that she can access the Account folder and the Sales folder? [Check all correct answers]

Folder	Group Membership
Account	Accounts, Administrators
Accounting	Temp2, Administrators
Sale	Sales
Sales	Sales2

❑ a. Accounts

❑ b. Accounting

❑ c. Sales

❑ d. Sales2

Question 43

Which options should be implemented before you use an ERD? [Check all correct answers]

❑ a. A boot disk

❑ b. Last Known Good Configuration

❑ c. Safe Mode

❑ d. Safe Mode With Networking

❑ e. Recovery Console

❑ f. Reinstall the server

Question 44

You are working on a server that has a striped volume with parity on dynamic disks. Two of the four disks in the volume fail. What recovery options can you employ?

○ a. Reactivate the disks and repair the volume

○ b. Reactivate the volume

○ c. Recover from a backup

○ d. Replace the failed disks and Disk Management recreates the volume

Question 45

The following users have just saved a file to the D: drive. Highlight the users in Figure 14.4 who will receive a warning when they save their file?

Logon Name	File Size
Bob	45MB
Ira	36MB
Mike	32MB
Nancy	54MB

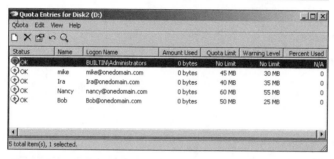

Status	Name	Logon Name	Amount Used	Quota Limit	Warning Level	Percent Used
OK		BUILTIN\Administrators	0 bytes	No Limit	No Limit	N/A
OK	mike	mike@onedomain.com	0 bytes	45 MB	30 MB	0
OK	Ira	Ira@onedomain.com	0 bytes	40 MB	35 MB	0
OK	Nancy	nancy@onedomain.com	0 bytes	60 MB	55 MB	0
OK	Bob	Bob@onedomain.com	0 bytes	50 MB	25 MB	0

5 total item(s), 1 selected.

Figure 14.4   Quota Entry screen.

Question 46

Jennifer has encrypted the annualsales.doc file that needs to be presented at the annual sales meeting. She then copies the file into the Presentation folder on the Marketing computer that will be shipped to the convention. Nancy logs onto the Marketing computer and has Full Control of the Presentation folder. What will happen when Nancy tries to present the annualsales.doc file?

○ a. She has Full Control of the file.

○ b. She has Read access to the file.

○ c. She decrypts the file and has access to it.

○ d. She cannot decrypt the file and does not have access to it.

Question 47

A new server arrives that has four 75GB hard drives. Your boss wants you to configure the server with the boot partition as large as possible, and the server should have the least amount of drive letters possible. What is the best way to meet the boss's expectations?

○ a. Configure a 25GB boot partition with one hard drive, label it C: drive, and configure the rest of the free space as drive D:

○ b. Configure a 75GB boot partition with one hard drive, label it C: drive, and configure the rest of the free space as drive D:

○ c. Configure a 25GB boot partition with one hard drive, label it C: drive, and configure the rest of the free space as a mounted volume

○ d. Configure a 75GB boot partition with one hard drive, label it C: drive, and configure the rest of the free space as a mounted volume

Question 48

The network consists of 52 Windows 2000 Servers and 25 NetWare Servers. You have been assigned the task of enabling communication between the two different operating systems. Five of the Windows 2000 Servers need be able to access the NetWare resources, and occasionally about 20 Windows 2000 Professional computers may also need to access the NetWare resources. What is the simplest way to configure the Windows 2000 Servers?

○ a. Install CNWS

○ b. Install CSNW

○ c. Install GNWS

○ d. Install GSNW

Question 49

Put the following policies in the order that they are implemented on the client.

The child OU policy

The domain policy

The local group policy

The OU policy

The site policy

The Windows NT system policies

Question 50

Zoe and Tim have been working for the onedomain.com corporation for many years. In those years they have both excelled in sales and marketing. Tim is a member of more groups in the forest than Zoe. Because the domain has moved to native mode, Zoe wants to know more about the forest structure. Their group memberships are listed below. What are Zoe and Tim's local domains? [Check all correct answers]

- Tim is a member of the Domain Local Group corp in sales.onedomain.com.

- Zoe is a member of the Global Group salesg in marketing.onedomain.com.

- Zoe is a member of the Global Group salesh in marketing.onedomain.com

- Zoe and Tim are both members of the Domain Local Group sales in domain sales.onedomain.com.

- Zoe and Tim are both members of the Domain Local Group marketing in sales.onedomain.com.

❑ a. Zoe's local domain is marketing.onedomain.com.

❑ b. Zoe's local domain is sales.onedomain.com.

❑ c. Tim's local domain is marketing.onedomain.com.

❑ d. Tim's local domain is sales.onedomain.com.

❑ e. There is not enough information to define Tim's local domain.

❑ f. There is not enough information to define Zoe's local domain.

Answer Key

1. a, d	18. b, c	35. a
2. b	19. a	36. b
3. a, b	20. d	37. a
4. See Figure 15.1	21. a	38. a
5. a, d	22. c	39. c
6. a, c	23. b, e	40. See Figure 15.3
7. See Figure 15.2	24. c	41. b, c
8. d	25. c	42. a, d
9. d	26. a	43. a, b, c, d, and e
10. d	27. a	44. c
11. d	28. a	45. See Figure 15.4
12. b	29. c	46. d
13. d	30. b	47. d
14. b	31. c	48. d
15. a, c	32. d	49. Refer to answer
16. a, c, and f	33. d	50. a, e
17. a, d	34. e	

Question 1

Answers a and d are correct. Answer b is incorrect because you cannot revert to a dynamic disk, you can only upgrade to a dynamic disk. Answer c is incorrect because the other server's hard drive has to be a basic disk to repair the mirrored set. The question states that the added hard drive was from a volume on another system, which indicates that it is a dynamic disk. Answer e is incorrect because Repair Set is not a Windows 2000 repair option.

Question 2

Answer b is correct. Active Directory Integrated Zones are replicated throughout Active Directory to provide fault tolerance for DNS. Answer a is incorrect because DHCP/BOOTP is used to transport DHCP traffic over a router. Answer c is incorrect because there is not a feature that is called an incremental zone for DNS, there are however incremental zone transfers. Answer d is incorrect because RIP is a routing protocol.

Question 3

Answers a and b are correct. Answer c is incorrect because a striped volume with parity is fault tolerant if one disk fails; therefore, data does not need to be recovered from a backup. Answer d is incorrect because Disk Management does not automatically recreate the failed volume.

Question 4

Answer: Place the check over Directory Browsing, as seen in Figure 15.1.

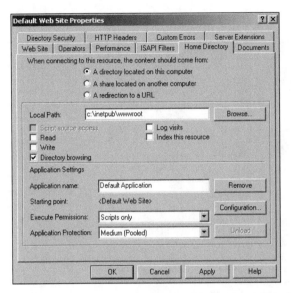

Figure 15.1   Directory Browsing enabled for the default Web site.

Question 5

Answers a and d are correct. Answer b is incorrect because the unattended.txt file is used for generic system information that can be implemented for multiple servers; therefore, no computer-specific information is used in this file. Answer c is incorrect because winnt32 is the upgrade version of Windows 2000, and the new server did not have a pervious 32-bit operating system. Also, the winnt32 program uses the **/unattend** switch, not the **/u** switch.

Question 6

Answers a and c are correct. Answer b is incorrect because the Recovery Console does not enable access to Safe Mode. To access Safe Mode, press F8 on startup. Answer d is incorrect because you need to press F8 to access the Advanced Startup options.

Question 7

Answer: Place a check in the box marked Integrated Windows Authentication.

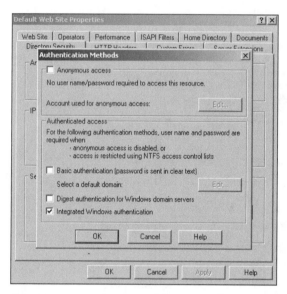

Figure 15.2 Authentication methods.

Question 8

Answer d is correct. When files or folders are copied to a new location on a different volume, they inherit the permission of the new location. Therefore, when the files are copied from a Full Control - Everyone directory to a Read - Administrators directory, they inherit the Read - Administrators permissions.

Question 9

Answer d is correct. Answers a and b are incorrect because Safe Mode and Safe Mode With Networking does not let you restore Active Directory using the System State data. Answer c is incorrect because to restore Active Directory using the System State data you must run the **ntdsutil** command so that restored information is not deleted from Active Directory because of the outdated USN.

Question 10

Answer d is correct. Answers a and c are incorrect because you cannot create a new striped set on basic disks in Windows 2000; you must convert the disks to dynamic disks to create a new striped volume. Answer b is incorrect because the striped set was part of the NT 4.0 upgrade and thus, already basic disks because of the upgrade. You cannot revert back to dynamic disks you must upgrade to dynamic disks, also the information cannot be regenerated because there is no fault tolerance in a striped set, the data must be restored from a backup.

Question 11

Answer d is correct. Answers a and b are incorrect because the clients using SQL do not need to slow their processes down by starting in Low, and processes are automatically started at Normal. Answer c is incorrect because by default Word starts at Normal, and starting it at Normal does not affect the system.

Question 12

Answer b is correct. Answers a and c are incorrect because /**definition** is not a winnt switch. Answers c and d are incorrect because /**unattend** is not a winnt switch. The /**unattend** switch is used for winnt32.

Question 13

Answer d is correct. Answers a and b are incorrect because rdisk(2) is the third disk on the first controller. Answer c is incorrect because partition(0) does not exist. Partitions always start with (1). Answers e and f are incorrect because rdisk (4) is the fifth disk on the first controller.

Question 14

Answer b is correct. Answer a is incorrect because IRQ 8 is used for the realtime clock. Answer c is incorrect because IRQ 10 is used for the primary SCSI controller. Answer d is incorrect because IRQ 11 is used for the secondary SCSI controller.

Question 15

Answers a and c are correct. Answer b is incorrect because the Setup Manager is used to automatically install Windows 2000 Server, and you were instructed to manually configure the server. Answer d is incorrect because the Add/Remove Hardware Wizard does not enable you to install the HAL; you must use Device Manager.

Question 16

Answers a, c, and f are correct. Answer b is incorrect because Disk Management does not assist you in managing disk quotas. Answer d is incorrect because the default limit should be set for the largest number of users, the Designers, not the least number of users. Answer e is incorrect because the Managers should be limited to 100MB, not 45MB.

Question 17

Answers a and d are correct. Answer b is incorrect because files that are moved keep their attributes from the original location; therefore, the files had to be compressed in their original location if they were moved and are still compressed. Answer c is incorrect because only the account folder was compressed. This indicates that the drive has to be uncompressed because of the copied folders.

Question 18

Answers b and c are correct. Answer a is incorrect because there is still a working part of the mirror, and it doesn't need to be recovered from a backup. Answer d is incorrect because reinitiate the mirror is not a function of dynamic disks.

Question 19

Answer a is correct. The policies are implemented in this order: a Windows NT policy, a system policy, a local group policy, a site policy, a domain policy, an OU policy, and then a child OU policy.

Question 20

Answer d is correct. Answer a is incorrect because after you press Enter you receive the same message. Answer b is incorrect because there is not an NTLDR selection on the screen. Answer c is incorrect because putting the NTLDR on a disk does not ensure that the system will boot. The boot floppy contains the NTLDR, boot.ini and ntdetect.com, which are all the files need to boot the server.

Question 21

Answer a is correct. The printer page is accessed by using the server name and the word "printers": **http://*servername*/printers**.

Question 22

Answer c is correct. Answers a and b are incorrect because her combined permissions give her Read and Write access. Answer d is incorrect because she is not a member of a group that gives her Full Control. Answer e is incorrect because she in not a member of a group that is denied access.

Question 23

Answers b and e are correct. Answers a and c are incorrect because the Windows Installer extension is .msi. Answer d is incorrect because a Global Catalog Server does not participate in the Software Installation And Maintenance program. Answer f is incorrect because RIS is used to remotely install Windows 2000 Professional.

Question 24

Answer c is correct. Answer a is incorrect because setting a process to Low slows it down and gives it less priority. Answer b is incorrect because processes start at Normal, and there is no time advantage. Answer d is incorrect because setting a process to Realtime only allows that process to run, leaving the server useless to everyone else.

Question 25

Answer c is correct. Answers a and b are incorrect because you are not able to log on, and you will be unable to find the Display icon or the Registry to edit. If you were to logon by memory, you would overwrite your Last Known Good Configuration with the bad driver configuration. Answer d is incorrect because Safe Mode loads the newly installed video drivers and the display will still be unreadable.

Question 26

Answer a is correct. Answer b is incorrect because Setup Manager is used to automatically install Windows 2000, but not the added software packages. Answer c is incorrect because Setup Wizard is used to individually install Windows 2000. Answer d is incorrect because Software Installation And Maintenance is used to install the software packages, but not Windows 2000 Professional.

Question 27

Answer a is correct. The URL for a printer is **http://*servername*/printers/*share_name*.print**. So the users need to access **http://webo/printers/webos.print**.

Question 28

Answer a is correct. Answers b, d, and e are incorrect because these are also members of the Sales folder. If she became a member of any of these groups, she would have access to both folders. Answer c is incorrect because the Sales2 group does not have permission to the Sales2 folder.

Question 29

Answer c is correct. Answers a and b are incorrect because you cannot reactivate or repair a failed striped volume; you can only recover from a backup because striped volumes do not include fault tolerance. Answer d is incorrect because Disk Management does not recreate a volume, and a striped volume cannot be recreated because only a striped volume with parity provides fault tolerance.

Question 30

Answer b is correct. Answer a is incorrect because the Adhocs group has not been assigned any special permissions, and by default, they only have print access. Answer c is incorrect because the Designers group can manage and change printer permissions, which you do not what Scott to be able to do. Answer d is incorrect because the LaserMaster has been restricted to the three groups, and if Scott is not a member of one of those three groups he will not be able to print or control job settings.

Question 31

Answer c is correct. Before Nancy can access all of the resources, she must first be a member of the global group Account3, then the global group Account3 should be added to the domain local group Account2. Answers a and b are incorrect because you cannot add domain local groups into global groups. Answer d is incorrect because Account and Account4 do not have access to the Accounting folder.

Question 32

Answer d is correct. Answers a, b, and c are incorrect because she is a member of the Sales and Planning groups and the security permissions for the Sales group is Read-Deny. This signifies that she does not have access to the resources.

Question 33

Answer d is correct. If Jennifer accesses the Accounting folder on the local machine, she has Full Control of the folder because there is no reference to security permissions. Answers a, b, c, and e are incorrect because these are the share permissions and they do not affect local machine access.

Question 34

Answer e is correct. Answer a is incorrect because the Recovery Console is accessible from bootup after you run **winnt32 /cmdcons**. Answers b and c are incorrect because the recoveryc is not a real program. Answer d is incorrect because winnt is a 16-bit program.

Question 35

Answer a is correct. Answer b is incorrect because adding two more DHCP servers is not the easiest way to solve this redundancy problem. Answer c is incorrect because adding a DNS server does not assist in DHCP redundancy. Answer d is incorrect because you can enable the DHCP/BOOTP Relay Agent to help with the problem.

Question 36

Answer b is correct. Answer a is incorrect because the internal network number is used to identify a specific server. The question states that none of the servers are accessible. Answer c is incorrect because GSNW does not have a network frame associated with it. Answer d is incorrect because GSNW automatically installs NWLink; it does not need to be manually installed.

Question 37

Answer a is correct. Zoe combined share permissions of Read and the combined security permissions of Modify and Read. This gives her a combined permission of Read because it is the most restrictive between her share and security permissions.

Question 38

Answer a is correct. Answers b and c are incorrect because when files or folders are moved to a new location on a local directory, they retain their original locations permissions. Therefore, the new files retain their Read permissions. Answer d is incorrect because the file is accessible in its new location with the Read attribute.

Question 39

Answer c is correct. Answer a is incorrect because manually installing each Service Pack on 300 servers is not easy. Answer b is incorrect because setting up a distribution server still requires you to manually configure the Service Packs for 300 servers. Answer d is incorrect because RIS is used to remotely install Windows 2000 Professional.

Question 40

Answer: The Sales group should be highlighted because the higher the group is on the GPO list the higher priority is has.

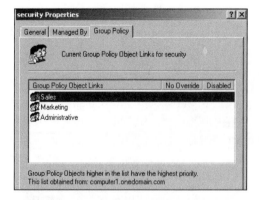

Figure 15.3   Group Policy Properties screen.

Question 41

Answers b and c are correct. Answer a is incorrect because the compressed file was copied to a remote volume, which signifies that the file inherits the permissions of the new location. Answer d is incorrect because the file is accessible due to its inherited permissions. Do not confuse compression with encryption. An encrypted file that was moved is accessible only to the person who encrypted the file, which is not the case for this question.

Question 42

Answers a and d are correct. Answers b and c are incorrect because the Accounting group doesn't exist, and the Sales group does not have group membership in Account or the Sales folder.

Question 43

Answers a, b, c, d, and e are correct. Answer f is incorrect because the ERD should be used before attempting to reinstall the server.

Question 44

Answer c is correct. Answers a and b are incorrect because although a striped volume with parity is fault tolerant, you can only lose one disk. If two disks in a striped volume with parity fail, you must recover from a backup. Answer d is incorrect because Disk Management does not recreate the volume for you, and there are two disks that failed which means you must recover from a backup.

Question 45

Answer: Mike, Ira, and Bob should all be highlighted because when they saved their file they exceeded their warning level.

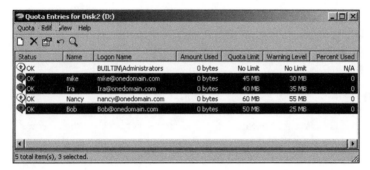

Figure 15.4 Quota Entry screen.

Question 46

Answer d is correct. Answers a, b, and c are incorrect because Jennifer encrypted the file. Only Jennifer can decrypt the file, no matter what permissions Nancy has to the folder the file is in. Jennifer is the only person who can access the file no matter where it is copied or moved.

Question 47

Answer d is correct. Answers a and b are incorrect because the question states that the least amount of drives letters be used. The least amount of drives letters is one, and answers a and b configure two drive letters. Answer c is incorrect because the question states that the largest boot partition possible be configured, 25GB is not the largest boot partition possible, 75GB is the largest.

Question 48

Answer d is correct. Answers a and c are incorrect because CNWS and GNWS are the incorrect acronym. Answer b is incorrect because only installing CSNW on the servers would not enable them to act as gateways for the client computers, therefore the clients would not have access to the NetWare servers.

Question 49

Answer:

The Windows NT system policies

The local group policy

The site policy

The domain policy

The OU policy

The child OU policy

Question 50

Answers a and e are correct. Answers b, c, and d are incorrect because group membership cannot be determined by the domain local group. Answer f is incorrect because Zoe is a member of a global group and this defines her local domain.

Glossary

Active Directory
A directory service database that hierarchically orders objects.

Active Directory Users And Computers
The snap-in used for administrating Organizational Units (OU), users, groups, computers, and objects.

adapter, network
A hardware device inserted into the computer to allow input and output of network communication.

Alerts
A program inside of the Performance tool that notifies the administrator when a defined counter falls above or below a specified range.

ANDing
The process by which two binary numbers are compared to determine whether two computers are on the same subnet.

answer file
A file used to supply answers to general questions during an unattended installation.

Application Server
A server that provides applications to the users on the network. Examples of an application server include a dedicated Terminal Server or a broad range of applications in a client/server environment.

ARC (Advanced RISC Computing) naming path
A path in the boot.ini file. The path informs the server which controller, disk, and partition the system and boot files are for Windows 2000 Server operating system.

ARPANET
An experimental network, the predecessor of the Internet, developed by the Advanced Research Projects Agency Network.

ASP (Active Server Pages)
A server-side scripting language for creating interactive and dynamic Web applications.

auditing

The process of monitoring security procedures that were implemented. The administrator can monitor users, file access, folder access, system events, system changes, and Active Directory.

Automatic Private IP Addressing (APIPA)

A new feature for Windows 2000 operating systems that enables a computer that cannot obtain an IP address from a DHCP server to automatically assign itself one. The assigned IP address is in a range of IPs from 169.254.0.1 to 169.254.255.254, with a subnet mask of 255.255.0.0.

Backup

The program used to protect against data loss, disk failures, viruses, power failure damage, and, if stored off site, natural disasters.

backup domain controllers (BDC)

Only used in NT 4.0, a computer that keeps a backup copy of the security information stored on the primary domain controller (PDC).

basic authentication

Authentication that transmits passwords in clear text. It is supported by most browsers but is not secure. Secure Socket Layer (SSL) must also be used to secure basic authentication.

Basic Input Output System (BIOS)

The computer's initial software program that tests hardware and transfers data to hardware devices.

basic storage

A storage device that can use either four primary partitions or three primary partitions with an extended partition as space allows. Used for disk partitioning and extended partitioning.

blocking inheritance

Preventing child OUs from inheriting the parent's permissions, security, or GPOs.

boot disk

Floppy used to start a Windows 2000 Server computer that has a corrupt master boot record (MBR), a corrupt boot sector, a missing NTLDR, a missing ntdetect.com, or a failed mirror. The floppy contains a copy of the ntldr, boot.ini, and dtdetct.com.

cipher

The command-line utility that is used by an administrator to manage encryption and decryption.

class A address

An IP address range that is defined by the first octet ranging from 1-126. This address enables each network to have 16 million hosts.

class B address

An IP address range that is defined by the first octet ranging from 128-191. This address enables each network to have 65,534 hosts.

class C address

An IP address range that is defined by the first octet ranging from 192-223. This address enables each network to have 254 hosts.

client service

The software that assists in communication with computer systems.

Examples of services include Client Services For Microsoft, Client Services For NetWare, and Gateway Services For NetWare.

code signing
The process of a digital signature being added to a drivers or operating system files by Microsoft to verify authenticity.

common name (CN)
An object's name that is included in the naming conventions of Active Directory.

compact.exe
The command used to change and display compressed files and directories.

compression
The compacting of a file, folder, or drive to save hard drive space.

computer accounts
Active Directory Users And Computer objects that uniquely identify computers in the domain.

contact accounts
Active Directory Users And Computers objects that are used for information and email purposes only.

containers
A unit that groups objects together, different from OUs because they cannot have group policies applied to them.

counter
Data associated with an object's performance in the Performance tool's System Monitor.

counter logs
A program inside of the Performance tool that an administrator uses to

record and collect data about specified counts and then logs the information to a file.

CSNW (Client Services For NetWare)
A service that allows Microsoft clients to connect and authenticate to file and print resources of a NetWare server.

DACL (Discretionary Access Control List)
A list of permissions that allows or denies users access to resources.

data compression
Attribute available on a drive formatted in NTFS that can save and conserve space on a hard drive.

DCPROMO
The command used to promote a member server to a domain controller. It can also be used to demote a domain controller to a member server.

default gateway
The IP address of a computer or piece of hardware that routes the TCP/IP packets between subnets.

Delegation Of Control Wizard
Program used in Active Directory to assign permissions to users or groups to manage OUs.

Device Manager
A program that supplies information about installed system devices, configurations, drivers, and their status.

differential backup
The type of backup that backs up the files that have changed since the last normal or incremental backup. It does not mark the files as being backed up.

Digest Authentication

Authentication protocol that uses a process called hashing to authenticate. Hashing converts the password into a numeric value that corresponds with one found in a server's hashing table.

digital signature

A code added to drivers and system files that verifies they have been tested by Microsoft and are in their original condition. A digital signature indicates that the driver, and its device, have been approved by Microsoft.

directory service

A database that keeps track of objects in a domain, and the programs that make the information in the database available.

Disk Cleanup

A utility that scans a selected hard drive, reports how much disk space it can free up, and then prompts for input on files to delete.

Disk Defragmenter

The program used to arrange files, programs, and free space on a hard drive.

disk duplication

Allows one installation to be duplicated to other computers. During the duplication process a program called *System Preparation Tool* is used.

disk quotas

A new technology implemented on Windows 2000 Server that uses NTFS as their file system. It is used to set space restrictions on users or groups and it enables an administrator to control disk utilization.

disk striping

Also referred to as RAID 0, this is a process which evenly writes data across the participating drives. Requires between 2 and 32 hard drives. If one drive fails, however, all of the data is lost. The main reason to implement it is to increased the read and write or input and out performance of your hardware.

disk striping with parity

Also referred to as RAID 5, this is the process of data that is written evenly across each of the drives in the volume. Parity information is stored for fault tolerance. It requires at least three hard drives and has an overhead proportional to the amount of hard drives used. If three drives are used, there is a one-third disk overhead for the parity information.

Diskperf

The command that must be executed before disk counters can collect data in Performance Tools System Monitor.

Distributed file system (Dfs)

Program used to create a logical hierarchical file system for users. This logical hierarchy is made up of shared folders from different locations, but they are seen by the users as one common logical file system. This makes it easier for users to locate and use shared network resources.

distinguished name

A unique name identifying where in the domain that object can be located. An example of a distinguished name is: CN=JohnDoe, CN=Users, DC=onedomain, DC=com.

distribution groups
Groups that are used only for email distribution.

Distribution Server
A computer responsible for sharing files that will be accessibly over the network for remote installations.

DNS (Domain Name System)
A service that provides TCP/IP clients with resolution of computer and domain names to IP addresses. It is also a service required to install Active Directory.

domain
A group of computers that is assigned by an administrator that shares a common Active Directory database.

domain Dfs
A distributed file system that is used to create a logical hierarchical file system that makes it easy for users to access shared network resources. It can be configured to be fault tolerant and is integrated into Active Directory.

domain component (DC)
The domain information included in the naming conventions of Active Directory.

domain controller
A computer responsible for Active Directory and security information.

domain local group
A Windows 2000 group that can have users from any domain in the forest, but they can only access resources in the local domain.

Domain Name System (DNS)
A service that provides TCP/IP clients with resolution of computer and domain names to IP addresses. It is also a service responsible for keeping track of name space for Active Directory.

domain security policy
A policy that is applied to the domain using Group Policy Objects (GPOs).

driver
Software that enables the operating system to control a hardware device.

driver signing
The process of a digital signature being added to a drivers or operating system files by Microsoft.

dual boot
The process of setting up your hard drive to boot to multiple operating systems on a single hardware system. You can then select which operating system will run at startup.

Dynamic Host Configuration Protocol (DHCP)
A networking service that dynamically assigns TCP/IP addresses to client computers.

dynamic storage
A new storage system for Windows 2000. It is used to create volumes, spanned volumes, mirrored volumes, striped volumes, and striped volumes with parity, commonly referred to as RAID 5. It was developed to expand storage, increase fault tolerance in the storage, and improve your ability to recover damaged storage. Allows for

options not available with a basic disk, and it extends the capability to repair, regenerate, and resynchronize a volume.

emergency repair disk (ERD)
A floppy that contains information about the Windows 2000 Server system settings that will help repair a damaged boot sector and system files.

Encrypting File System (EFS)
A Windows 2000 addition that enables the use of public key encryption to secure files and folders on an NTFS volume.

encryption
The process of encoding data so that unauthorized users cannot access the data.

explicit permissions
Permissions that are attached directly to an object or Organizational Unit (OU), which can include file and folder permissions.

FAT (File Allocation Table)
An older 16-bit file system that defines how a hard drive is segmented. It is limited in its operation and does not provide security.

FAT32 (File Allocation Table 32)
A newer 32-bit file system that defines how a hard drive is segmented; it supports larger files and larger disk sizes than FAT. It is limited in its operations and does not provide security.

file and print server
A server that supports file storage, while still providing access to networked printers.

file encryption
The process of making a file unreadable to unauthorized users, through the use of an encoding mechanism.

File Signature Verification Tool (sigverif.exe)
A wizard that scans the Windows 2000 file system and starts a log file that reports which files are signed, which files are unsigned, the modified date, and the version of each file.

file system
The definition of how the files are organized on storage media, Windows 2000 supports FAT, FAT32, and NTFS.

Flexible Single Master Operation (FSMO)
A server that acts as the master for a particular operation. There are five types: the Schema master, Domain Naming Master, Infrastructure Master, PDC Emulator, and the RID Master.

forest
A group of trees that may or may not share the same name space.

frame type
The format in which the packets are sent over NWLink and IPX/SPX. Computers that need to communicate must have the same frame type. Computers with different frame types cannot transmit data between themselves. The frame types that are available with NWLink are Ethernet 802.2, Ethernet 802.3, Ethernet II, and Ethernet SNAP.

FTP (File Transfer Protocol)
Program provided with IIS 5.0 that enables users to have a central location for uploading and downloading files. It enables users to move files between computers over a TCP/IP network.

global catalog
A partial copy of the Active Directory database that allows searches of the entire forest regardless of the location.

global group
A Windows 2000 group that can only have uses from the local domain, but they can access resources in any domain in the forest.

group
A unit that is used to organize users for the purpose of assigning permissions to resources or, in the case of distribution groups, for sending messages to each user in the group.

group policies
Rules that are applied to users and groups for security in Windows 2000. They can be applied to a site, a domain, an OU, or a computer.

GSNW (Gateway Services For NetWare)
A service that enables a Microsoft server to act as a gateway for Microsoft clients to access and authenticate to a NetWare file and print server. When it is configured it installs Client Services for NetWare and NWLink

HAL (hardware abstraction layer)
A file or files that are supplied by the hardware manufacture that specify how to set up a hardware device on a

particular platform. It enables device drivers to function on a variety of platforms without modifying the driver software.

hardware device
A piece of equipment that is physically connected to a computer.

hardware profile
A configuration that tells the computer which device drivers and services to load when the computer starts.

HCL (Hardware Compatibility List)
A Microsoft list of supported and approved hardware devices.

incremental backup
The type of backup that backs up files that have changed since the last normal or incremental backup. The files are marked as backed up.

Infrastructure Master
A domain controller that records changes made concerning users and groups in a domain. There is only one infrastructure master per domain.

inherited permissions
Permissions that propagate from a parent folder, container, or OU to child files, folders, containers, or OUs.

Integrated Windows Authentication
Authentication protocol that uses the logon user name and password so that passwords are not sent over the network.

internal network number
A unique eight-digit hexadecimal identifier that distinguishes a NetWare server, used for configuring NWLink or IPS/SPX.

Internet Information Server (IIS) 5.0
The Web server provided with Windows 2000.

IP address
A unique 32-bit binary number that identifies a computer, represented in a decimal notation.

IPP (Internet Printing Protocol)
The protocol that is used for management of printers on a Web page, and enables users to send jobs to a printer over a TCP/IP network.

IP Security (IPSec)
The protocol that can provide encryption and secure communication between computers using Kerberos authentication on a TCP/IP network.

IRQ (Interrupt request)
A specific hardware channel that is used to send signals to the processor. Each device has its own unique IRQ that is a number from 0-15.

IUSR_computername
The account created as a built-in anonymous access account for IIS.

IWAM_computername
The account created during the installation of IIS to start process applications such as accounting, monitoring, and scripting.

Kerberos
A popular security protocol used for authentication. The most current version is V5.

licensing mode
The type of licenses that are defined for the organization: per server or per seat.

Lightweight Directory Access Protocol (LDAP)
An Internet standard used for defining a directory service and the protocols for interacting with that directory service.

local user profile
Files that are created the first time a user logs on to a specific computer. It is stored on the local computer and can only be accessed from that computer.

local security policy
A policy used to protect and secure the local computer. There are three categories to a policy: audit polices, user rights assignment, and security options.

logical structure
The setup for a domain defined for administrative purposes. This structure is centered around objects, organizational units, domains, trees, and forests.

LPD (Line Printer Daemon)
A Unix-compatible print server program that listens for printing requests (LPR) to the Unix server and controls the Unix print spool (LPQ).

LPQ (Line Printer Queue)
The place where the print device holds the print jobs until they are ready to process by the Unix server.

LPR (Line Printer Remote)
The command for sending a print job to a print device in Unix.

makeboot.exe
The command used to make the 4 boot floppies for Windows 2000 Server Setup.

mandatory user profile

Files stored on the server that hold configuration information specific to a user that cannot be updated by the user. When a user tries to change it, the changes are not updated on the server; they will continue to get the same stored mandatory profile.

mirrored volume or partition

Also referred to as RAID 1, occurs when two physical disks have replicas of one set of data. Requires two hard drives—one for the original data and the other to hold a copy of the original data. There is a 50 percent disk overhead because one drive holds a copy of the information. If one disk in a mirror fails, a copy of the data is available on the other disk in the mirror.

mixed mode

A network that consists of Windows 2000 servers and Windows NT servers. A network can remain in mixed mode indefinitely. Windows 2000 domains are mixed-mode domains by default. A one-way conversion to native mode allows enhanced capabilities but means no more NT 4 domain controllers (PDC or BDC) can exist on the network.

modems

A hardware device used to dial directly to other computers over an analog telephone line or to an Internet Service Provider (ISP).

mounted volume

A folder that is attached to an existing directory. It is used to add more space to an existing hierarchy without using a drive letter.

multiple master

A model for replication that ensures all the domain controllers in the domain have the same information. All Windows 2000 domain controllers use the multiple master model.

Microsoft Management Console (MMC)

The main console of Windows 2000 that uses a variety of snap-ins to manage a Windows 2000 Server.

naming conventions

A common way to refer to objects in an Active Directory hierarchy.

native mode

The way to define a network where all the domain controllers in the domain are Windows 2000 Servers. Only the domain controllers need to be Windows 2000; member servers and client computers can be running any operating system.

Network Monitor

The program used to view network statistics and packet information.

network number

A number used in AppleTalk, IPX/SPX, IP, and other protocol to differentiate one network or subnet from another.

network router

A program or piece of hardware that is used to provide communication between different networks.

NNTP (Network News Transfer Protocol)

The program that enables users to have a centralized database of discussion groups over the Web.

nontransitive

The way that information does not flow through computer to computer. For example, if computer A has a nontransitive trust relationship to computer B, and computer B has a nontransitive trust with computer C, computer A does not necessarily trust computer C.

NTFS 5.0

The preferred file system for Windows 2000 Server because of its reliability, fault tolerance, and security.

NWLink

Microsoft's version of IPX/SPX, used to communicate with Novell's NetWare servers or other operating systems that use IPX/SPX.

objects

The most basic unit of organization in Active Directory. Objects are items such as a user, a printer, a group, a computer, or a policy.

offline files

Files that can be worked on by a user whether they are connected to the network or not. If files are being worked on offline, the files are automatically updated when the computer is reconnected to the network.

operation masters

The servers assigned to complete certain tasks for the domain or forest which are handled by one server.

Organizational Unit (OU)

A container in Active Directory that is used to organize objects.

partition

A section of the hard drive that is used to store data that is accessible by a drive letter.

per seat

A type of licensing that is purchased for each client on a network. In large networks with multiple servers it is more economical.

per server

A type of licensing that is purchased for number of clients connected to each server. In a network with only one or two servers, this can be more economical than "per seat" licensing.

Performance tool

The program that is used to monitor, collect, and store information about local and remote servers.

permissions

Rights used to control who can and cannot have access to a resource.

physical structure

The location of computers and network connections to those computers. It is used to determine network traffic and how it is configured and managed. It configured with sites and domain controllers.

ping

A command used to test connectivity of devices running the TCP/IP protocol.

Plug and Play

The program that automatically detects, installs, and loads the correct drivers for a hardware device.

primary domain controllers (PDC)

Only used in NT 4.0, the computer that is responsible for the writable copy of the domain database and domain security.

Primary Domain Controller (PDC) Emulator

The Windows 2000 domain computer responsible for emulating an NT 4.0 PDC in a mixed-mode environment There is only one per domain.

Printer

The software that is installed on the print server.

print device

The hardware device that produces the printed output.

print server

The server to which users send their documents to be printed.

protocol

A standard that regulates the transmission of data between computers. Examples of protocols include TCP/IP and NWLink.

quotas

A technology new to Windows 2000 Servers that can be implemented on an NTFS file system. It is used to set space restrictions on users or groups and it enables an administrator to control disk utilization.

RAID 0

Also referred to as disk striping, the process of evenly writing data across the participating drives. Requires between 2 and 32 hard drives. If one drive fails, however, all of the data is lost. The main reason to implement it is to increase the read and write or input and output performance of your hardware.

RAID 1

Also referred to as disk mirroring, two physical disks have replicas of one set of data. Requires two hard drives—one for the original data and the other to hold a copy of the original data. There is a 50 percent overhead, because one drive holds a copy of the information. If one disk in a mirror fails, a copy of the data is available on the other disk in the mirror.

RAID 5

Also referred to as disk striping with parity, data is written across each of the drives in the volume. Parity information is stored for fault tolerance. Requires at least three hard drives and has overhead proportional to the number of hard drives used. If three drives are used, there is a one-third disk overhead for the parity information.

Recovery Console

The program used after all attempts at repairing the operating system using the Advanced Startup options have failed. A command prompt utility that enables an administrator to start and stop services, access the server's drives, copy files, delete files, logon to the server, and format a server's hard drives.

Regedit, Regedt32

The programs that are used to edit the Windows 2000 registry.

Relative Distinguished Name (RDN)

Uniquely distinguishes an object within a container. John Doe is the RDN that distinguishes the object "John Doe" within the Users container for CN=John Doe, CN=Users, DC=onedomain, DC=com

Relative Identifier (RID) Master

A server in a domain that is responsible for assigning blocks of unique identifiers to all domain controller in a domain.

Remote Access Server (RAS)

A set of programs used to enable dial-in access to the network.

Remote Desktop Protocol (RDP)

The protocol used to enable communication between a Terminal Services server and a client.

Remote Installation Services (RIS)

The server program that provides preconfigured images to remotely install Windows 2000 Professional.

Resource Kit

A purchased product that supplies extra documentation and software to help you support your Windows 2000 Server.

roaming user profile

Files maintained on the server that hold configuration information specific to a user, and available to the user regardless of which computer they use to log onto in the domain. When changes are made to the user's configuration or desktop setup, the changes are updated and stored in the roaming profile on the server.

Routing And Remote Access Services (RRAS)

The program that provides routing, Virtual Private Networking (VPN), and Remote Access Server (RAS) over the network, phone lines, or ISPs.

schema

A definition of all objects stored in Active Directory for a forest that specifies which attributes an object may have, and the proper syntax for those attributes. There is only one schema and one Schema Master per forest.

Schema Master

The domain controller that maintains and can update the schema for the forest.

Security Configuration And Analysis Tool

The program used to configure your server against security holes and attacks. It uses different security templates to assist in analyzing and securing the computer.

security groups

Groups that are used to specify security for a collection of objects. Groups are listed in the Discretionary Access Control List (DACL) that allows or denies users access to resources.

security permissions

Permissions assigned to files and folders that are formatted in NTFS. They protect files and folders at the local computer and over network shares.

Setup Wizard

The program that runs when installing Windows 2000 Server. It is started by running winnt or winnt32.

Setup Manager

A new tool provided in the *Windows 2000 Server Resource Kit*. It assists you in creating scripting files for automatically installing Windows 2000 Professional and Windows 2000 Server.

share permissions

Permissions that are assigned to a folder that make it accessible to users over the network.

SID (security identifier)

A number assigned to a user, group, or computer that uniquely identifies the object.

simple volume

Space that is used from one hard drive.

site

A combination of one or more IP subnets connected by a high speed link. They are used to segment a network into manageable parts, particularly for replication purposes, depending on the LAN or WAN speeds. They are representatives of the physical structure of an organization.

SMTP (Simple Mail Transfer Protocol)

The protocol that sends mail between servers.

Software Installation And Maintenance

The program used to deploy and manage software throughout an organization in accordance with Group Policy Objects (GPOs). It can install a software package, upgrade different versions of software, and remove software, all by adding information to the software section of a GPO.

spanned volume

Space that is combined from at least two dynamic disks, but is limited to 32 dynamic disks.

standalone Dfs

The program used to create a logical hierarchical file system that is installed on the same server that houses the shared network resources.

subnet mask

A 32-bit binary number that determines which bits identify the segment of the network where a host (e.g., a computer or other networked device) is located.

switches

Used when running a command to execute or add to the commands instructions.

system file checker

A command-line-utility, sfc.exe, that verifies the correct system files versions are in use.

System Monitor

A program inside of the Performance tool that an administrator uses to add performance counters to be charted, logged, or reported.

System Preparation Tool

The program that allows one installation to be duplicated to other computers. The tool is run by executing the sysprep command, which removes the installation-specific SIDs before a third-party tool is used to create an image file.

system state data

A combination of important Windows 2000 Server system components packaged together for easy backup and restoration. Includes the Registry, System Startup files, Component Services Class Registration, Certificate Services database (if installed), Active Directory (if a domain controller), and Sysvol (if a domain controller).

Task Manager

A tool used to monitor programs, track system performance, and maintain processes.

TCP/IP (Transmission Control Protocol/Internet Protocol)

The default protocol for Windows 2000. It is a suite of protocols that provides reliable transmission of data between computers.

TechNet

A resource provided by Microsoft with technical and troubleshooting information about all of Microsoft's products. It includes service packs and hot fixes, and is available on CD (by subscription) or via Microsoft's Web site.

Terminal Services

The program that is loaded on a server for clients and administrators to run applications on the server's desktop without using client re-sources. A terminal emulator enables a very low-end client machine to

display the server's desktop and lets the client control the desktop using a keyboard and a mouse. It can also be configured in such a way as to allow administrators to provide remote administration and support.

trace logs

A program inside of the Performance tool that an administrator uses to record and collect data about the operating system and programs and send that to a file.

transitive

The way that information flows through from computer to computer. For example, if computer A has a transitive trust relationship with computer B, and computer B has a transitive trust relationship with computer C, then computer A also trusts computer C because of the transitive trust relationships.

tree

A logical organization comprised of more than one domain that shares a common name space.

trust relationship

An agreement of two computers to authorize authenticated users, so that their resources can be accessed.

uniqueness database files (UDF)

A file that provides answers to questions that are unique to the individual computer being installed. The file contains information such as computer name and computer IP that are unique to each computer specified in the UDF.

universal group
A new group type with Windows 2000 that can contain users and groups from any domain in the forest, and they can access resources in any domain in the forest. This group is only available in native mode.

update sequence numbers (USN)
Numbers that keep track of changes in Active Directory. Each domain tracks the numbers for all domain controllers in the domain, and uses them to determine which information to replicate, and which replication changes take precedence. For example, by comparing USNs, a domain controller can tell whether information replicated by another domain controller is newer than information contained in its own copy of the Active Directory.

User
An object that represents a person who uses a computer.

user principle name (UPN)
A unique name for a user that can be thought of as the user's logon name.

user profile
A file that stores the users' settings such as desktop configurations, background settings, and printer configurations. They are located in the Documents and Settings folder.

Virtual Private Network (VPN) Server
The server implementing special protocols used to connect to the network over a secure Internet connection using Routing And Remote Access Services (RRAS). It provides secure encrypted transmission used to connect to a remote access server.

volume
A section of a hard drive, or group of hard drives, that is used to store data and is accessible by a drive letter or a mount point.

Web server
A server whose function is to provide Web services, file transfer protocol (FTP) services, Network News Transfer Protocol (NNTP), and Simple Mail Transfer Protocol (SMTP) to clients.

Windows File Protection
A program that monitors system files, verifies the digital signatures, and replaces non-Microsoft files with the original copies that are backed up in the dllcache folder.

Windows Installer
The program used to manage the installation of software packages on remote computers. It determines how packages are installed and uninstalled on computers or for users. The package that is created uses a file with a .msi extension, which replaces the setup.exe program that normally controlled software installation prior to Windows 2000.

Windows Update
A program that scans your computer for outdated files and drivers and then accesses the Microsoft Web site to automatically replace them with the most current versions.

winnt

The command to install Windows
2000 Server on Windows 3.x or DOS
operating systems, or from a command
prompt on any 16-bit operating
platform.

winnt32

The command used for upgrading to
Windows 2000 Server from Windows 95, Windows 98, Windows NT
Server 4.0, Windows NT Server 3.51,
or a server with Windows 2000
already installed.

X.500

Standards for accessing a directory
service upon which Active Directory
is based.

Index

The Coriolis Exam Cram Personal Trainer
An exciting new category in certification training products

The Exam Cram Personal Trainer is the first certification-specific testing product that completely links learning with testing to:

- **Increase your comprehension**
- **Decrease the time it takes you to learn**

No system blends learning content with test questions as effectively as the Exam Cram Personal Trainer.

Only the Exam Cram Personal Trainer offers this much power at this price.

Its unique Personalized Practice Test Engine provides a real-time test environment and an authentic representation of what you will encounter during your actual certification exams.

Much More than Just Another CBT!

Most current CBT learning systems offer simple review questions at the end of a chapter with an overall test at the end of the course, with no links back to the lessons. But Exam Cram Personal Trainer takes learning to a higher level.

Its four main components are:

- The complete text of an Exam Cram study guide in HTML format
- A Personalized Practice Test Engine with multiple test methods
- A database of 150 questions linked directly to an Exam Cram chapter

Plus, additional features include:

- **Hint:** Not sure of your answer? Click Hint and the software goes to the text that covers that topic.
- **Lesson:** Still not enough detail? Click Lesson and the software goes to the beginning of the chapter.
- **Update feature:** Need even more questions? Click Update to download more questions from the Coriolis Web site.
- **Notes:** Create your own memory joggers.

- **Graphic analysis:** How did you do? View your score, the required score to pass, and other information.
- **Personalized Cram Sheet:** Print unique study information just for you.

Windows 2000 Server
Exam Cram Personal Trainer
ISBN: 1-57610-735-3

Windows 2000 Professional
Exam Cram Personal Trainer
ISBN: 1-57610-734-5

Windows 2000 Directory Services
Exam Cram Personal Trainer
ISBN: 1-57610-732-9

Windows 2000 Security Design
Exam Cram Personal Trainer
ISBN: 1-57610-772-8

Windows 2000 Network
Exam Cram Personal Trainer
ISBN: 1-57610-733-7

Windows 2000 Migrating from NT4
Exam Cram Personal Trainer
ISBN: 1-57610-773-6

MCSE Networking Essentials
Exam Cram Personal Trainer
ISBN:1-57610-644-6

A+ Exam Cram Personal Trainer
ISBN: 1-57610-658-6

CCNA Routing and Switching
Exam Cram Personal Trainer
ISBN: 1-57610-781-7

$99.99 U.S. • $149.99 Canada

Available: November 2000

CORIOLIS™
Certification Insider Press

The _Smartest_ Way to Get Certified
Just Got Smarter™

Look for All of the Exam Cram Brand Certification Study Systems

ALL NEW! Exam Cram Personal Trainer Systems

The Exam Cram Personal Trainer systems are an exciting new category in certification training products. These CD-ROM based systems offer extensive capabilities at a moderate price and are the first certification-specific testing product to completely link learning with testing.

This Exam Cram study guide turned interactive course lets you customize the way you learn.

Each system includes:

- A Personalized Practice Test engine with multiple test methods
- A database of nearly 300 questions linked directly to the subject matter within the Exam Cram

Exam Cram Audio Review Systems

Written and read by certification instructors, each set contains four cassettes jam-packed with the certification exam information you must have. Designed to be used on their own or as a complement to our Exam Cram study guides, Flash Cards, and Practice Tests.

Each system includes:

- Study preparation tips with an essential last-minute review for the exam
- Hours of lessons highlighting key terms and techniques
- A comprehensive overview of all exam objectives
- 45 minutes of review questions, complete with answers and explanations

Exam Cram Flash Cards

These pocket-sized study tools are 100% focused on exams. Key questions appear on side one of each card and in-depth answers on side two. Each card features either a cross-reference to the appropriate Exam Cram study guide chapter or to another valuable resource. Comes with a CD-ROM featuring electronic versions of the flash cards and a complete practice exam.

Exam Cram Practice Tests

Our readers told us that extra practice exams were vital to certification success, so we created the perfect companion book for certification study material.

Each book contains:

- Several practice exams
- Electronic versions of practice exams on the accompanying CD-ROM presented in an interactive format, enabling practice in an environment similar to that of the actual exam
- Each practice question is followed by the corresponding answer (why the right answers are right and the wrong answers are wrong)
- References to the Exam Cram study guide chapter or other resource for that topic

CORIOLIS™

Certification Insider Press

The Smartest Way to Get Certified™